The Complete
Tower Air Fryer Cookbook

1000 Super-Easy, Tasty & Healthy Recipes with Just 5 Ingredients to Fit Your Budget

Janice S. Landis

CONTENTS

Chapter 4 Poultry Recipes 34

Chapter 5 Beef , pork & Lamb Recipes..44

Chapter 6 Fish And Seafood Recipes..55

Chapter 7 Vegetarians Recipes 66

Chapter 8 Vegetable Side Dishes Recipes 76

Chapter 9 Desserts And Sweets Recipes 87

Appendix : Recipes Index 98

INTRODUCTION

With a rise in popularity over the last decade, air fryers have been in the spotlight for their ability to quickly give your food a crispy taste without the use of oil and other additional fat. It is the healthy alternative to deep frying, and it is a cooking method that takes very little time when you compare it to most others. As quickly as you can microwave a meal, you can also use your air fryer to give the ingredients a more gourmet feel. The Towe model is an air fryer and toaster oven in one. Because it does so much, many people are quick to say that it is their favorite model on the market -even Oprah!

You are going to love your Towe air fryer oven because of its notable versatility. You can bake, broil, fry, toast, and convection cook at the press of a button! But, I'm getting ahead of myself. Let's take a step back, and I'll tell you what an air fryer is. In essence, air-fried food is a healthy option to deep-fried food—you use 95% less oil.

The delicious air fryer recipes are categorized by breakfast, lunch, dinner, seafood, and desserts. This book used trials and tested recipes to ensure that each recipe tastes good. You will get the crispness, fried aroma, browning, and, most importantly, delicious taste. I have taken special care to include simple, flavorful, and easy to prepare recipes for people with a busy schedule and life.

I hope that trying the recipes in this cookbook will spark some ideas, and you'll be brave enough to come up with your own masterpieces. If you already have a Towe Air Fryer Oven, it's time to fry, toast, bake, broil, or cook to your heart's content. I'm sure you'll find quite a few recipes you want to try in between the ones included in this book! For those readers who are still undecided if the Towe is the kitchen appliance for them, I suggest you browse through the recipes to see what mouth-watering dishes await you when you use this air fryer, toaster, and oven combo. It'll turn you into a master chef in no time!

Chapter 1 Preparing for Your Towe Air Fryer Meals

What a Towe Air Fryer Oven is

The Towe brand was founded in the 1970s. Its founders (The Sontheimer) visited a home goods fair in France. This fateful journey led to the introduction of the American food processor, which was modeled on a similar device that the French called a robotic coupe. For many years after that, Towe only made kitchen machines. Towe did not develop further until the 1990s and offered other items to make life in the kitchen easier. The name Towe has stood for quality, innovative products, and design for many years.

The Towe Air Fryer Oven is the newest addition to the line of innovative kitchen appliances of Towe. It serves as an air fryer and a fast and efficient electric oven, and a toaster. It is an electric air fryer that has rapid airflow technology. This appliance is perfect for people who love to cook crispy food in a large amount. The Towe Air Fryer is readily available on its online stores and Amazon, and this countertop convection oven comes with accessories including Towe air fryer, baking pan and air fry basket. It boasts the following features:

- 1800-watt motor, fan, and heater.

- Wide temperature range: 80°F to 450°F.

- Selecting presets, temperature, time, and function has never been easier with an extensive digital display and intuitive programming options.

- Adaptable Thermostat, 60 Minutes Auto shut off, Selector-Timer of Toast Shade Internally.

- A range of 7 functions: Air fry, Convection bake, Convection broil, Bake, Broil, Warm & Toast

- Easy cleanup: nonstick interior, dishwasher-safe Baking Tray, Oven Rack, Air Fryer Basket, Whisper for Quiet Operation

Advantages of the Towe Air Fryer Oven

1. When you are cooking for a family, you need a device that has a larger capacity—the Towe is the device for you. It is larger than your standard air fryer or toaster oven without taking up too much extra space on your countertop. You will easily be able to cook meals that are meant to be eaten by multiple people without having to put in a lot of extra time or effort.

2. Because this device is multi-functional, it eliminates the need for you to have a separate air fryer and toaster oven. It is a 2-in-1 that will end up saving you money. Even if your budget isn't tight, it makes sense to save as much money as possible with the rising costs of food and other appliances like this on the market.

3. Nothing is worse than a cluttered countertop. It can become cumbersome when you have too many appliances to choose from. When you want to fry, bake, toast, or broil, you won't have to get out any additional appliances from your cupboards. The Towe fits neatly on your kitchen countertop, and it still leaves plenty of room for the rest of your appliances and kitchen items.

4. When you are cooking in large batches, one big problem that you encounter is unevenness in the final result. Even putting a large batch of veggies in the oven might result in some being well done while other pieces are undercooked. The air fryer element of the Towe eliminates this problem for you. With this device, you get even cooking every time. There is also no need to flip anything or adjust anything—all you need to do is put your ingredients inside and set the dials; it doesn't get any easier than this.

5. You are going to become a more efficient cook when you use your Towe. Because you do not have to constantly stand around to monitor if your food is going to burn or overcook, you can go about your day without any worries. It is a controlled method for cooking that offers you great results every time.

Main Functions of the Towe Air Fryer Oven

- **Air fry**

Place the Air Fryer Basket on the Baking Pan. Select the Air Fry on the Function Dial and set the Temperature Dial to the desired temperature. Turn the on/Oven Timer Dial to set the expected cooking time. When air frying, you can use a little oil but only spritz the surface of your food with oil, then massage to distribute the oil evenly. You can also use an assortment of coatings such as corn flakes, potato chips, breadcrumbs, and panko to make your air-fried favorites more flavorful. Moreover, it is also important to flip your food halfway through the cooking time for even cooking.

- **Bake/ Convection bake**

When using this function, place the Baking Pan on the Oven Rack. Set the Function Dial to Bake or Convection Bake and turn on the on/Oven Timer Dial to choose the desired cooking time. You must preheat the oven for 5 minutes before baking custards, cakes, and other pastries. For more oversized items such as chicken, place the baking pan in rack near the bottom of the oven. On the other hand, there is a big difference when using Baking and Convection Baking (this is also true for Broiling and Convection Broiling). Select Convection Bake if you require browning on your food. If you are using this setting, reduce the temperature to 250 F as the temperature gets evenly distributed inside the oven.

- **Broil / Convection broil**

When using this function, place the Air Fryer basket above the baking pan. Select the 'Broil' or 'Convection Broil' function and turn on the on/Oven Timer Dial to choose the desired cooking time. For best results, do not use glass oven dishes to broil, and always keep an eye on your food while cooking to avoid over broiling. Use this function for cooking all types of meats.

- **Warm**

Fit the Baking Pan or Oven Rack. Set the Temperature Dial and Function Dial to Warm before turning the on/Oven Timer Dial to the preferred warming time. Once the timer is off, turn off the oven.

- **Toast**

Fit the Oven Rack, then place the items on the rack. If you are going to toast a slice of bread, make sure to put it in the middle of the rack. For more items, make sure that they are evenly spaced. Set the Function Dial to Toast, then the on/Toast Timer Dial to choose the desired color setting of your toast.

Cleaning Instructions

Knowing how to clean your Towe air fryer is important because it will last longer the better you take care of it.

● Allow the air fryer to cool down after using it.

● Unplug the unit before starting.

● Use a damp cloth to clean any debris from the outside of the fryer.

● Prepare a sink of water with dishwashing liquid.

● Thoroughly wash the basket tray and pan. (The removable components of the deep fryer can be washed in the dishwasher if you prefer not to wash them by hand).

● Use a cleaning sponge or rag and warm water to clean the inside of the fryer.

● Keep a small brush handy to clean the food stuck on the heating element above the food basket.

● Ensure the basket, tray, and pan are completely dry before returning to the air fryer.

Several Tips on Making Your Towe Air Fryer Shine

An air fryer oven is pretty straight forward to use, but with a few tips you can really make it shine for you.

1. Find the right place for your air fryer oven in your kitchen. Make sure you have some clearance around the oven so that the hot air can escape from the vent at the back.

2. Pre-heat your air fryer before adding your food. Because an air fryer heats up so quickly, it isn't critical to wait for the oven to pre-heat before putting food inside, but it's a good habit to get into. Sometimes a recipe requires a hot start and putting food into a less than hot oven will give you less than perfect results. For instance, pastry bakes better if cold pastry is placed into a hot oven. Pizza dough works better with a burst of heat at the beginning of baking. It only takes a few minutes to pre-heat the oven, so unless you're in a real rush, just wait to put your food inside.

3. Invest in a kitchen spray bottle. Spraying oil on the food is easier than drizzling or brushing, and allows you to use less oil overall. It will be worth it!

4. Think about lining your drip tray with aluminum foil for easy clean up.

5. Use the proper breading technique. Breading is an important step in many air fryer recipes. Don't skip a step! It is important to coat foods with flour first, then egg and then the breadcrumbs. Be diligent about the breadcrumbs and press them onto the food with your hands. Because the air fryer has a powerful fan as part of its mechanism, breading can sometimes blow off the food. Pressing those crumbs on firmly will help the breading adhere.

6. If you're cooking very fatty foods, add a little water to the drip pan below the basket tray to help prevent grease from getting too hot and smoking.

7. Don't overcrowd the mesh tray, but cook foods on one layer instead. I can't stress this enough. It's tempting to try to cook more at one time, but over-crowding will prevent foods from crisping and browning evenly and take more time over all.

8. Spray with oil part way through. If you are trying to get the food to brown and crisp more, try spritzing it with oil part way through the cooking process. This will also help the food to brown more evenly.

9. Place delicate items lower in the oven so they don't over brown or brown too quickly. Foods with ingredients like cheese or pastry on top can get too hot being too close to the upper element, so take advantage of the versatility of your air fryer oven and move the tray lower in the oven.

Measurement Conversions

BASIC KITCHEN CONVERSIONS & EQUIVALENTS

DRY MEASUREMENTS CONVERSION CHART

3 TEASPOONS = 1 TABLESPOON = 1/16 CUP

6 TEASPOONS = 2 TABLESPOONS = 1/8 CUP

12 TEASPOONS = 4 TABLESPOONS = 1/4 CUP

24 TEASPOONS = 8 TABLESPOONS = 1/2 CUP

36 TEASPOONS = 12 TABLESPOONS = 3/4 CUP

48 TEASPOONS = 16 TABLESPOONS = 1 CUP

METRIC TO US COOKING CONVERSIONS

OVEN TEMPERATURES

120 °C = 250 °F

160 °C = 320 °F

180° C = 350 °F

205 °C = 400 °F

220 °C = 425 °F

LIQUID MEASUREMENTS CONVERSION CHART

8 FLUID OUNCES = 1 CUP = 1/2 PINT = 1/4 QUART

16 FLUID OUNCES = 2 CUPS = 1 PINT = 1/2 QUART

32 FLUID OUNCES = 4 CUPS = 2 PINTS = 1 QUART

= 1/4 GALLON

128 FLUID OUNCES = 16 CUPS = 8 PINTS = 4 QUARTS = 1 GALLON

BAKING IN GRAMS

1 CUP FLOUR = 140 GRAMS

1 CUP SUGAR = 150 GRAMS

1 CUP POWDERED SUGAR = 160 GRAMS

1 CUP HEAVY CREAM = 235 GRAMS

VOLUME

1 MILLILITER = 1/5 TEASPOON

5 ML = 1 TEASPOON

15 ML = 1 TABLESPOON

240 ML = 1 CUP OR 8 FLUID OUNCES

1 LITER = 34 FL. OUNCES

WEIGHT

1 GRAM = .035 OUNCES

100 GRAMS = 3.5 OUNCES

500 GRAMS = 1.1 POUNDS

1 KILOGRAM = 35 OUNCES

US TO METRIC COOKING CONVERSIONS

1/5 TSP = 1 ML

1 TSP = 5 ML

1 TBSP = 15 ML

1 FL OUNCE = 30 ML

1 CUP = 237 ML

1 PINT (2 CUPS) = 473 ML

1 QUART (4 CUPS) = .95 LITER

1 GALLON (16 CUPS) = 3.8 LITERS

1 OZ = 28 GRAMS

1 POUND = 454 GRAMS

BUTTER

1 CUP BUTTER = 2 STICKS = 8 OUNCES = 230 GRAMS = 8 TABLESPOONS

WHAT DOES 1 CUP EQUAL

1 CUP = 8 FLUID OUNCES

1 CUP = 16 TABLESPOONS

1 CUP = 48 TEASPOONS

1 CUP = 1/2 PINT

1 CUP = 1/4 QUART

1 CUP = 1/16 GALLON

1 CUP = 240 ML

BAKING PAN CONVERSIONS

1 CUP ALL-PURPOSE FLOUR = 4.5 OZ

1 CUP ROLLED OATS = 3 OZ 1 LARGE EGG = 1.7 OZ

1 CUP BUTTER = 8 OZ 1 CUP MILK = 8 OZ

1 CUP HEAVY CREAM = 8.4 OZ

1 CUP GRANULATED SUGAR = 7.1 OZ

1 CUP PACKED BROWN SUGAR = 7.75 OZ

1 CUP VEGETABLE OIL = 7.7 OZ

1 CUP UNSIFTED POWDERED SUGAR = 4.4 OZ

BAKING PAN CONVERSIONS

9-INCH ROUND CAKE PAN = 12 CUPS

10-INCH TUBE PAN =16 CUPS

11-INCH BUNDT PAN = 12 CUPS

9-INCH SPRINGFORM PAN = 10 CUPS

9 X 5 INCH LOAF PAN = 8 CUPS

9-INCH SQUARE PAN = 8 CUPS

Chapter 2 Appetizers And Snacks Recipes

Chapter 2 Appetizers And Snacks Recipes

Sweet Apple Fries

Servings: 3 | Cooking Time: 8 Minutes

Ingredients:
- 2 Medium-size sweet apple(s), such as Gala or Fuji
- 1 Large egg white(s)
- 2 tablespoons Water
- 1½ cups Finely ground gingersnap crumbs (gluten-free, if a concern)
- Vegetable oil spray

Directions:
1. Preheat the air fryer to 375°F .
2. Peel and core an apple, then cut it into 12 slices. Repeat with more apples as necessary.
3. Whisk the egg white(s) and water in a medium bowl until foamy. Add the apple slices and toss well to coat.
4. Spread the gingersnap crumbs across a dinner plate. Using clean hands, pick up an apple slice, let any excess egg white mixture slip back into the rest, and dredge the slice in the crumbs, coating it lightly but evenly on all sides. Set it aside and continue coating the remaining apple slices.
5. Lightly coat the slices on all sides with vegetable oil spray, then set them curved side down in the basket in one layer. Air-fry undisturbed for 6 minutes, or until browned and crisp. You may need to air-fry the slices for 2 minutes longer if the temperature is at 360°F.
6. Use kitchen tongs to transfer the slices to a wire rack. Cool for 2 to 3 minutes before serving.

Homemade French Fries

Servings: 2 | Cooking Time: 25 Minutes

Ingredients:
- 2 to 3 russet potatoes, peeled and cut into ½-inch sticks
- 2 to 3 teaspoons olive or vegetable oil
- salt

Directions:
1. Bring a large saucepan of salted water to a boil on the stovetop while you peel and cut the potatoes. Blanch the potatoes in the boiling salted water for 4 minutes while you Preheat the air fryer to 400°F. Strain the potatoes and rinse them with cold water. Dry them well with a clean kitchen towel.
2. Toss the dried potato sticks gently with the oil and place them in the air fryer basket. Air-fry for 25 minutes, shaking the basket a few times while the fries cook to help them brown evenly. Season the fries with salt mid-way through cooking and serve them warm with tomato ketchup, Sriracha mayonnaise or a mix of lemon zest, Parmesan cheese and parsley.

Curly's Cauliflower

Servings: 4 | Cooking Time: 30 Minutes

Ingredients:
- 4 cups bite-sized cauliflower florets
- 1 cup friendly bread crumbs, mixed with 1 tsp. salt
- ¼ cup melted butter [vegan/other]
- ¼ cup buffalo sauce [vegan/other]
- Mayo [vegan/other] or creamy dressing for dipping

Directions:
1. In a bowl, combine the butter and buffalo sauce to create a creamy paste.
2. Completely cover each floret with the sauce.
3. Coat the florets with the bread crumb mixture. Cook the florets in the Air Fryer for approximately 15 minutes at 350°F, shaking the basket occasionally.
4. Serve with a raw vegetable salad, mayo or creamy dressing.

Sugar-glazed Walnuts

Servings: 6 | Cooking Time: 5 Minutes

Ingredients:
- 1 Large egg white(s)
- 2 tablespoons Granulated white sugar
- ⅛ teaspoon Table salt
- 2 cups Walnut halves

Directions:
1. Preheat the air fryer to 400°F.
2. Use a whisk to beat the egg white(s) in a large bowl until quite foamy, more so than just well combined but certainly not yet a meringue.
3. If you're working with the quantities for a small batch, remove half of the foamy egg white.
4. If you're working with the quantities for a large batch, remove a quarter of it. It's fine to eyeball the amounts.
5. You can store the removed egg white in a sealed container to save for another use.
6. Stir in the sugar and salt. Add the walnut halves and toss to coat evenly and well, including the nuts' crevasses.
7. When the machine is at temperature, use a slotted spoon to transfer the walnut halves to the basket, taking care not to dislodge any coating. Gently spread the nuts into as close to one layer as you can. Air-fry undisturbed for 2 minutes.
8. Break up any clumps, toss the walnuts gently but well, and air-fry for 3 minutes more, tossing after 1 minute, then every 30 seconds thereafter, until the nuts are browned in spots and very aromatic. Watch carefully so they don't burn.
9. Gently dump the nuts onto a lipped baking sheet and spread them into one layer. Cool for at least 10 minutes before serving, separating any that stick together. The walnuts can be stored in a sealed container at room temperature for up to 5 days.

Spicy Cheese-stuffed Mushrooms

Servings:20 | Cooking Time: 8 Minutes

Ingredients:
- 4 ounces cream cheese, softened
- 6 tablespoons shredded pepper jack cheese
- 2 tablespoons chopped pickled jalapeños
- 20 medium button mushrooms, stems removed
- 2 tablespoons olive oil
- ¼ teaspoon salt
- ⅛ teaspoon ground black pepper

Directions:
1. In a large bowl, mix cream cheese, pepper jack, and jalapeños together.
2. Drizzle mushrooms with olive oil, then sprinkle with salt and pepper. Spoon 2 tablespoons cheese mixture into each mushroom and place in a single layer into ungreased air fryer basket. Adjust the temperature to 370°F and set the timer for 8 minutes, checking halfway through cooking to ensure even cooking, rearranging if some are darker than others. When they're golden and cheese is bubbling, mushrooms will be done. Serve warm.

Bacon-wrapped Mozzarella Sticks

Servings:6 | Cooking Time: 12 Minutes

Ingredients:
- 6 sticks mozzarella string cheese
- 6 slices sugar-free bacon

Directions:
1. Place mozzarella sticks on a medium plate, cover, and place into freezer 1 hour until frozen solid.
2. Wrap each mozzarella stick in 1 piece of bacon and secure with a toothpick. Place into ungreased air fryer basket. Adjust the temperature to 400°F and set the timer for 12 minutes, turning sticks once during cooking. Bacon will be crispy when done. Serve warm.

Bacon-wrapped Goat Cheese Poppers

Servings: 10 | Cooking Time: 10 Minutes

Ingredients:
- 10 large jalapeño peppers
- 8 ounces goat cheese
- 10 slices bacon

Directions:
1. Preheat the air fryer to 380°F.
2. Slice the jalapeños in half. Carefully remove the veins and seeds of the jalapeños with a spoon.
3. Fill each jalapeño half with 2 teaspoons goat cheese.
4. Cut the bacon in half lengthwise to make long strips. Wrap the jalapeños with bacon, trying to cover the entire length of the jalapeño.
5. Place the bacon-wrapped jalapeños into the air fryer basket. Cook the stuffed jalapeños for 10 minutes or until bacon is crispy.

Bacon-wrapped Jalapeño Poppers

Servings:4 | Cooking Time: 12 Minutes

Ingredients:
- 3 ounces full-fat cream cheese
- ½ cup shredded sharp Cheddar cheese
- ¼ teaspoon garlic powder
- 6 jalapeño peppers, trimmed and halved lengthwise, seeded and membranes removed
- 12 slices bacon

Directions:
1. Preheat the air fryer to 400°F.
2. In a large microwave-safe bowl, place cream cheese, Cheddar, and garlic powder. Microwave 20 seconds until softened and stir. Spoon cheese mixture into hollow jalapeño halves.
3. Wrap a bacon slice around each jalapeño half, completely covering pepper.
4. Place in the air fryer basket and cook 12 minutes, turning halfway through cooking time. Serve warm.

Beet Chips

Servings: 4 | Cooking Time: 20 Minutes

Ingredients:
- 2 large red beets, washed and skinned
- 1 tablespoon avocado oil
- ¼ teaspoon salt

Directions:
1. Preheat the air fryer to 330°F.
2. Using a mandolin or sharp knife, slice the beets in ⅛-inch slices. Place them in a bowl of water and let them soak for 30 minutes. Drain the water and pat the beets dry with a paper towel or kitchen cloth.
3. In a medium bowl, toss the beets with avocado oil and sprinkle them with salt.
4. Lightly spray the air fryer basket with olive oil mist and place the beet chips into the basket. To allow for even cooking, don't overlap the beets; cook in batches if necessary.
5. Cook the beet chips 15 to 20 minutes, shaking the basket every 5 minutes, until the outer edges of the beets begin to flip up like a chip. Remove from the basket and serve warm. Repeat with the remaining chips until they're all cooked.

Taquito Quesadillas

Servings: 4 | Cooking Time: 35 Minutes

Ingredients:
- 8 tbsp Mexican blend shredded cheese
- 8 soft corn tortillas
- 2 tsp olive oil
- ¼ cup chopped cilantro

Directions:
1. Preheat air fryer at 350°F. Spread cheese and coriander over 4 tortillas; top each with the remaining tortillas and brush the tops lightly with oil. Place quesadillas in the frying basket and Air Fry for 6 minutes. Serve warm.

Onion Rings

Servings: 4 | Cooking Time: 12 Minutes

Ingredients:
- 1 cup all-purpose flour
- 1 tablespoon seasoned salt
- 1 cup whole milk
- 1 large egg
- 1 cup panko bread crumbs
- 1 large Vidalia onion, peeled and sliced into ¼"-thick rings

Directions:
1. Preheat the air fryer to 350°F.
2. In a large bowl, whisk together flour and seasoned salt.
3. In a medium bowl, whisk together milk and egg. Place bread crumbs in a separate large bowl.
4. Dip onion rings into flour mixture to coat and set them aside. Pour milk mixture into the bowl of flour and stir to combine.
5. Dip onion rings into wet mixture and then press into bread crumbs to coat.
6. Place onion rings in the air fryer basket and spritz with cooking spray. Cook 12 minutes until the edges are crispy and golden. Serve warm.

Potato Chips

Servings: 2 | Cooking Time: 15 Minutes

Ingredients:
- 2 medium potatoes
- 2 teaspoons extra-light olive oil
- oil for misting or cooking spray
- salt and pepper

Directions:
1. Peel the potatoes.
2. Using a mandoline or paring knife, shave potatoes into thin slices, dropping them into a bowl of water as you cut them.
3. Dry potatoes as thoroughly as possible with paper towels or a clean dish towel. Toss potato slices with the oil to coat completely.
4. Spray air fryer basket with cooking spray and add potato slices.
5. Stir and separate with a fork.
6. Cook 390°F for 5minutes. Stir and separate potato slices. Cook 5 more minutes. Stir and separate potatoes again. Cook another 5 minutes.
7. Season to taste.

Sweet Chili Peanuts

Servings: 6 | Cooking Time: 5 Minutes

Ingredients:
- 2 cups Shelled raw peanuts
- 2 tablespoons Granulated white sugar
- 2 teaspoons Hot red pepper sauce, such as Cholula or Tabasco (gluten-free, if a concern)

Directions:
1. Preheat the air fryer to 400°F.
2. Toss the peanuts, sugar, and hot pepper sauce in a bowl until the peanuts are well coated.
3. When the machine is at temperature, pour the peanuts into the basket, spreading them into one layer as much as you can. Air-fry undisturbed for 3 minutes.
4. Shake the basket to rearrange the peanuts. Continue air-frying for 2 minutes more, shaking and stirring the peanuts every 30 sec-onds, until golden brown.
5. Pour the peanuts onto a large lipped baking sheet. Spread them into one layer and cool for 5 minutes before serving.

Homemade Pretzel Bites

Servings: 8 | Cooking Time: 6 Minutes

Ingredients:
- 4¾ cups filtered water, divided
- 1 tablespoon butter
- 1 package fast-rising yeast
- ½ teaspoon salt
- 2⅓ cups bread flour
- 2 tablespoons baking soda
- 2 egg whites
- 1 teaspoon kosher salt

Directions:
1. Preheat the air fryer to 370°F.
2. In a large microwave-safe bowl, add ¾ cup of the water. Heat for 40 seconds in the microwave. Remove and whisk in the butter; then mix in the yeast and salt. Let sit 5 minutes.
3. Using a stand mixer with a dough hook attachment, add the yeast liquid and mix in the bread flour ⅓ cup at a time until all the flour is added and a dough is formed.
4. Remove the bowl from the stand; then let the dough rise 1 hour in a warm space, covered with a kitchen towel.
5. After the dough has doubled in size, remove from the bowl and punch down a few times on a lightly floured flat surface.
6. Divide the dough into 4 balls; then roll each ball out into a long, skinny, sticklike shape. Using a sharp knife, cut each dough stick into 6 pieces.
7. Repeat Step 6 for the remaining dough balls until you have about 24 bites formed.
8. Heat the remaining 4 cups of water over the stovetop in a medium pot with the baking soda stirred in.
9. Drop the pretzel bite dough into the hot water and let boil for 60 seconds, remove, and let slightly cool.
10. Lightly brush the top of each bite with the egg whites, and then cover with a pinch of kosher salt.
11. Spray the air fryer basket with olive oil spray and place the pretzel bites on top. Cook for 6 to 8 minutes, or until lightly browned. Remove and keep warm.
12. Repeat until all pretzel bites are cooked.
13. Serve warm.

Okra Chips

Servings: 4 | Cooking Time: 16 Minutes

Ingredients:
- 1¼ pounds Thin fresh okra pods, cut into 1-inch pieces
- 1½ tablespoons Vegetable or canola oil
- ¾ teaspoon Coarse sea salt or kosher salt

Directions:
1. Preheat the air fryer to 400°F.
2. Toss the okra, oil, and salt in a large bowl until the pieces are well and evenly coated.
3. When the machine is at temperature, pour the contents of the bowl into the basket. Air-fry, tossing several times, for 16 minutes, or until crisp and quite brown.
4. Pour the contents of the basket onto a wire rack. Cool for a couple of minutes before serving.

Wrapped Shrimp Bites

Servings: 4 | Cooking Time: 15 Minutes

Ingredients:
- 2 jumbo shrimp, peeled
- 2 bacon strips, sliced
- 2 tbsp lemon juice
- ½ tsp chipotle powder
- ½ tsp garlic salt

Directions:
1. Preheat air fryer to 350°F. Wrap the bacon around the shrimp and place the shrimp in the foil-lined frying basket, seam side down. Drizzle with lemon juice, chipotle powder and garlic salt. Air Fry for 10 minutes, turning the shrimp once until cooked through and bacon is crispy. Serve hot.

Fried Ranch Pickles

Servings:4 | Cooking Time: 10 Minutes

Ingredients:
- 4 dill pickle spears, halved lengthwise
- ¼ cup ranch dressing
- ½ cup blanched finely ground almond flour
- ½ cup grated Parmesan cheese
- 2 tablespoons dry ranch seasoning

Directions:
1. Wrap spears in a kitchen towel 30 minutes to soak up excess pickle juice.
2. Pour ranch dressing into a medium bowl and add pickle spears. In a separate medium bowl, mix flour, Parmesan, and ranch seasoning.
3. Remove each spear from ranch dressing and shake off excess. Press gently into dry mixture to coat all sides. Place spears into ungreased air fryer basket. Adjust the temperature to 400°F and set the timer for 10 minutes, turning spears three times during cooking. Serve warm.

Crispy Tofu Bites

Servings: 4 | Cooking Time: 20 Minutes

Ingredients:
- 1 pound Extra firm unflavored tofu
- Vegetable oil spray

Directions:
1. Wrap the piece of tofu in a triple layer of paper towels. Place it on a wooden cutting board and set a large pot on top of it to press out excess moisture. Set aside for 10 minutes.
2. Preheat the air fryer to 400°F.
3. Remove the pot and unwrap the tofu. Cut it into 1-inch cubes. Place these in a bowl and coat them generously with vegetable oil spray. Toss gently, then spray generously again before tossing, until all are glistening.
4. Gently pour the tofu pieces into the basket, spread them into as close to one layer as possible, and air-fry for 20 minutes, using kitchen tongs to gently rearrange the pieces at the 7- and 14-minute marks, until light brown and crisp.
5. Gently pour the tofu pieces onto a wire rack. Cool for 5 minutes before serving warm.

Cheesy Tortellini Bites

Servings: 8 | Cooking Time: 10 Minutes

Ingredients:
- 1 large egg
- ½ teaspoon black pepper
- ½ teaspoon garlic powder
- 1 teaspoon Italian seasoning
- 12 ounces frozen cheese tortellini
- ½ cup panko breadcrumbs

Directions:
1. Preheat the air fryer to 380°F.
2. Spray the air fryer basket with an olive-oil-based spray.
3. In a medium bowl, whisk the egg with the pepper, garlic powder, and Italian seasoning.
4. Dip the tortellini in the egg batter and then coat with the breadcrumbs. Place each tortellini in the basket, trying not to overlap them. You may need to cook in batches to ensure the even crisp all around.
5. Bake for 5 minutes, shake the basket, and bake another 5 minutes.
6. Remove and let cool 5 minutes. Serve with marinara sauce, ranch, or your favorite dressing.

Bacon Butter

Servings:5 | Cooking Time: 2 Minutes

Ingredients:
- ½ cup butter
- 3 oz bacon, chopped

Directions:
1. Preheat the air fryer to 400°F and put the bacon inside. Cook it for 8 minutes. Stir the bacon every 2 minutes. Meanwhile, soften the butter in the oven and put it in the butter mold. Add cooked bacon and churn the butter. Refrigerate the butter for 30 minutes.

Plantain Chips

Servings: 2 | Cooking Time: 14 Minutes

Ingredients:
- 1 large green plantain
- 2½ cups filtered water, divided
- 2 teaspoons sea salt, divided
- Cooking spray

Directions:
1. Slice the plantain into 1-inch pieces. Place the plantains into a large bowl, cover with 2 cups water and 1 teaspoon salt. Soak the plantains for 30 minutes; then remove and pat dry.
2. Preheat the air fryer to 390°F.
3. Place the plantain pieces into the air fryer basket, leaving space between the plantain rounds. Cook the plantains for 5 minutes, and carefully remove them from the air fryer basket.
4. Add the remaining water to a small bowl.
5. Using a small drinking glass, dip the bottom of the glass into the water and mash the warm plantains until they're ¼-inch thick. Return the plantains to the air fryer basket, sprinkle with the remaining sea salt, and spray lightly with cooking spray.
6. Cook for another 6 to 8 minutes, or until lightly golden brown edges appear.

Italian Dip

Servings:8 | Cooking Time: 12 Minutes

Ingredients:
- 8 oz cream cheese, softened
- 1 cup mozzarella cheese, shredded
- 1/2 cup roasted red peppers
- 1/3 cup basil pesto
- 1/4 cup parmesan cheese, grated

Directions:
1. Add parmesan cheese and cream cheese into the food processor and process until smooth.
2. Transfer cheese mixture into the air fryer pan and spread evenly.
3. Pour basil pesto on top of cheese layer.
4. Sprinkle roasted pepper on top of basil pesto layer.
5. Sprinkle mozzarella cheese on top of pepper layer and place dish in air fryer basket.
6. Cook dip at 250°F for 12 minutes.
7. Serve and enjoy.

Skinny Fries

Servings: 2 | Cooking Time: 15 Minutes

Ingredients:
- 2 to 3 russet potatoes, peeled and cut into ¼-inch sticks
- 2 to 3 teaspoons olive or vegetable oil
- salt

Directions:
1. Cut the potatoes into ¼-inch strips. Rinse the potatoes with cold water several times and let them soak in cold water for at least 10 minutes or as long as overnight.
2. Preheat the air fryer to 380°F.
3. Drain and dry the potato sticks really well, using a clean kitchen towel. Toss the fries with the oil in a bowl and then air-fry the fries in two batches at 380°F for 15 minutes, shaking the basket a couple of times while they cook.
4. Add the first batch of French fries back into the air fryer basket with the finishing batch and let everything warm through for a few minutes. As soon as the fries are done, season them with salt and transfer to a plate or basket. Serve them warm with ketchup or your favorite dip.

Root Vegetable Crisps

Servings: 4 | Cooking Time: 8 Minutes

Ingredients:
- 1 small taro root, peeled and washed
- 1 small yucca root, peeled and washed
- 1 small purple sweet potato, washed
- 2 cups filtered water
- 2 teaspoons extra-virgin olive oil
- ½ teaspoon salt

Directions:
1. Using a mandolin, slice the taro root, yucca root, and purple sweet potato into ⅛-inch slices.
2. Add the water to a large bowl. Add the sliced vegetables and soak for at least 30 minutes.
3. Preheat the air fryer to 370°F.
4. Drain the water and pat the vegetables dry with a paper towel or kitchen cloth. Toss the vegetables with the olive oil and sprinkle with salt. Liberally spray the air fryer basket with olive oil mist.
5. Place the vegetables into the air fryer basket, making sure not to overlap the pieces.
6. Cook for 8 minutes, shaking the basket every 2 minutes, until the outer edges start to turn up and the vegetables start to brown. Remove from the basket and serve warm. Repeat with the remaining vegetable slices until all are cooked.

Parmesan Pizza Nuggets

Servings: 8 | Cooking Time: 6 Minutes

Ingredients:
- ¾ cup warm filtered water
- 1 package fast-rising yeast
- ½ teaspoon salt
- 2 cups all-purpose flour
- ¼ cup finely grated Parmesan cheese
- 1 teaspoon Italian seasoning
- 2 tablespoon extra-virgin olive oil
- 1 teaspoon kosher salt

Directions:
1. Preheat the air fryer to 370°F.
2. In a large microwave-safe bowl, add the water. Heat for 40 seconds in the microwave. Remove and mix in the yeast and salt. Let sit 5 minutes.
3. Meanwhile, in a medium bowl, mix the flour with the Parmesan cheese and Italian seasoning. Set aside.
4. Using a stand mixer with a dough hook attachment, add the yeast liquid and then mix in the flour mixture ⅓ cup at a time until all the flour mixture is added and a dough is formed.
5. Remove the bowl from the stand, and then let the dough rise for 1 hour in a warm space, covered with a kitchen towel.
6. After the dough has doubled in size, remove it from the bowl and punch it down a few times on a lightly floured flat surface.
7. Divide the dough into 4 balls, and then roll each ball out into a long, skinny, sticklike shape.
8. Using a sharp knife, cut each dough stick into 6 pieces. Repeat for the remaining dough balls until you have about 24 nuggets formed.
9. Lightly brush the top of each bite with the egg whites and cover with a pinch of sea salt.
10. Spray the air fryer basket with olive oil spray and place the pizza nuggets on top. Cook for 6 minutes, or until lightly browned. Remove and keep warm.
11. Repeat until all the nuggets are cooked.
12. Serve warm.

Bacon-wrapped Cabbage Bites

Servings:6 | Cooking Time: 12 Minutes

Ingredients:
- 3 tablespoons sriracha hot chili sauce, divided
- 1 medium head cabbage, cored and cut into 12 bite-sized pieces
- 2 tablespoons coconut oil, melted
- ½ teaspoon salt
- 12 slices sugar-free bacon
- ½ cup mayonnaise
- ¼ teaspoon garlic powder

Directions:
1. Evenly brush 2 tablespoons sriracha onto cabbage pieces. Drizzle evenly with coconut oil, then sprinkle with salt.
2. Wrap each cabbage piece with bacon and secure with a toothpick. Place into ungreased air fryer basket. Adjust the temperature to 375°F and set the timer for 12 minutes, turning cabbage

halfway through cooking. Bacon will be cooked and crispy when done.

3. In a small bowl, whisk together mayonnaise, garlic powder, and remaining sriracha. Use as a dipping sauce for cabbage bites.

Fried Goat Cheese

Servings: 3 | Cooking Time: 4 Minutes

Ingredients:
• 7 ounces 1- to 1½-inch-diameter goat cheese log
• 2 Large egg(s)
• 1¾ cups Plain dried bread crumbs (gluten-free, if a concern)
• Vegetable oil spray

Directions:
1. Slice the goat cheese log into ½-inch-thick rounds. Set these flat on a small cutting board, a small baking sheet, or a large plate. Freeze uncovered for 30 minutes.
2. Preheat the air fryer to 400°F.
3. Set up and fill two shallow soup plates or small pie plates on your counter: one in which you whisk the egg(s) until uniform and the other for the bread crumbs.
4. Take the goat cheese rounds out of the freezer. With clean, dry hands, dip one round in the egg(s) to coat it on all sides. Let the excess egg slip back into the rest, then dredge the round in the bread crumbs, turning it to coat all sides, even the edges. Repeat this process—egg, then bread crumbs—for a second coating. Coat both sides of the round and its edges with vegetable oil spray, then set it aside. Continue double-dipping, double-dredging, and spraying the remaining rounds.
5. Place the rounds in one layer in the basket. Air-fry undisturbed for 4 minutes, or until lightly browned and crunchy. Do not overcook. Some of the goat cheese may break through the crust. A few little breaks are fine but stop the cooking before the coating reaches structural failure.
6. Remove the basket from the machine and set aside for 3 minutes. Use a nonstick-safe spatula, and maybe a flatware fork for balance, to transfer the rounds to a wire rack. Cool for 5 minutes more before serving.

Sweet Plantain Chips

Servings: 4 | Cooking Time: 11 Minutes

Ingredients:
• 2 Very ripe plantain(s), peeled and sliced into 1-inch pieces
• Vegetable oil spray
• 3 tablespoons Maple syrup
• For garnishing Coarse sea salt or kosher salt

Directions:
1. Pour about ½ cup water into the bottom of your air fryer basket or into a metal tray on a lower rack in some models. Preheat the air fryer to 400°F.
2. Put the plantain pieces in a bowl, coat them with vegetable oil spray, and toss gently, spraying at least one more time and tossing repeatedly, until the pieces are well coated.
3. When the machine is at temperature, arrange the plantain pieces in the basket in one layer. Air-fry undisturbed for 5 minutes.
4. Remove the basket from the machine and spray the back of a metal spatula with vegetable oil spray. Use the spatula to press down on the plantain pieces, spraying it again as needed, to flatten the pieces to about half their original height. Brush the plantain pieces with maple syrup, then return the basket to the machine and continue air-frying undisturbed for 6 minutes, or until the plantain pieces are soft and caramelized.

5. Use kitchen tongs to transfer the pieces to a serving platter. Sprinkle the pieces with salt and cool for a couple of minutes before serving. Or cool to room temperature before serving, about 1 hour.

Grilled Cheese Sandwiches

Servings:2 | Cooking Time:5 Minutes

Ingredients:
• 4 white bread slices
• ½ cup melted butter, softened
• ½ cup sharp cheddar cheese, grated
• 1 tablespoon mayonnaise

Directions:
1. Preheat the Air fryer to 355°F and grease an Air fryer basket.
2. Spread the mayonnaise and melted butter over one side of each bread slice.
3. Sprinkle the cheddar cheese over the buttered side of the 2 slices.
4. Cover with the remaining slices of bread and transfer into the Air fryer basket.
5. Cook for about 5 minutes and dish out to serve warm.

Korean-style Wings

Servings: 4 | Cooking Time: 10 Minutes

Ingredients:
• 1 pound chicken wings, drums and flats separated
• ½ teaspoon salt
• ¼ teaspoon ground black pepper
• ¼ cup gochujang sauce
• 2 tablespoons soy sauce
• 1 teaspoon ground ginger
• ¼ cup mayonnaise

Directions:
1. Preheat the air fryer to 350°F.
2. Sprinkle wings with salt and pepper. Place wings in the air fryer basket and cook 15 minutes, turning halfway through cooking time.
3. In a medium bowl, mix gochujang sauce, soy sauce, ginger, and mayonnaise.
4. Toss wings in sauce mixture and adjust the air fryer temperature to 400°F.
5. Place wings back in the air fryer basket and cook an additional 5 minutes until the internal temperature reaches at least 165°F. Serve warm.

Ham And Cheese Sliders

Servings:3 | Cooking Time: 10 Minutes

Ingredients:
• 6 Hawaiian sweet rolls
• 12 slices thinly sliced Black Forest ham
• 6 slices sharp Cheddar cheese
• ⅓ cup salted butter, melted
• 1 ½ teaspoons minced garlic

Directions:
1. Preheat the air fryer to 350°F.
2. For each slider, slice horizontally through the center of a roll without fully separating the two halves. Place 2 slices ham and 2 slices cheese inside roll and close. Repeat with remaining rolls, ham, and cheese.
3. In a small bowl, mix butter and garlic and brush over all sides

of rolls.

4. Place in the air fryer and cook 10 minutes until rolls are golden on top and cheese is melted. Serve warm.

Crispy Curried Sweet Potato Fries

Servings: 4 | Cooking Time: 20 Minutes

Ingredients:
- ½ cup sour cream
- ½ cup peach chutney
- 3 tsp curry powder
- 2 sweet potatoes, julienned
- 1 tbsp olive oil
- Salt and pepper to taste

Directions:
1. Preheat air fryer to 390°F. Mix together sour cream, peach chutney, and 1 ½ tsp curry powder in a small bowl. Set aside. In a medium bowl, add sweet potatoes, olive oil, the rest of the curry powder, salt, and pepper. Toss to coat. Place the potatoes in the frying basket. Bake for about 6 minutes, then shake the basket once. Cook for an additional 4 -6 minutes or until the potatoes are golden and crispy. Serve the fries hot in a basket along with the chutney sauce for dipping.

Asian Five-spice Wings

Servings: 4 | Cooking Time: 15 Minutes

Ingredients:
- 2 pounds chicken wings
- ½ cup Asian-style salad dressing
- 2 tablespoons Chinese five-spice powder

Directions:
1. Cut off wing tips and discard or freeze for stock. Cut remaining wing pieces in two at the joint.
2. Place wing pieces in a large sealable plastic bag. Pour in the Asian dressing, seal bag, and massage the marinade into the wings until well coated. Refrigerate for at least an hour.
3. Remove wings from bag, drain off excess marinade, and place wings in air fryer basket.
4. Cook at 360°F for 15minutes or until juices run clear. About halfway through cooking time, shake the basket or stir wings for more even cooking.
5. Transfer cooked wings to plate in a single layer. Sprinkle half of the Chinese five-spice powder on the wings, turn, and sprinkle other side with remaining seasoning.

Zucchini Chips

Servings: 3 | Cooking Time: 17 Minutes

Ingredients:
- 1½ small Zucchini, washed but not peeled, and cut into ¼-inch-thick rounds
- Olive oil spray
- ¼ teaspoon Table salt

Directions:
1. Preheat the air fryer to 375°F.
2. Lay some paper towels on your work surface. Set the zucchini rounds on top, then set more paper towels over the rounds. Press gently to remove some of the moisture. Remove the top layer of paper towels and lightly coat the rounds with olive oil spray on both sides.
3. When the machine is at temperature, set the rounds in the basket, overlapping them a bit as needed. Air-fry for 15 minutes,

tossing and rearranging the rounds at the 5- and 10-minute marks, until browned, soft, yet crisp at the edges.

4. Gently pour the contents of the basket onto a wire rack. Cool for at least 10 minutes or up to 2 hours before serving.

Sausage-stuffed Mushrooms

Servings:6 | Cooking Time: 20 Minutes

Ingredients:
- ½ pound ground pork sausage
- ¼ teaspoon salt
- ¼ teaspoon garlic powder
- 2 medium scallions, trimmed and chopped
- ½ ounce plain pork rinds, finely crushed
- 1 pound cremini mushrooms, stems removed

Directions:
1. In a large bowl, mix sausage, salt, garlic powder, scallions, and pork rinds. Scoop 1 tablespoon mixture into center of each mushroom cap.
2. Place mushrooms into ungreased air fryer basket. Adjust the temperature to 375°F and set the timer for 20 minutes. Pork will be fully cooked to at least 145°F in the center and browned when done. Serve warm.

Baba Ghanouj

Servings: 2 | Cooking Time: 40 Minutes

Ingredients:
- 2 Small purple Italian eggplant(s)
- ¼ cup Olive oil
- ¼ cup Tahini
- ½ teaspoon Ground black pepper
- ¼ teaspoon Onion powder
- ¼ teaspoon Mild smoked paprika (optional)
- Up to 1 teaspoon Table salt

Directions:
1. Preheat the air fryer to 400°F.
2. Prick the eggplant(s) on all sides with a fork. When the machine is at temperature, set the eggplant(s) in the basket in one layer. Air-fry undisturbed for 40 minutes, or until blackened and soft.
3. Remove the basket from the machine. Cool the eggplant(s) in the basket for 20 minutes.
4. Use a nonstick-safe spatula, and perhaps a flatware tablespoon for balance, to gently transfer the eggplant(s) to a bowl. The juices will run out. Make sure the bowl is close to the basket. Split the eggplant(s) open.
5. Scrape the soft insides of half an eggplant into a food processor. Repeat with the remaining piece(s). Add any juices from the bowl to the eggplant in the food processor, but discard the skins and stems.
6. Add the olive oil, tahini, pepper, onion powder, and smoked paprika. Add about half the salt, then cover and process until smooth, stopping the machine at least once to scrape down the inside of the canister. Check the spread for salt and add more as needed. Scrape the baba ghanouj into a bowl and serve warm, or set aside at room temperature for up to 2 hours, or cover and store in the refrigerator for up to 4 days.

Thyme Sweet Potato Chips

Servings: 2 | Cooking Time: 20 Minutes

Ingredients:
• 1 tbsp olive oil
• 1 sweet potato, sliced
• ¼ tsp dried thyme
• Salt to taste

Directions:
1. Preheat air fryer to 390°F. Spread the sweet potato slices in the greased basket and brush with olive oil. Air Fry for 6 minutes. Remove the basket, shake, and sprinkle with thyme and salt. Cook for 6 more minutes or until lightly browned. Serve warm and enjoy!

Fiery Bacon-wrapped Dates

Servings: 16 | Cooking Time: 6 Minutes

Ingredients:
• 8 Thin-cut bacon strips, halved widthwise (gluten-free, if a concern)
• 16 Medium or large Medjool dates, pitted
• 3 tablespoons (about ¾ ounce) Shredded semi-firm mozzarella
• 32 Pickled jalapeño rings

Directions:
1. Preheat the air fryer to 400°F.
2. Lay a bacon strip half on a clean, dry work surface. Split one date lengthwise without cutting through it, so that it opens like a pocket. Set it on one end of the bacon strip and open it a bit. Place 1 teaspoon of the shredded cheese and 2 pickled jalapeño rings in the date, then gently squeeze it together without fully closing it. Roll up the date in the bacon strip and set it bacon seam side down on a cutting board. Repeat this process with the remaining bacon strip halves, dates, cheese, and jalapeño rings.
3. Place the bacon-wrapped dates bacon seam side down in the basket. Air-fry undisturbed for 6 minutes, or until crisp and brown.
4. Use kitchen tongs to gently transfer the wrapped dates to a wire rack or serving platter. Cool for a few minutes before serving.

Bacon Wrapped Onion Rings

Servings: 2 | Cooking Time: 30 Minutes

Ingredients:
• 1 onion, cut into 1/2-inch slices
• 1 teaspoon curry powder
• 1 teaspoon cayenne pepper
• Salt and ground black pepper, to your liking
• 8 strips bacon
• 1/4 cup spicy ketchup

Directions:
1. Place the onion rings in the bowl with cold water; let them soak approximately 20 minutes; drain the onion rings and pat dry using a kitchen towel.
2. Sprinkle curry powder, cayenne pepper, salt, and black pepper over onion rings.
3. Wrap one layer of bacon around onion, trimming any excess. Secure the rings with toothpicks.
4. Spritz the Air Fryer basket with cooking spray; arrange the breaded onion rings in the Air Fryer basket.
5. Cook in the preheated Air Fryer at 360 °F for 15 minutes, turning them over halfway through the cooking time. Serve with spicy

ketchup. Bon appétit!

Cauliflower Buns

Servings:8 | Cooking Time: 12 Minutes

Ingredients:
• 1 steamer bag cauliflower, cooked according to package instructions
• ½ cup shredded mozzarella cheese
• ¼ cup shredded mild Cheddar cheese
• ¼ cup blanched finely ground almond flour
• 1 large egg
• ½ teaspoon salt

Directions:
1. Let cooked cauliflower cool about 10 minutes. Use a kitchen towel to wring out excess moisture, then place cauliflower in a food processor.
2. Add mozzarella, Cheddar, flour, egg, and salt to the food processor and pulse twenty times until mixture is combined. It will resemble a soft, wet dough.
3. Divide mixture into eight piles. Wet your hands with water to prevent sticking, then press each pile into a flat bun shape, about ½" thick.
4. Cut a sheet of parchment to fit air fryer basket. Working in batches if needed, place the formed dough onto ungreased parchment in air fryer basket. Adjust the temperature to 350°F and set the timer for 12 minutes, turning buns halfway through cooking.
5. Let buns cool 10 minutes before serving. Serve warm.

Home-style Taro Chips

Servings: 2 | Cooking Time: 20 Minutes

Ingredients:
• 1 tbsp olive oil
• 1 cup thinly sliced taro
• Salt to taste
• ½ cup hummus

Directions:
1. Preheat air fryer to 325°F. Put the sliced taro in the greased frying basket, spread the pieces out, and drizzle with olive oil. Air Fry for 10-12 minutes, shaking the basket twice. Sprinkle with salt and serve with hummus.

Crispy Deviled Eggs

Servings:12 | Cooking Time: 25 Minutes

Ingredients:
• 7 large eggs, divided
• 1 ounce plain pork rinds, finely crushed
• 2 tablespoons mayonnaise
• ¼ teaspoon salt
• ¼ teaspoon ground black pepper

Directions:
1. Place 6 whole eggs into ungreased air fryer basket. Adjust the temperature to 220°F and set the timer for 20 minutes. When done, place eggs into a bowl of ice water to cool 5 minutes.
2. Peel cool eggs, then cut in half lengthwise. Remove yolks and place aside in a medium bowl.
3. In a separate small bowl, whisk remaining raw egg. Place pork rinds in a separate medium bowl. Dip each egg white into whisked egg, then gently coat with pork rinds. Spritz with cooking spray and place into ungreased air fryer basket. Adjust the temperature to 400°F and set the timer for 5 minutes, turning eggs

halfway through cooking. Eggs will be golden when done.

4. Mash yolks in bowl with mayonnaise until smooth. Sprinkle with salt and pepper and mix.

5. Spoon 2 tablespoons yolk mixture into each fried egg white. Serve warm.

Fried Dill Pickle Chips

Servings: 4 | Cooking Time: 12 Minutes

Ingredients:
- 1 cup All-purpose flour or tapioca flour
- 1 Large egg white(s)
- 1 tablespoon Brine from a jar of dill pickles
- 1 cup Seasoned Italian-style dried bread crumbs (gluten-free, if a concern)
- 2 Large dill pickle(s), cut into ½-inch-thick rounds
- Vegetable oil spray

Directions:
1. Preheat the air fryer to 400°F.
2. Set up and fill three shallow soup plates or small pie plates on your counter: one for the flour, one for the egg white(s) whisked with the pickle brine, and one for the bread crumbs.
3. Set a pickle round in the flour and turn it to coat all sides, even the edge. Gently shake off the excess flour, then dip the round into the egg-white mixture and turn to coat both sides and the edge. Let any excess egg white mixture slip back into the rest, then set the round in the bread crumbs and turn it to coat both sides as well as the edge. Set aside on a cutting board and soldier on, dipping and coating the remaining rounds. Lightly coat the coated rounds on both sides with vegetable oil spray.
4. Set the pickle rounds in the basket in one layer. Air-fry undisturbed for 7 minutes, or until golden brown and crunchy. Cool in the basket for a few minutes before using kitchen tongs to transfer the rounds to a serving platter.

Croutons

Servings:4 | Cooking Time: 5 Minutes

Ingredients:
- 4 slices sourdough bread, diced into small cubes
- 2 tablespoons salted butter, melted
- 1 teaspoon chopped fresh parsley
- 2 tablespoons grated Parmesan cheese

Directions:
1. Preheat the air fryer to 400°F.
2. Place bread cubes in a large bowl.
3. Pour butter over bread cubes. Add parsley and Parmesan. Toss bread cubes until evenly coated.
4. Place bread cubes in the air fryer basket in a single layer. Cook 5 minutes until well toasted. Serve cooled for maximum crunch.

Sausage And Cheese Rolls

Servings: 3 | Cooking Time: 18 Minutes

Ingredients:
- 3 3- to 3½-ounce sweet or hot Italian sausage links
- 2 1-ounce string cheese stick(s), unwrapped and cut in half lengthwise
- Three quarters from one thawed sheet A 17.25-ounce box frozen puff pastry

Directions:
1. Preheat the air fryer to 400°F.
2. When the machine is at temperature, set the sausage links in the basket and air-fry undisturbed for 12 minutes, or until cooked through.
3. Use kitchen tongs to transfer the links to a wire rack. Cool for 15 minutes.
4. Cut the sausage links in half lengthwise. Sandwich half a string cheese stick between two sausage halves, trimming the ends so the cheese doesn't stick out beyond the meat.
5. Roll each piece of puff pastry into a 6 x 6-inch square on a clean, dry work surface. Set the sausage-cheese sandwich at one edge and roll it up in the dough. The ends will be open like a pig-in-a-blanket. Repeat with the remaining puff pastry, sausage, and cheese.
6. Set the rolls seam side down in the basket. Air-fry undisturbed for 6 minutes, or until puffed and golden brown.
7. Use a nonstick-safe spatula, and perhaps a flatware fork for balance, to transfer the rolls to a wire rack. Cool for at least 5 minutes before serving.

Amazing Blooming Onion

Servings: 4 | Cooking Time: 40 Minutes

Ingredients:
- 4 medium/small onions
- 1 tbsp. olive oil
- 4 dollops of butter

Directions:
1. Peel the onion. Cut off the top and bottom.
2. To make it bloom, cut as deeply as possible without slicing through it completely. 4 cuts should do it.
3. Place the onions in a bowl of salted water and allow to absorb for 4 hours to help eliminate the sharp taste and induce the blooming process.
4. Pre-heat your Air Fryer to 355°F.
5. Transfer the onions to the Air Fryer. Pour over a light drizzle of olive oil and place a dollop of butter on top of each onion.
6. Cook or roast for 30 minutes. Remove the outer layer before serving if it is too brown.

Basil Pork Bites

Servings: 6 | Cooking Time: 25 Minutes

Ingredients:
- 2 pounds pork belly, cut into strips
- 2 tablespoons olive oil
- 2 teaspoons fennel seeds
- A pinch of salt and black pepper
- A pinch of basil, dried

Directions:
1. In a bowl, mix all the ingredients, toss and put the pork strips in your air fryer's basket and cook at 425°F for 25 minutes. Divide into bowls and serve as a snack.

Roasted Red Salsa

Servings: 4 | Cooking Time: 10 Minutes

Ingredients:
- 10 medium Roma tomatoes, quartered
- 1 medium white onion, peeled and sliced
- 2 medium cloves garlic, peeled
- 2 tablespoons olive oil
- ¼ cup chopped fresh cilantro
- ½ teaspoon salt

Directions:
1. Preheat the air fryer to 340°F.
2. Place tomatoes, onion, and garlic into a 6" round baking dish. Drizzle with oil and toss to coat.
3. Place in the air fryer basket and cook 10 minutes, stirring twice during cooking, until vegetables start to turn dark brown and caramelize.
4. In a food processor, add roasted vegetables, cilantro, and salt. Pulse five times until vegetables are mostly broken down. Serve immediately.

Avocado Fries

Servings: 4 | Cooking Time: 20 Minutes

Ingredients:
- ½ cup panko
- ½ tsp. salt
- 1 whole avocado
- 1 oz. aquafaba

Directions:
1. In a shallow bowl, stir together the panko and salt.
2. In a separate shallow bowl, add the aquafaba.
3. Dip the avocado slices into the aquafaba, before coating each one in the panko.
4. Place the slices in your Air Fryer basket, taking care not to overlap any. Air fry for 10 minutes at 390°F.

Cheese Wafers

Servings: 4 | Cooking Time: 6 Minutes Per Batch

Ingredients:
- 4 ounces sharp Cheddar cheese, grated
- ¼ cup butter
- ½ cup flour
- ¼ teaspoon salt
- ½ cup crisp rice cereal
- oil for misting or cooking spray

Directions:
1. Cream the butter and grated cheese together. You can do it by hand, but using a stand mixer is faster and easier.
2. Sift flour and salt together. Add it to the cheese mixture and mix until well blended.
3. Stir in cereal.
4. Place dough on wax paper and shape into a long roll about 1 inch in diameter. Wrap well with the wax paper and chill for at least 4 hours.
5. When ready to cook, preheat air fryer to 360°F.
6. Cut cheese roll into ¼-inch slices.
7. Spray air fryer basket with oil or cooking spray and place slices in a single layer, close but not touching.
8. Cook for 6minutes or until golden brown. When done, place them on paper towels to cool.
9. Repeat previous step to cook remaining cheese bites.

Chili Kale Chips

Servings:4 | Cooking Time: 5 Minutes

Ingredients:
- 1 teaspoon nutritional yeast
- 1 teaspoon salt
- 2 cups kale, chopped
- ½ teaspoon chili flakes
- 1 teaspoon sesame oil

Directions:
1. Mix up kale leaves with nutritional yeast, salt, chili flakes, and sesame oil. Shake the greens well. Preheat the air fryer to 400°F and put the kale leaves in the air fryer basket. Cook them for 3 minutes and then give a good shake. Cook the kale leaves for 2 minutes more.

Bacon Candy

Servings: 6 | Cooking Time: 6 Minutes

Ingredients:
- 1½ tablespoons Honey
- 1 teaspoon White wine vinegar
- 3 Extra thick–cut bacon strips, halved widthwise (gluten-free, if a concern)
- ½ teaspoon Ground black pepper

Directions:
1. Preheat the air fryer to 350°F .
2. Whisk the honey and vinegar in a small bowl until incorporated.
3. When the machine is at temperature, remove the basket. Lay the bacon strip halves in the basket in one layer. Brush the tops with the honey mixture; sprinkle each bacon strip evenly with black pepper.
4. Return the basket to the machine and air-fry undisturbed for 6 minutes, or until the bacon is crunchy. Or a little less time if you prefer bacon that's still pliable, an extra minute if you want the bacon super crunchy. Take care that the honey coating doesn't burn. Remove the basket from the machine and set aside for 5 minutes. Use kitchen tongs to transfer the bacon strips to a serving plate.

Tortilla Chips

Servings: 4 | Cooking Time: 5 Minutes

Ingredients:
- 8 white corn tortillas
- ¼ cup olive oil
- 2 tablespoons lime juice
- ½ teaspoon salt

Directions:
1. Preheat the air fryer to 350°F.
2. Cut each tortilla into fourths and brush lightly with oil.
3. Place chips in a single layer in the air fryer basket, working in batches as necessary. Cook 5 minutes, shaking the basket halfway through cooking time.
4. Sprinkle with lime juice and salt. Serve warm.

Halloumi Fries

Servings: 3 | Cooking Time: 12 Minutes

Ingredients:
- 1½ tablespoons Olive oil
- 1½ teaspoons Minced garlic
- ⅛ teaspoon Dried oregano
- ⅛ teaspoon Dried thyme
- ⅛ teaspoon Table salt
- ⅛ teaspoon Ground black pepper
- ¾ pound Halloumi

Directions:
1. Preheat the air fryer to 400°F.
2. Whisk the oil, garlic, oregano, thyme, salt, and pepper in a medium bowl.
3. Lay the piece of halloumi flat on a cutting board. Slice it widthwise into ½-inch-thick sticks. Cut each stick lengthwise into ½-inch-thick batons.
4. Put these batons into the olive oil mixture. Toss gently but well to coat.
5. Place the batons in the basket in a single layer. Air-fry undisturbed for 12 minutes, or until lightly browned, particularly at the edges.
6. Dump the fries out onto a wire rack. They may need a little coaxing with a nonstick-safe spatula to come free. Cool for a couple of minutes before serving hot.

Pizza Bagel Bites

Servings: 2 | Cooking Time: 5 Minutes

Ingredients:
- 2 Mini bagel(s), split into two rings
- ¼ cup Purchased pizza sauce
- ½ cup Finely grated or shredded cheese, such as Parmesan cheese, semi-firm mozzarella, fontina, or (preferably) a cheese blend

Directions:
1. Preheat the air fryer to 375°F.
2. Spread the cut side of each bagel half with 1 tablespoon pizza sauce; top each half with 2 tablespoons shredded cheese.
3. When the machine is at temperature, put the bagels cheese side up in the basket in one layer. Air-fry undisturbed for 4 minutes, or until the cheese has melted and is gooey. You may need to air-fry the pizza bagel bites for 1 minute extra if the temperature is at 360°F.
4. Use a nonstick-safe spatula to transfer the topped bagel halves to a wire rack. Cool for at least 5 minutes before serving.

Chapter 3 Bread And Breakfast Recipes

Chapter 3 Bread And Breakfast Recipes

Crust-less Quiche

Servings:2 | Cooking Time:30 Minutes

Ingredients:
- 4 eggs
- ¼ cup onion, chopped
- ½ cup tomatoes, chopped
- ½ cup milk
- 1 cup Gouda cheese, shredded
- Salt, to taste

Directions:
1. Preheat the Air fryer to 340°F and grease 2 ramekins lightly.
2. Mix together all the ingredients in a ramekin until well combined.
3. Place in the Air fryer and cook for about 30 minutes.
4. Dish out and serve.

Strawberry Bread

Servings: 6 | Cooking Time: 28 Minutes

Ingredients:
- ½ cup frozen strawberries in juice, completely thawed (do not drain)
- 1 cup flour
- ½ cup sugar
- 1 teaspoon cinnamon
- ½ teaspoon baking soda
- ⅛ teaspoon salt
- 1 egg, beaten
- ⅓ cup oil
- cooking spray

Directions:
1. Cut any large berries into smaller pieces no larger than ½ inch.
2. Preheat air fryer to 330°F.
3. In a large bowl, stir together the flour, sugar, cinnamon, soda, and salt.
4. In a small bowl, mix together the egg, oil, and strawberries. Add to dry ingredients and stir together gently.
5. Spray 6 x 6-inch baking pan with cooking spray.
6. Pour batter into prepared pan and cook at 330°F for 28 minutes.
7. When bread is done, let cool for 10minutes before removing from pan.

Seasoned Herbed Sourdough Croutons

Servings: 4 | Cooking Time: 7 Minutes

Ingredients:
- 4 cups cubed sourdough bread, 1-inch cubes
- 1 tablespoon olive oil
- 1 teaspoon fresh thyme leaves
- ¼ – ½ teaspoon salt
- freshly ground black pepper

Directions:
1. Combine all ingredients in a bowl and taste to make sure it is seasoned to your liking.
2. Preheat the air fryer to 400°F.
3. Toss the bread cubes into the air fryer and air-fry for 7 min-utes, shaking the basket once or twice while they cook.
4. Serve warm or store in an airtight container.

Chocolate Chip Scones

Servings:8 | Cooking Time:15 Minutes

Ingredients:
- ½ cup cold salted butter, divided
- 2 cups all-purpose flour
- ½ cup brown sugar
- ½ teaspoon baking powder
- 1 large egg
- ¾ cup buttermilk
- ½ cup semisweet chocolate chips

Directions:
1. Preheat the air fryer to 320°F. Cut parchment paper to fit the air fryer basket.
2. Chill 6 tablespoons butter in the freezer 10 minutes. In a small microwave-safe bowl, microwave remaining 2 tablespoons butter 30 seconds until melted, and set aside.
3. In a large bowl, mix flour, brown sugar, and baking powder.
4. Remove butter from freezer and grate into bowl. Use a wooden spoon to evenly distribute.
5. Add egg and buttermilk and stir gently until a soft, sticky dough forms. Gently fold in chocolate chips.
6. Turn dough out onto a lightly floured surface. Fold a couple of times and gently form into a 6" round. Cut into eight triangles.
7. Place scones on parchment in the air fryer basket, leaving at least 2" space between each, working in batches as necessary.
8. Brush each scone with melted butter. Cook 15 minutes until scones are dark golden brown and crispy on the edges, and a toothpick inserted into the center comes out clean. Serve warm.

Cheddar Soufflés

Servings:4 | Cooking Time: 12 Minutes

Ingredients:
- 3 large eggs, whites and yolks separated
- ¼ teaspoon cream of tartar
- ½ cup shredded sharp Cheddar cheese
- 3 ounces cream cheese, softened

Directions:
1. In a large bowl, beat egg whites together with cream of tartar until soft peaks form, about 2 minutes.
2. In a separate medium bowl, beat egg yolks, Cheddar, and cream cheese together until frothy, about 1 minute. Add egg yolk mixture to whites, gently folding until combined.
3. Pour mixture evenly into four 4" ramekins greased with cooking spray. Place ramekins into air fryer basket. Adjust the temperature to 350°F and set the timer for 12 minutes. Eggs will be browned on the top and firm in the center when done. Serve warm.

Cheese Pie

Servings: 4 | Cooking Time: 16 Minutes

Ingredients:
- 8 eggs
- 1 1/2 cups heavy whipping cream
- 1 lb cheddar cheese, grated
- Pepper
- Salt

Directions:
1. Preheat the air fryer to 325°F.
2. In a bowl, whisk together cheese, eggs, whipping cream, pepper, and salt.
3. Spray air fryer baking dish with cooking spray.
4. Pour egg mixture into the prepared dish and place in the air fryer basket.
5. Cook for 16 minutes or until the egg is set.
6. Serve and enjoy.

Scotch Eggs

Servings:6 | Cooking Time: 15 Minutes

Ingredients:
- 1 pound ground pork breakfast sausage
- 6 large hard-boiled eggs, peeled
- 1 cup all-purpose flour
- 2 large eggs, beaten
- 2 cups plain bread crumbs

Directions:
1. Preheat the air fryer to 375°F.
2. Separate sausage into six equal amounts and flatten into patties.
3. Form sausage patties around hard-boiled eggs, completely enclosing them.
4. In three separate small bowls, place flour, eggs, and bread crumbs.
5. Roll each sausage-covered egg first in flour, then egg, and finally bread crumbs. Place rolled eggs in the air fryer basket and spritz them with cooking spray.
6. Cook 15 minutes, turning halfway through cooking time and spraying any dry spots with additional cooking spray. Serve warm.

Whole-grain Cornbread

Servings: 6 | Cooking Time: 25 Minutes

Ingredients:
- 1 cup stoneground cornmeal
- ½ cup brown rice flour
- 1 teaspoon sugar
- 2 teaspoons baking powder
- ¼ teaspoon salt
- 1 cup milk
- 2 tablespoons oil
- 2 eggs
- cooking spray

Directions:
1. Preheat the air fryer to 360°F.
2. In a medium mixing bowl, mix cornmeal, brown rice flour, sugar, baking powder, and salt together.
3. Add the remaining ingredients and beat with a spoon until batter is smooth.
4. Spray air fryer baking pan with nonstick cooking spray and add the cornbread batter.
5. Bake at 360°F for 25 minutes, until center is done.

Strawberry Toast

Servings: 4 | Cooking Time: 8 Minutes

Ingredients:
- 4 slices bread, ½-inch thick
- butter-flavored cooking spray
- 1 cup sliced strawberries
- 1 teaspoon sugar

Directions:
1. Spray one side of each bread slice with butter-flavored cooking spray. Lay slices sprayed side down.
2. Divide the strawberries among the bread slices.
3. Sprinkle evenly with the sugar and place in the air fryer basket in a single layer.
4. Cook at 390°F for 8minutes. The bottom should look brown and crisp and the top should look glazed.

Bunless Breakfast Turkey Burgers

Servings:4 | Cooking Time: 15 Minutes

Ingredients:
- 1 pound ground turkey breakfast sausage
- ½ teaspoon salt
- ¼ teaspoon ground black pepper
- ¼ cup seeded and chopped green bell pepper
- 2 tablespoons mayonnaise
- 1 medium avocado, peeled, pitted, and sliced

Directions:
1. In a large bowl, mix sausage with salt, black pepper, bell pepper, and mayonnaise. Form meat into four patties.
2. Place patties into ungreased air fryer basket. Adjust the temperature to 370°F and set the timer for 15 minutes, turning patties halfway through cooking. Burgers will be done when dark brown and they have an internal temperature of at least 165°F.
3. Serve burgers topped with avocado slices on four medium plates.

Strawberry Pastry

Servings:8 | Cooking Time: 15 Minutes Per Batch

Ingredients:
- 1 package refrigerated piecrust
- 1 cup strawberry jam
- 1 large egg, whisked
- ½ cup confectioners' sugar
- 2 tablespoons whole milk
- ½ teaspoon vanilla extract

Directions:
1. Preheat the air fryer to 320°F. Cut parchment paper to fit the air fryer basket.
2. On a lightly floured surface, lay piecrusts out flat. Cut each piecrust round into six 4" × 3" rectangles, reserving excess dough.
3. Form remaining dough into a ball, then roll out and cut four additional 4" × 3" rectangles, bringing the total to sixteen.
4. For each pastry, spread 2 tablespoons jam on a pastry rectangle, leaving a 1" border around the edges. Top with a second pastry rectangle and use a fork to gently press all four edges together. Repeat with remaining jam and pastry.
5. Brush tops of each pastry with egg and cut an X in the center of each to prevent excess steam from building up.

6. Place pastries on parchment in the air fryer basket, working in batches as necessary. Cook 12 minutes, then carefully flip and cook an additional 3 minutes until each side is golden brown. Let cool 10 minutes.

7. In a small bowl, whisk confectioners' sugar, milk, and vanilla. Brush each pastry with glaze, then place in the refrigerator 5 minutes to set before serving.

Sausage-crusted Egg Cups

Servings:6 | Cooking Time: 15 Minutes

Ingredients:
- 12 ounces ground pork breakfast sausage
- 6 large eggs
- ½ teaspoon salt
- ¼ teaspoon ground black pepper
- ½ teaspoon crushed red pepper flakes

Directions:
1. Place sausage in six 4" ramekins greased with cooking oil. Press sausage down to cover bottom and about ½" up the sides of ramekins. Crack one egg into each ramekin and sprinkle evenly with salt, black pepper, and red pepper flakes.

2. Place ramekins into air fryer basket. Adjust the temperature to 350°F and set the timer for 15 minutes. Egg cups will be done when sausage is fully cooked to at least 145°F and the egg is firm. Serve warm.

Mini Bagels

Servings:6 | Cooking Time: 10 Minutes

Ingredients:
- 2 cups blanched finely ground almond flour
- 2 cups shredded mozzarella cheese
- 3 tablespoons salted butter, divided
- 1½ teaspoons baking powder
- 1 teaspoon apple cider vinegar
- 2 large eggs, divided

Directions:
1. In a large microwave-safe bowl, combine flour, mozzarella, and 1 tablespoon butter. Microwave on high 90 seconds, then form into a soft ball of dough.

2. Add baking powder, vinegar, and 1 egg to dough, stirring until fully combined.

3. Once dough is cool enough to work with your hands, about 2 minutes, divide evenly into six balls. Poke a hole in each ball of dough with your finger and gently stretch each ball out to be 2" in diameter.

4. In a small microwave-safe bowl, melt remaining butter in microwave on high 30 seconds, then let cool 1 minute. Whisk with remaining egg, then brush mixture over each bagel.

5. Line air fryer basket with parchment paper and place bagels onto ungreased parchment, working in batches if needed.

6. Adjust the temperature to 350°F and set the timer for 10 minutes. Halfway through, use tongs to flip bagels for even cooking.

7. Allow bagels to set and cool completely, about 15 minutes, before serving. Store leftovers in a sealed bag in the refrigerator up to 4 days.

Jalapeño And Bacon Breakfast Pizza

Servings:2 | Cooking Time: 10 Minutes

Ingredients:
- 1 cup shredded mozzarella cheese
- 1 ounce cream cheese, broken into small pieces
- 4 slices cooked sugar-free bacon, chopped
- ¼ cup chopped pickled jalapeños
- 1 large egg, whisked
- ¼ teaspoon salt

Directions:
1. Place mozzarella in a single layer on the bottom of an ungreased 6" round nonstick baking dish. Scatter cream cheese pieces, bacon, and jalapeños over mozzarella, then pour egg evenly around baking dish.

2. Sprinkle with salt and place into air fryer basket. Adjust the temperature to 330°F and set the timer for 10 minutes. When cheese is brown and egg is set, pizza will be done.

3. Let cool on a large plate 5 minutes before serving.

Garlic Bread Knots

Servings: 8 | Cooking Time: 5 Minutes

Ingredients:
- ¼ cup melted butter
- 2 teaspoons garlic powder
- 1 teaspoon dried parsley
- 1 tube of refrigerated French bread dough

Directions:
1. Mix the melted butter, garlic powder and dried parsley in a small bowl and set it aside.

2. To make smaller knots, cut the long tube of bread dough into 16 slices. If you want to make bigger knots, slice the dough into 8 slices. Shape each slice into a long rope about 6 inches long by rolling it on a flat surface with the palm of your hands. Tie each rope into a knot and place them on a plate.

3. Preheat the air fryer to 350°F.

4. Transfer half of the bread knots into the air fryer basket, leaving space in between each knot. Brush each knot with the butter mixture using a pastry brush.

5. Air-fry for 5 minutes. Remove the baked knots and brush a little more of the garlic butter mixture on each. Repeat with the remaining bread knots and serve warm.

French Toast Sticks

Servings:4 | Cooking Time: 8 Minutes

Ingredients:
- 4 slices Texas toast, or other thick-sliced bread
- 2 large eggs
- ¼ cup heavy cream
- 4 tablespoons salted butter, melted
- ½ cup granulated sugar
- 1 ½ tablespoons ground cinnamon

Directions:
1. Preheat the air fryer to 350°F. Cut parchment paper to fit the air fryer basket.

2. Slice each piece of bread into four even sticks.

3. In a medium bowl, whisk together eggs and cream. Dip each bread stick into mixture and place on parchment in the air fryer basket.

4. Cook 5 minutes, then carefully turn over and cook an additional 3 minutes until golden brown on both sides.

5. Drizzle sticks with butter and toss to ensure they're covered on all sides.
6. In a medium bowl, mix sugar and cinnamon. Dip both sides of each stick into the mixture and shake off excess. Serve warm.

Smoked Salmon Croissant Sandwich

Servings: 1 | Cooking Time: 30 Minutes

Ingredients:
- 1 croissant, halved
- 2 eggs
- 1 tbsp guacamole
- 1 smoked salmon slice
- Salt and pepper to taste

Directions:
1. Preheat air fryer to 360°F. Place the croissant, crusty side up, in the frying basket side by side. Whisk the eggs in a small ceramic dish until fluffy. Place in the air fryer. Bake for 10 minutes. Gently scramble the half-cooked egg in the baking dish with a fork. Flip the croissant and cook for another 10 minutes until the scrambled eggs are cooked, but still fluffy, and the croissant is toasted.
2. Place one croissant on a serving plate, then spread the guacamole on top. Scoop the scrambled eggs onto guacamole, then top with smoked salmon. Sprinkle with salt and pepper. Top with the second slice of toasted croissant, close sandwich, and serve hot.

Puffed Egg Tarts

Servings:4 | Cooking Time:42 Minutes

Ingredients:
- 1 sheet frozen puff pastry half, thawed and cut into 4 squares
- ¾ cup Monterey Jack cheese, shredded and divided
- 4 large eggs
- 1 tablespoon fresh parsley, minced
- 1 tablespoon olive oil

Directions:
1. Preheat the Air fryer to 390°F
2. Place 2 pastry squares in the air fryer basket and cook for about 10 minutes.
3. Remove Air fryer basket from the Air fryer and press each square gently with a metal tablespoon to form an indentation.
4. Place 3 tablespoons of cheese in each hole and top with 1 egg each.
5. Return Air fryer basket to Air fryer and cook for about 11 minutes.
6. Remove tarts from the Air fryer basket and sprinkle with half the parsley.
7. Repeat with remaining pastry squares, cheese and eggs.
8. Dish out and serve warm.

Mini Bacon Egg Quiches

Servings:6 | Cooking Time: 30 Minutes

Ingredients:
- 3 eggs
- 2 tbsp heavy cream
- ¼ tsp Dijon mustard
- Salt and pepper to taste
- 3 oz cooked bacon, crumbled
- ¼ cup grated cheddar

Directions:
1. Preheat air fryer to 350ºF. Beat the eggs with salt and pepper in a bowl until fluffy. Stir in heavy cream, mustard, cooked bacon, and cheese. Divide the mixture between 6 greased muffin cups and place them in the frying basket. Bake for 8-10 minutes. Let cool slightly before serving.

Green Onion Pancakes

Servings: 4 | Cooking Time: 8 Minutes

Ingredients:
- 2 cup all-purpose flour
- ½ teaspoon salt
- ¾ cup hot water
- 1 tablespoon vegetable oil
- 1 tablespoon butter, melted
- 2 cups finely chopped green onions
- 1 tablespoon black sesame seeds, for garnish

Directions:
1. In a large bowl, whisk together the flour and salt. Make a well in the center and pour in the hot water. Quickly stir the flour mixture together until a dough forms. Knead the dough for 5 minutes; then cover with a warm, wet towel and set aside for 30 minutes to rest.
2. In a small bowl, mix together the vegetable oil and melted butter.
3. On a floured surface, place the dough and cut it into 8 pieces. Working with 1 piece of dough at a time, use a rolling pin to roll out the dough until it's ¼ inch thick; then brush the surface with the oil and butter mixture and sprinkle with green onions. Next, fold the dough in half and then in half again. Roll out the dough again until it's ¼ inch thick and brush with the oil and butter mixture and green onions. Fold the dough in half and then in half again and roll out one last time until it's ¼ inch thick. Repeat this technique with all 8 pieces.
4. Meanwhile, preheat the air fryer to 400°F.
5. Place 1 or 2 pancakes into the air fryer basket, and cook for 2 minutes or until crispy and golden brown. Repeat until all the pancakes are cooked. Top with black sesame seeds for garnish, if desired.

Bagels

Servings:4 | Cooking Time: 10 Minutes

Ingredients:
- 1 cup self-rising flour
- 1 cup plain full-fat Greek yogurt
- 2 tablespoons granulated sugar
- 1 large egg, whisked

Directions:
1. Preheat the air fryer to 320°F.
2. In a large bowl, mix flour, yogurt, and sugar together until a ball of dough forms.
3. Turn dough out onto a lightly floured surface. Knead dough for 3 minutes, then form into a smooth ball. Cut dough into four sections. Roll each piece into an 8" rope, then shape into a circular bagel shape. Brush top and bottom of each bagel with egg.
4. Place in the air fryer basket and cook 10 minutes, turning halfway through cooking time to ensure even browning. Let cool 5 minutes before serving.

Chives Omelet

Servings: 4 | Cooking Time: 20 Minutes

Ingredients:
- 6 eggs, whisked
- 1 cup chives, chopped
- Cooking spray
- 1 cup mozzarella, shredded
- Salt and black pepper to the taste

Directions:
1. In a bowl, mix all the ingredients except the cooking spray and whisk well. Grease a pan that fits your air fryer with the cooking spray, pour the eggs mix, spread, put the pan into the machine and cook at 350°F for 20 minutes. Divide the omelet between plates and serve for breakfast.

Coconut Pudding

Servings: 4 | Cooking Time: 20 Minutes

Ingredients:
- 1 cup cauliflower rice
- ½ cup coconut, shredded
- 3 cups coconut milk
- 2 tablespoons stevia

Directions:
1. In a pan that fits the air fryer, combine all the ingredients and whisk well. Introduce the in your air fryer and cook at 360°F for 20 minutes. Divide into bowls and serve for breakfast.

Bacon Eggs

Servings: 2 | Cooking Time: 5 Minutes

Ingredients:
- 2 eggs, hard-boiled, peeled
- 4 bacon slices
- ½ teaspoon avocado oil
- 1 teaspoon mustard

Directions:
1. Preheat the air fryer to 400°F. Then sprinkle the air fryer basket with avocado oil and place the bacon slices inside. Flatten them in one layer and cook for 2 minutes from each side. After this, cool the bacon to the room temperature. Wrap every egg into 2 bacon slices. Secure the eggs with toothpicks and place them in the air fryer. Cook the wrapped eggs for 1 minute at 400°F.

Mushroom Frittata

Servings: 1 | Cooking Time: 13 Minutes

Ingredients:
- 1 cup egg whites
- 1 cup spinach, chopped
- 2 mushrooms, sliced
- 2 tbsp parmesan cheese, grated
- Salt

Directions:
1. Spray pan with cooking spray and heat over medium heat.
2. Add mushrooms and sauté for 2-3 minutes. Add spinach and cook for 1-2 minutes or until wilted.
3. Transfer mushroom spinach mixture into the air fryer pan.
4. Whisk egg whites in a mixing bowl until frothy. Season with a pinch of salt.
5. Pour egg white mixture into the spinach and mushroom mixture and sprinkle with parmesan cheese.

6. Place pan in air fryer basket and cook frittata at 350°F for 8 minutes.
7. Slice and serve.

Spinach Eggs And Cheese

Servings: 2 | Cooking Time: 40 Minutes

Ingredients:
- 3 whole eggs
- 3 oz cottage cheese
- 3-4 oz chopped spinach
- ¼ cup parmesan cheese
- ¼ cup of milk

Directions:
1. Preheat your fryer to 375°F.
2. In a large bowl, whisk the eggs, cottage cheese, the parmesan and the milk.
3. Mix in the spinach.
4. Transfer to a small, greased, fryer dish.
5. Sprinkle the cheese on top.
6. Bake for 25-30 minutes.
7. Let cool for 5 minutes and serve.

Cheesy Bell Pepper Eggs

Servings:4 | Cooking Time: 15 Minutes

Ingredients:
- 4 medium green bell peppers, tops removed, seeded
- 1 tablespoon coconut oil
- 3 ounces chopped cooked no-sugar-added ham
- ¼ cup peeled and chopped white onion
- 4 large eggs
- ½ teaspoon salt
- 1 cup shredded mild Cheddar cheese

Directions:
1. Place peppers upright into ungreased air fryer basket. Drizzle each pepper with coconut oil. Divide ham and onion evenly among peppers.
2. In a medium bowl, whisk eggs, then sprinkle with salt. Pour mixture evenly into each pepper. Top each with ¼ cup Cheddar.
3. Adjust the temperature to 320°F and set the timer for 15 minutes. Peppers will be tender and eggs will be firm when done.
4. Serve warm on four medium plates.

Sausage Bacon Fandango

Servings:4 | Cooking Time:20 Minutes

Ingredients:
- 8 bacon slices
- 8 chicken sausages
- 4 eggs
- Salt and black pepper, to taste

Directions:
1. Preheat the Air fryer to 320°F and grease 4 ramekins lightly.
2. Place bacon slices and sausages in the Air fryer basket.
3. Cook for about 10 minutes and crack 1 egg in each prepared ramekin.
4. Season with salt and black pepper and cook for about 10 more minutes.
5. Divide bacon slices and sausages in serving plates.
6. Place 1 egg in each plate and serve warm.

Sausage Egg Muffins

Servings: 4 | Cooking Time: 30 Minutes

Ingredients:
- 6 oz Italian sausage
- 6 eggs
- 1/8 cup heavy cream
- 3 oz cheese

Directions:
1. Preheat the fryer to 350°F.
2. Grease a muffin pan.
3. Slice the sausage links and place them two to a tin.
4. Beat the eggs with the cream and season with salt and pepper.
5. Pour over the sausages in the tin.
6. Sprinkle with cheese and the remaining egg mixture.
7. Cook for 20 minutes or until the eggs are done and serve!

Sausage Solo

Servings:4 | Cooking Time:22 Minutes

Ingredients:
- 6 eggs
- 4 cooked sausages, sliced
- 2 bread slices, cut into sticks
- ½ cup mozzarella cheese, grated
- ½ cup cream

Directions:
1. Preheat the Air fryer to 355°F and grease 4 ramekins lightly.
2. Whisk together eggs and cream in a bowl and beat well.
3. Transfer the egg mixture into ramekins and arrange the bread sticks and sausage slices around the edges.
4. Top with mozzarella cheese evenly and place the ramekins in Air fryer basket.
5. Cook for about 22 minutes and dish out to serve warm.

Mini Tomato Quiche

Servings:2 | Cooking Time:30 Minutes

Ingredients:
- 4 eggs
- ¼ cup onion, chopped
- ½ cup tomatoes, chopped
- ½ cup milk
- 1 cup Gouda cheese, shredded
- Salt, to taste

Directions:
1. Preheat the Air fryer to 340°F and grease a large ramekin with cooking spray.
2. Mix together all the ingredients in a ramekin and transfer into the air fryer basket.
3. Cook for about 30 minutes and dish out to serve hot.

Quiche Cups

Servings: 10 | Cooking Time: 16 Minutes

Ingredients:
- ¼ pound all-natural ground pork sausage
- 3 eggs
- ¼ cup milk
- 20 foil muffin cups
- cooking spray
- 4 ounces sharp Cheddar cheese, grated

Directions:

1. Divide sausage into 3 portions and shape each into a thin patty.
2. Place patties in air fryer basket and cook 390°F for 6minutes.
3. While sausage is cooking, prepare the egg mixture. A large measuring cup or bowl with a pouring lip works best. Combine the eggs and milk and whisk until well blended. Set aside.
4. When sausage has cooked fully, remove patties from basket, drain well, and use a fork to crumble the meat into small pieces.
5. Double the foil cups into 10 sets. Remove paper liners from the top muffin cups and spray the foil cups lightly with cooking spray.
6. Divide crumbled sausage among the 10 muffin cup sets.
7. Top each with grated cheese, divided evenly among the cups.
8. Place 5 cups in air fryer basket.
9. Pour egg mixture into each cup, filling until each cup is at least ⅔ full.
10. Cook for 8 minutes and test for doneness. A knife inserted into the center shouldn't have any raw egg on it when removed.
11. If needed, cook 2 more minutes, until egg completely sets.
12. Repeat steps 8 through 11 for the remaining quiches.

Onion Marinated Skirt Steak

Servings:3 | Cooking Time: 45 Minutes

Ingredients:
- 1 large red onion, grated or pureed
- 2 tablespoons brown sugar
- 1 tablespoon vinegar
- 1 ½ pounds skirt steak
- Salt and pepper to taste

Directions:
1. Place all ingredients in a Ziploc bag and allow to marinate in the fridge for at least 2 hours.
2. Preheat the air fryer at 390°F.
3. Place the grill pan accessory in the air fryer.
4. Grill for 15 minutes per batch.
5. Flip every 8 minutes for even grilling.

Roasted Golden Mini Potatoes

Servings:4 | Cooking Time: 22 Minutes

Ingredients:
- 6 cups water
- 1 pound baby Dutch yellow potatoes, quartered
- 2 tablespoons olive oil
- ½ teaspoon garlic powder
- ¾ teaspoon seasoned salt
- ¼ teaspoon salt
- ½ teaspoon ground black pepper

Directions:
1. In a medium saucepan over medium-high heat bring water to a boil. Add potatoes and boil 10 minutes until fork-tender, then drain and gently pat dry.
2. Preheat the air fryer to 400°F.
3. Drizzle oil over potatoes, then sprinkle with garlic powder, seasoned salt, salt, and pepper.
4. Place potatoes in the air fryer basket and cook 12 minutes, shaking the basket three times during cooking. Potatoes will be done when golden brown and edges are crisp. Serve warm.

Bacon And Cheese Quiche

Servings:2 | Cooking Time: 12 Minutes

Ingredients:
- 3 large eggs
- 2 tablespoons heavy whipping cream
- ¼ teaspoon salt
- 4 slices cooked sugar-free bacon, crumbled
- ½ cup shredded mild Cheddar cheese

Directions:
1. In a large bowl, whisk eggs, cream, and salt together until combined. Mix in bacon and Cheddar.
2. Pour mixture evenly into two ungreased 4" ramekins. Place into air fryer basket. Adjust the temperature to 320°F and set the timer for 12 minutes. Quiche will be fluffy and set in the middle when done.
3. Let quiche cool in ramekins 5 minutes. Serve warm.

Cinnamon Rolls

Servings:12 | Cooking Time: 20 Minutes

Ingredients:
- 2½ cups shredded mozzarella cheese
- 2 ounces cream cheese, softened
- 1 cup blanched finely ground almond flour
- ½ teaspoon vanilla extract
- ½ cup confectioners' erythritol
- 1 tablespoon ground cinnamon

Directions:
1. In a large microwave-safe bowl, combine mozzarella cheese, cream cheese, and flour. Microwave the mixture on high 90 seconds until cheese is melted.
2. Add vanilla extract and erythritol, and mix 2 minutes until a dough forms.
3. Once the dough is cool enough to work with your hands, about 2 minutes, spread it out into a 12" × 4" rectangle on ungreased parchment paper. Evenly sprinkle dough with cinnamon.
4. Starting at the long side of the dough, roll lengthwise to form a log. Slice the log into twelve even pieces.
5. Divide rolls between two ungreased 6" round nonstick baking dishes. Place one dish into air fryer basket. Adjust the temperature to 375°F and set the timer for 10 minutes.
6. Cinnamon rolls will be done when golden around the edges and mostly firm. Repeat with second dish. Allow rolls to cool in dishes 10 minutes before serving.

Eggs Salad

Servings: 4 | Cooking Time: 10 Minutes

Ingredients:
- 1 tablespoon lime juice
- 4 eggs, hard boiled, peeled and sliced
- 2 cups baby spinach
- Salt and black pepper to the taste
- 3 tablespoons heavy cream
- 2 tablespoons olive oil

Directions:
1. In your Air Fryer, mix the spinach with cream, eggs, salt and pepper, cover and cook at 360°F for 6 minutes. Transfer this to a bowl, add the lime juice and oil, toss and serve for breakfast.

Scones

Servings: 9 | Cooking Time: 8 Minutes Per Batch

Ingredients:
- 2 cups self-rising flour, plus ¼ cup for kneading
- ⅓ cup granulated sugar
- ¼ cup butter, cold
- 1 cup milk

Directions:
1. Preheat air fryer at 360°F.
2. In large bowl, stir together flour and sugar.
3. Cut cold butter into tiny cubes, and stir into flour mixture with fork.
4. Stir in milk until soft dough forms.
5. Sprinkle ¼ cup of flour onto wax paper and place dough on top. Knead lightly by folding and turning the dough about 6 to 8 times.
6. Pat dough into a 6 x 6-inch square.
7. Cut into 9 equal squares.
8. Place all squares in air fryer basket or as many as will fit in a single layer, close together but not touching.
9. Cook at 360°F for 8minutes. When done, scones will be lightly browned on top and will spring back when pressed gently with a dull knife.
10. Repeat steps 8 and 9 to cook remaining scones.

Pizza Eggs

Servings:2 | Cooking Time: 10 Minutes

Ingredients:
- 1 cup shredded mozzarella cheese
- 7 slices pepperoni, chopped
- 1 large egg, whisked
- ¼ teaspoon dried oregano
- ¼ teaspoon dried parsley
- ¼ teaspoon garlic powder
- ¼ teaspoon salt

Directions:
1. Place mozzarella in a single layer on the bottom of an ungreased 6" round nonstick baking dish. Scatter pepperoni over cheese, then pour egg evenly around baking dish.
2. Sprinkle with remaining ingredients and place into air fryer basket. Adjust the temperature to 330°F and set the timer for 10 minutes. When cheese is brown and egg is set, dish will be done.
3. Let cool in dish 5 minutes before serving.

Mini Pita Breads

Servings: 8 | Cooking Time: 6 Minutes

Ingredients:
- 2 teaspoons active dry yeast
- 1 tablespoon sugar
- 1¼ to 1½ cups warm water
- 3¼ cups all-purpose flour
- 2 teaspoons salt
- 1 tablespoon olive oil, plus more for brushing
- kosher salt (optional)

Directions:
1. Dissolve the yeast, sugar and water in the bowl of a stand mixer. Let the mixture sit for 5 minutes to make sure the yeast is active – it should foam a little. Combine the flour and salt in a bowl, and add it to the water, along with the olive oil. Mix with the dough hook until combined. Add a little more flour if needed

to get the dough to pull away from the sides of the mixing bowl, or add a little more water if the dough seems too dry.

2. Knead the dough until it is smooth and elastic. Transfer the dough to a lightly oiled bowl, cover and let it rise in a warm place until doubled in bulk. Divide the dough into 8 portions and roll each portion into a circle about 4-inches in diameter. Don't roll the balls too thin, or you won't get the pocket inside the pita.

3. Preheat the air fryer to 400°F.

4. Brush both sides of the dough with olive oil, and sprinkle with kosher salt if desired. Air-fry one at a time at 400°F for 6 minutes, flipping it over when there are two minutes left in the cooking time.

Hashbrown Potatoes Lyonnaise

Servings: 4 | Cooking Time: 33 Minutes

Ingredients:
- 1 Vidalia (or other sweet) onion, sliced
- 1 teaspoon butter, melted
- 1 teaspoon brown sugar
- 2 large russet potatoes, sliced ½-inch thick
- 1 tablespoon vegetable oil
- salt and freshly ground black pepper

Directions:
1. Preheat the air fryer to 370°F.
2. Toss the sliced onions, melted butter and brown sugar together in the air fryer basket. Air-fry for 8 minutes, shaking the basket occasionally to help the onions cook evenly.
3. While the onions are cooking, bring a 3-quart saucepan of salted water to a boil on the stovetop. Par-cook the potatoes in boiling water for 3 minutes. Drain the potatoes and pat them dry with a clean kitchen towel.
4. Add the potatoes to the onions in the air fryer basket and drizzle with vegetable oil. Toss to coat the potatoes with the oil and season with salt and freshly ground black pepper.
5. Increase the air fryer temperature to 400°F and air-fry for 22 minutes tossing the vegetables a few times during the cooking time to help the potatoes brown evenly. Season to taste again with salt and freshly ground black pepper and serve warm.

Bacon, Egg, And Cheese Calzones

Servings:4 | Cooking Time: 12 Minutes

Ingredients:
- 2 large eggs
- 1 cup blanched finely ground almond flour
- 2 cups shredded mozzarella cheese
- 2 ounces cream cheese, softened and broken into small pieces
- 4 slices cooked sugar-free bacon, crumbled

Directions:
1. Beat eggs in a small bowl. Pour into a medium nonstick skillet over medium heat and scramble. Set aside.
2. In a large microwave-safe bowl, mix flour and mozzarella. Add cream cheese to bowl.
3. Place bowl in microwave and cook 45 seconds on high to melt cheese, then stir with a fork until a soft dough ball forms.
4. Cut a piece of parchment to fit air fryer basket. Separate dough into two sections and press each out into an 8" round.
5. On half of each dough round, place half of the scrambled eggs and crumbled bacon. Fold the other side of the dough over and press to seal the edges.
6. Place calzones on ungreased parchment and into air fryer basket. Adjust the temperature to 350°F and set the timer for 12

minutes, turning calzones halfway through cooking. Crust will be golden and firm when done.

7. Let calzones cool on a cooking rack 5 minutes before serving.

Peppered Maple Bacon Knots

Servings: 6 | Cooking Time: 8 Minutes

Ingredients:
- 1 pound maple smoked center-cut bacon
- ¼ cup maple syrup
- ¼ cup brown sugar
- coarsely cracked black peppercorns

Directions:
1. Tie each bacon strip in a loose knot and place them on a baking sheet.
2. Combine the maple syrup and brown sugar in a bowl. Brush each knot generously with this mixture and sprinkle with coarsely cracked black pepper.
3. Preheat the air fryer to 390°F.
4. Air-fry the bacon knots in batches. Place one layer of knots in the air fryer basket and air-fry for 5 minutes. Turn the bacon knots over and air-fry for an additional 3 minutes.
5. Serve warm.

Taj Tofu

Servings: 4 | Cooking Time: 40 Minutes

Ingredients:
- 1 block firm tofu, pressed and cut into 1-inch thick cubes
- 2 tbsp. soy sauce
- 2 tsp. sesame seeds, toasted
- 1 tsp. rice vinegar
- 1 tbsp. cornstarch

Directions:
1. Set your Air Fryer at 400°F to warm.
2. Add the tofu, soy sauce, sesame seeds and rice vinegar in a bowl together and mix well to coat the tofu cubes. Then cover the tofu in cornstarch and put it in the basket of your fryer.
3. Cook for 25 minutes, giving the basket a shake at five-minute intervals to ensure the tofu cooks evenly.

Goat Cheese, Beet, And Kale Frittata

Servings: 6 | Cooking Time: 20 Minutes

Ingredients:
- 6 large eggs
- ½ teaspoon garlic powder
- ¼ teaspoon black pepper
- ¼ teaspoon salt
- 1 cup chopped kale
- 1 cup cooked and chopped red beets
- ⅓ cup crumbled goat cheese

Directions:
1. Preheat the air fryer to 320°F.
2. In a medium bowl, whisk the eggs with the garlic powder, pepper, and salt. Mix in the kale, beets, and goat cheese.
3. Spray an oven-safe 7-inch springform pan with cooking spray. Pour the egg mixture into the pan and place it in the air fryer basket.
4. Cook for 20 minutes, or until the internal temperature reaches 145°F.
5. When the frittata is cooked, let it set for 5 minutes before removing from the pan.
6. Slice and serve immediately.

Parmesan Breakfast Casserole

Servings: 3 | Cooking Time: 20 Minutes

Ingredients:
- 5 eggs
- 2 tbsp heavy cream
- 3 tbsp chunky tomato sauce
- 2 tbsp parmesan cheese, grated

Directions:
1. Preheat the air fryer to 325°F.
2. In mixing bowl, combine together cream and eggs.
3. Add cheese and tomato sauce and mix well.
4. Spray air fryer baking dish with cooking spray.
5. Pour mixture into baking dish and place in the air fryer basket.
6. Cook for 20 minutes.
7. Serve and enjoy.

Banana Baked Oatmeal

Servings:2 | Cooking Time:10 Minutes

Ingredients:
- 1 cup quick-cooking oats
- 1 cup whole milk
- 2 tablespoons unsalted butter, melted
- 1 medium banana, peeled and mashed
- 2 tablespoons brown sugar
- ½ teaspoon vanilla extract
- ½ teaspoon salt

Directions:
1. Preheat the air fryer to 360°F.
2. In a 6" round pan, add oats. Pour in milk and butter.
3. In a medium bowl, mix banana, brown sugar, vanilla, and salt until combined. Add to pan and mix until well combined.
4. Place in the air fryer and cook 10 minutes until the top is brown and oats feel firm to the touch. Serve warm.

Grilled Bbq Sausages

Servings:3 | Cooking Time: 30 Minutes

Ingredients:
- 6 sausage links
- ½ cup prepared BBQ sauce

Directions:
1. Preheat the air fryer at 390°F.
2. Place the grill pan accessory in the air fryer.
3. Place the sausage links and grill for 30 minutes.
4. Flip halfway through the cooking time.
5. Before serving brush with prepared BBQ sauce.

Cream Cheese Danish

Servings:4 | Cooking Time: 10 Minutes

Ingredients:
- 1 sheet frozen puff pastry dough, thawed
- 1 large egg, beaten
- 4 ounces full-fat cream cheese, softened
- ¼ cup confectioners' sugar
- 1 teaspoon vanilla extract
- ½ teaspoon lemon juice

Directions:
1. Preheat the air fryer to 320°F.
2. Unfold puff pastry and cut into four equal squares. For each pastry, fold all four corners partway to the center, leaving a 1"

square in the center.
3. Brush egg evenly over folded puff pastry.
4. In a medium bowl, mix cream cheese, confectioners' sugar, vanilla, and lemon juice. Scoop 2 tablespoons of mixture into the center of each pastry square.
5. Place danishes directly in the air fryer basket and cook 10 minutes until puffy and golden brown. Cool 5 minutes before serving.

Breakfast Chimichangas

Servings: 4 | Cooking Time: 8 Minutes

Ingredients:
- Four 8-inch flour tortillas
- ½ cup canned refried beans
- 1 cup scrambled eggs
- ½ cup grated cheddar or Monterey jack cheese
- 1 tablespoon vegetable oil
- 1 cup salsa

Directions:
1. Lay the flour tortillas out flat on a cutting board. In the center of each tortilla, spread 2 tablespoons refried beans. Next, add ¼ cup eggs and 2 tablespoons cheese to each tortilla.
2. To fold the tortillas, begin on the left side and fold to the center. Then fold the right side into the center. Next fold the bottom and top down and roll over to completely seal the chimichanga. Using a pastry brush or oil mister, brush the tops of the tortilla packages with oil.
3. Preheat the air fryer to 400°F for 4 minutes. Place the chimichangas into the air fryer basket, seam side down, and air fry for 4 minutes. Using tongs, turn over the chimichangas and cook for an additional 2 to 3 minutes or until light golden brown.

Creamy Parsley Soufflé

Servings:2 | Cooking Time:10 Minutes

Ingredients:
- 2 eggs
- 1 tablespoon fresh parsley, chopped
- 1 fresh red chili pepper, chopped
- 2 tablespoons light cream
- Salt, to taste

Directions:
1. Preheat the Air fryer to 390°F and grease 2 soufflé dishes.
2. Mix together all the ingredients in a bowl until well combined.
3. Transfer the mixture into prepared soufflé dishes and place in the Air fryer.
4. Cook for about 10 minutes and dish out to serve warm.

Ham And Egg Toast Cups

Servings:2 | Cooking Time:5 Minutes

Ingredients:
- 2 eggs
- 2 slices of ham
- 2 tablespoons butter
- Cheddar cheese, for topping
- Salt, to taste
- Black pepper, to taste

Directions:
1. Preheat the Air fryer to 400°F and grease both ramekins with melted butter.
2. Place each ham slice in the greased ramekins and crack each egg over ham slices.

3. Sprinkle with salt, black pepper and cheddar cheese and transfer into the Air fryer basket.
4. Cook for about 5 minutes and remove the ramekins from the basket.
5. Serve warm.

Pancake For Two

Servings:2 | Cooking Time: 30 Minutes

Ingredients:
- 1 cup blanched finely ground almond flour
- 2 tablespoons granular erythritol
- 1 tablespoon salted butter, melted
- 1 large egg
- ⅓ cup unsweetened almond milk
- ½ teaspoon vanilla extract

Directions:
1. In a large bowl, mix all ingredients together, then pour half the batter into an ungreased 6" round nonstick baking dish.
2. Place dish into air fryer basket. Adjust the temperature to 320°F and set the timer for 15 minutes. The pancake will be golden brown on top and firm, and a toothpick inserted in the center will come out clean when done. Repeat with remaining batter.
3. Slice in half in dish and serve warm.

Meaty Omelet

Servings: 4 | Cooking Time: 20 Minutes

Ingredients:
- 6 eggs
- ½ cup grated Swiss cheese
- 3 breakfast sausages, sliced
- 8 bacon strips, sliced
- Salt and pepper to taste

Directions:
1. Preheat air fryer to 360°F. In a bowl, beat the eggs and stir in Swiss cheese, sausages and bacon. Transfer the mixture to a baking dish and set in the fryer. Bake for 15 minutes or until golden and crisp. Season and serve.

Green Beans Bowls

Servings: 2 | Cooking Time: 20 Minutes

Ingredients:
- 1 cup green beans, halved
- 2 spring onions, chopped
- 4 eggs, whisked
- Salt and black pepper to the taste
- ¼ teaspoon cumin, ground

Directions:
1. Preheat the air fryer at 360°F, add all the ingredients, toss, cover, cook for 20 minutes, divide into bowls and serve for breakfast.

Chapter 4 Poultry Recipes

Chapter 4 Poultry Recipes

Mustardy Chicken Bites

Servings: 4 | Cooking Time: 20 Minutes + Chilling Time

Ingredients:
- 2 tbsp horseradish mustard
- 1 tbsp mayonnaise
- 1 tbsp olive oil
- 2 chicken breasts, cubes
- 1 tbsp parsley

Directions:
1. Combine all ingredients, excluding parsley, in a bowl. Let marinate covered in the fridge for 30 minutes. Preheat air fryer at 350°F. Place chicken cubes in the greased frying basket and Air Fry for 9 minutes, tossing once. Serve immediately sprinkled with parsley.

Buttermilk Brined Turkey Breast

Servings:8 | Cooking Time:20 Minutes

Ingredients:
- ¾ cup brine from a can of olives
- 3½ pounds boneless, skinless turkey breast
- 2 fresh thyme sprigs
- 1 fresh rosemary sprig
- ½ cup buttermilk

Directions:
1. Preheat the Air fryer to 350°F and grease an Air fryer basket.
2. Mix olive brine and buttermilk in a bowl until well combined.
3. Place the turkey breast, buttermilk mixture and herb sprigs in a resealable plastic bag.
4. Seal the bag and refrigerate for about 12 hours.
5. Remove the turkey breast from bag and arrange the turkey breast into the Air fryer basket.
6. Cook for about 20 minutes, flipping once in between.
7. Dish out the turkey breast onto a cutting board and cut into desired size slices to serve.

Yummy Stuffed Chicken Breast

Servings:4 | Cooking Time:15 Minutes

Ingredients:
- 2 chicken fillets, skinless and boneless, each cut into 2 pieces
- 4 brie cheese slices
- 1 tablespoon chive, minced
- 4 cured ham slices
- Salt and black pepper, to taste

Directions:
1. Preheat the Air fryer to 355°F and grease an Air fryer basket.
2. Make a slit in each chicken piece horizontally and season with the salt and black pepper.
3. Insert cheese slice in the slits and sprinkle with chives.
4. Wrap each chicken piece with one ham slice and transfer into the Air fryer basket.
5. Cook for about 15 minutes and dish out to serve warm.

Basic Chicken Breasts

Servings: 4 | Cooking Time: 15 Minutes

Ingredients:
- 2 tsp olive oil
- 4 chicken breasts
- Salt and pepper to taste
- 1 tbsp Italian seasoning

Directions:
1. Preheat air fryer at 350°F. Rub olive oil over chicken breasts and sprinkle with salt, Italian seasoning and black pepper. Place them in the frying basket and Air Fry for 8-10 minutes. Let rest for 5 minutes before cutting. Store it covered in the fridge for up to 1 week.

Lemon Sage Roast Chicken

Servings: 4 | Cooking Time: 60 Minutes

Ingredients:
- 1 chicken
- 1 bunch sage, divided
- 1 lemon, zest and juice
- salt and freshly ground black pepper

Directions:
1. Preheat the air fryer to 350°F and pour a little water into the bottom of the air fryer drawer.
2. Run your fingers between the skin and flesh of the chicken breasts and thighs. Push a couple of sage leaves up underneath the skin of the chicken on each breast and each thigh.
3. Push some of the lemon zest up under the skin of the chicken next to the sage. Sprinkle some of the zest inside the chicken cavity, and reserve any leftover zest. Squeeze the lemon juice all over the chicken and in the cavity as well.
4. Season the chicken, inside and out, with the salt and freshly ground black pepper. Set a few sage leaves aside for the final garnish. Crumple up the remaining sage leaves and push them into the cavity of the chicken, along with one of the squeezed lemon halves.
5. Place the chicken breast side up into the air fryer basket and air-fry for 20 minutes at 350°F. Flip the chicken over so that it is breast side down and continue to air-fry for another 20 minutes. Return the chicken to breast side up and finish air-frying for 20 more minutes. The internal temperature of the chicken should register 165°F in the thickest part of the thigh when fully cooked. Remove the chicken from the air fryer and let it rest on a cutting board for at least 5 minutes.
6. Cut the rested chicken into pieces, sprinkle with the reserved lemon zest and garnish with the reserved sage leaves.

Chicken Fajita Poppers

Servings:18 | Cooking Time: 20 Minutes

Ingredients:
- 1 pound ground chicken thighs
- ½ medium green bell pepper, seeded and finely chopped
- ¼ medium yellow onion, peeled and finely chopped
- ½ cup shredded pepper jack cheese
- 1 packet gluten-free fajita seasoning

Directions:
1. In a large bowl, combine all ingredients. Form mixture into eighteen 2" balls and place in a single layer into ungreased air fryer basket, working in batches if needed.
2. Adjust the temperature to 350°F and set the timer for 20 minutes. Carefully use tongs to turn poppers halfway through cooking. When 5 minutes remain on timer, increase temperature to 400°F to give the poppers a dark golden-brown color. Shake air fryer basket once more when 2 minutes remain on timer. Serve warm.

Bacon-wrapped Chicken

Servings: 6 | Cooking Time: 20 Minutes

Ingredients:
• 1 chicken breast, cut into 6 pieces
• 6 rashers back bacon
• 1 tbsp. soft cheese

Directions:
1. Put the bacon rashers on a flat surface and cover one side with the soft cheese.
2. Lay the chicken pieces on each bacon rasher. Wrap the bacon around the chicken and use a toothpick stick to hold each one in place. Put them in Air Fryer basket.
3. Air fry at 350°F for 15 minutes.

Chicken Gruyere

Servings:4 | Cooking Time: 20 Minutes

Ingredients:
• ¼ cup Gruyere cheese, grated
• 1 pound chicken breasts, boneless, skinless
• ½ cup flour
• 2 eggs, beaten
• Sea salt and black pepper to taste
• 4 lemon slices
• Cooking spray

Directions:
1. Preheat your Air Fryer to 370°F. Spray the air fryer basket with cooking spray.
2. Mix the breadcrumbs with Gruyere cheese in a bowl, pour the eggs in another bowl, and the flour in a third bowl. Toss the chicken in the flour, then in the eggs, and then in the breadcrumb mixture. Place in the fryer basket, close and cook for 12 minutes. At the 6-minute mark, turn the chicken over. Once golden brown, remove onto a serving plate and serve topped with lemon slices.

Sweet Lime 'n Chili Chicken Barbecue

Servings:2 | Cooking Time: 40 Minutes

Ingredients:
• ¼ cup soy sauce
• 1 cup sweet chili sauce
• 1-pound chicken breasts
• Juice from 2 limes, freshly squeezed

Directions:
1. In a Ziploc bag, combine all Ingredients and give a good shake. Allow to marinate for at least 2 hours in the fridge.
2. Preheat the air fryer to 390°F.
3. Place the grill pan accessory in the air fryer.
4. Place chicken on the grill and cook for 30 to 40 minutes. Make sure to flip the chicken every 10 minutes to cook evenly.
5. Meanwhile, use the remaining marinade and put it in a sauce-pan. Simmer until the sauce thickens.
6. Once the chicken is cooked, brush with the thickened marinade.

Betty's Baked Chicken

Servings: 1 | Cooking Time: 70 Minutes

Ingredients:
• ½ cup butter
• 1 tsp. pepper
• 3 tbsp. garlic, minced
• 1 whole chicken

Directions:
1. Pre-heat your fryer at 350°F.
2. Allow the butter to soften at room temperature, then mix well in a small bowl with the pepper and garlic.
3. Massage the butter into the chicken. Any remaining butter can go inside the chicken.
4. Cook the chicken in the fryer for half an hour. Flip, then cook on the other side for another thirty minutes.
5. Test the temperature of the chicken by sticking a meat thermometer into the fat of the thigh to make sure it has reached 165°F. Take care when removing the chicken from the fryer. Let sit for ten minutes before you carve it and serve.

Jerk Chicken Wings

Servings:4 | Cooking Time: 1 Hour 20 Minutes

Ingredients:
• ¼ cup Jamaican jerk marinade
• 1 teaspoon onion powder
• 1 teaspoon garlic powder
• 1 teaspoon salt
• 2 pounds chicken wings, flats and drums separated

Directions:
1. In a large bowl, combine jerk seasoning, onion powder, garlic powder, and salt. Add chicken wings and toss to coat well. Cover and let marinate in refrigerator at least 1 hour.
2. Preheat the air fryer to 400°F.
3. Place wings in the air fryer basket in a single layer, working in batches as necessary. Cook wings 20 minutes, turning halfway through cooking time, until internal temperature reaches at least 165°F. Cool 5 minutes before serving.

Herb Seasoned Turkey Breast

Servings: 4 | Cooking Time: 35 Minutes

Ingredients:
• 2 lbs turkey breast
• 1 tsp fresh sage, chopped
• 1 tsp fresh rosemary, chopped
• 1 tsp fresh thyme, chopped
• Pepper
• Salt

Directions:
1. Spray air fryer basket with cooking spray.
2. In a small bowl, mix together sage, rosemary, and thyme.
3. Season turkey breast with pepper and salt and rub with herb mixture.
4. Place turkey breast in air fryer basket and cook at 390°F for 30-35 minutes.
5. Slice and serve.

Creamy Onion Chicken

Servings:4 | Cooking Time: 20 Minutes

Ingredients:
- 1 ½ cup onion soup mix
- 1 cup mushroom soup
- ½ cup cream

Directions:
1. Preheat Fryer to 400°F. Add mushrooms, onion mix and cream in a frying pan. Heat on low heat for 1 minute. Pour the warm mixture over chicken slices and allow to sit for 25 minutes. Place the marinated chicken in the air fryer cooking basket and cook for 15 minutes. Serve with the remaining cream.

Buffalo Chicken Sandwiches

Servings:4 | Cooking Time: 20 Minutes

Ingredients:
- 4 boneless, skinless chicken thighs
- 1 packet dry ranch seasoning
- ¼ cup buffalo sauce
- 4 slices pepper jack cheese
- 4 sandwich buns

Directions:
1. Preheat the air fryer to 375°F.
2. Sprinkle each chicken thigh with ranch seasoning and spritz with cooking spray.
3. Place chicken in the air fryer basket and cook 20 minutes, turning chicken halfway through, until chicken is brown at the edges and internal temperature reaches at least 165°F.
4. Drizzle buffalo sauce over chicken, top with a slice of cheese, and place on buns to serve.

Easy & Crispy Chicken Wings

Servings: 8 | Cooking Time: 20 Minutes

Ingredients:
- 1 1/2 lbs chicken wings
- 2 tbsp olive oil
- Pepper
- Salt

Directions:
1. Toss chicken wings with oil and place in the air fryer basket.
2. Cook chicken wings at 370°F for 15 minutes.
3. Shake basket and cook at 400 F for 5 minutes more.
4. Season chicken wings with pepper and salt.
5. Serve and enjoy.

Breaded Chicken Patties

Servings:4 | Cooking Time: 15 Minutes

Ingredients:
- 1 pound ground chicken breast
- 1 cup shredded sharp Cheddar cheese
- ½ cup plain bread crumbs
- 1 teaspoon salt
- ½ teaspoon ground black pepper
- 2 tablespoons mayonnaise
- 1 cup panko bread crumbs
- Cooking spray

Directions:
1. Preheat the air fryer to 400°F.
2. In a large bowl, mix chicken, Cheddar, plain bread crumbs, salt, and pepper until well combined. Separate into four portions and form into patties ½" thick.
3. Brush each patty with mayonnaise, then press into panko bread crumbs to fully coat. Spritz with cooking spray.
4. Place in the air fryer basket and cook 15 minutes, turning halfway through cooking time, until patties are golden brown and internal temperature reaches at least 165°F. Serve warm.

Chicken Thighs In Salsa Verde

Servings: 4 | Cooking Time: 35 Minutes

Ingredients:
- 4 boneless, skinless chicken thighs
- 1 cup salsa verde
- 1 tsp mashed garlic

Directions:
1. Preheat air fryer at 350ºF. Add chicken thighs to a cake pan and cover with salsa verde and mashed garlic. Place cake pan in the frying basket and Bake for 30 minutes. Let rest for 5 minutes before serving.

Chicken Chunks

Servings: 4 | Cooking Time: 10 Minutes

Ingredients:
- 1 pound chicken tenders cut in large chunks, about 1½ inches
- salt and pepper
- ½ cup cornstarch
- 2 eggs, beaten
- 1 cup panko breadcrumbs
- oil for misting or cooking spray

Directions:
1. Season chicken chunks to your liking with salt and pepper.
2. Dip chicken chunks in cornstarch. Then dip in egg and shake off excess. Then roll in panko crumbs to coat well.
3. Spray all sides of chicken chunks with oil or cooking spray.
4. Place chicken in air fryer basket in single layer and cook at 390°F for 5minutes. Spray with oil, turn chunks over, and spray other side.
5. Cook for an additional 5minutes or until chicken juices run clear and outside is golden brown.
6. Repeat steps 4 and 5 to cook remaining chicken.

Dill Pickle–ranch Wings

Servings:4 | Cooking Time: 2 Hours 20 Minutes

Ingredients:
- 1 cup pickle juice
- 2 pounds chicken wings, flats and drums separated
- ½ teaspoon salt
- ½ teaspoon ground black pepper
- 2 teaspoons dry ranch seasoning

Directions:
1. In a large bowl or resealable plastic bag, combine pickle juice and wings. Cover and let marinate in refrigerator 2 hours.
2. Preheat the air fryer to 400°F.
3. In a separate bowl, mix salt, pepper, and ranch seasoning. Remove wings from marinade and toss in dry seasoning.
4. Place wings in the air fryer basket in a single layer, working in batches as necessary. Cook 20 minutes, turning halfway through cooking time, until wings reach an internal temperature of at least 165°F. Cool 5 minutes before serving.

Chicken Tenders With Basil-strawberry Glaze

Servings:4 | Cooking Time: 20 Minutes

Ingredients:
- 1 lb chicken tenderloins
- ¼ cup strawberry preserves
- 3 tbsp chopped basil
- 1 tsp orange juice
- ½ tsp orange zest
- Salt and pepper to taste

Directions:
1. Combine all ingredients, except for 1 tbsp of basil, in a bowl. Marinade in the fridge covered for 30 minutes.
2. Preheat air fryer to 350ºF. Place the chicken tenders in the frying basket and Air Fry for 4-6 minutes. Shake gently the basket and turn over the chicken. Cook for 5 more minutes. Top with the remaining basil to serve.

Perfect Grill Chicken Breast

Servings: 2 | Cooking Time: 12 Minutes

Ingredients:
- 2 chicken breast, skinless and boneless
- 2 tsp olive oil
- Pepper
- Salt

Directions:
1. Remove air fryer basket and replace it with air fryer grill pan.
2. Place chicken breast to the grill pan. Season chicken with pepper and salt. Drizzle with oil.
3. Cook chicken for 375°F for 12 minutes.
4. Serve and enjoy.

Peppery Lemon-chicken Breast

Servings:1 | Cooking Time:

Ingredients:
- 1 chicken breast
- 1 teaspoon minced garlic
- 2 lemons, rinds and juice reserved
- Salt and pepper to taste

Directions:
1. Preheat the air fryer.
2. Place all ingredients in a baking dish that will fit in the air fryer.
3. Place in the air fryer basket.
4. Close and cook for 20 minutes at 400°F.

Family Chicken Fingers

Servings: 4 | Cooking Time: 30 Minutes

Ingredients:
- 1 lb chicken breast fingers
- 1 tbsp chicken seasoning
- ½ tsp mustard powder
- Salt and pepper to taste
- 2 eggs
- 1 cup bread crumbs

Directions:
1. Preheat air fryer to 400°F. Add the chicken fingers to a large bowl along with chicken seasoning, mustard, salt, and pepper; mix well. Set up two small bowls. In one bowl, beat the eggs. In the second bowl, add the bread crumbs. Dip the chicken in the egg, then dredge in breadcrumbs. Place the nuggets in the air fryer. Lightly spray with cooking oil, then Air Fry for 8 minutes, shaking the basket once until crispy and cooked through. Serve warm.

Chicken Nuggets

Servings:4 | Cooking Time: 10 Minutes

Ingredients:
- 1 pound ground chicken breast
- 1 ½ teaspoons salt, divided
- ¾ teaspoon ground black pepper, divided
- 1 ½ cups plain bread crumbs, divided
- 2 large eggs

Directions:
1. Preheat the air fryer to 400°F.
2. In a large bowl, mix chicken, 1 teaspoon salt, ½ teaspoon pepper, and ½ cup bread crumbs.
3. In a small bowl, whisk eggs. In a separate medium bowl, mix remaining 1 cup bread crumbs with remaining ½ teaspoon salt and ¼ teaspoon pepper.
4. Scoop 1 tablespoon chicken mixture and flatten it into a nugget shape.
5. Dip into eggs, shaking off excess before rolling in bread crumb mixture. Repeat with remaining chicken mixture to make twenty nuggets.
6. Place nuggets in the air fryer basket and spritz with cooking spray. Cook 10 minutes, turning halfway through cooking time, until internal temperature reaches 165°F. Serve warm.

Chipotle Aioli Wings

Servings:6 | Cooking Time: 25 Minutes

Ingredients:
- 2 pounds bone-in chicken wings
- ½ teaspoon salt
- ¼ teaspoon ground black pepper
- 2 tablespoons mayonnaise
- 2 teaspoons chipotle powder
- 2 tablespoons lemon juice

Directions:
1. In a large bowl, toss wings in salt and pepper, then place into ungreased air fryer basket. Adjust the temperature to 400°F and set the timer for 25 minutes, shaking the basket twice while cooking. Wings will be done when golden and have an internal temperature of at least 165°F.
2. In a small bowl, whisk together mayonnaise, chipotle powder, and lemon juice. Place cooked wings into a large serving bowl and drizzle with aioli. Toss to coat. Serve warm.

Buffalo Chicken Wings

Servings: 3 | Cooking Time: 37 Minutes

Ingredients:
- 2 lb. chicken wings
- 1 tsp. salt
- ¼ tsp. black pepper
- 1 cup buffalo sauce

Directions:
1. Wash the chicken wings and pat them dry with clean kitchen towels.

2. Place the chicken wings in a large bowl and sprinkle on salt and pepper.
3. Pre-heat the Air Fryer to 380°F.
4. Place the wings in the fryer and cook for 15 minutes, giving them an occasional stir throughout.
5. Place the wings in a bowl. Pour over the buffalo sauce and toss well to coat.
6. Put the chicken back in the Air Fryer and cook for a final 5 – 6 minutes.

Chicken Adobo

Servings: 6 | Cooking Time: 12 Minutes

Ingredients:
- 6 boneless chicken thighs
- ¼ cup soy sauce or tamari
- ½ cup rice wine vinegar
- 4 cloves garlic, minced
- ⅛ teaspoon crushed red pepper flakes
- ½ teaspoon black pepper

Directions:
1. Place the chicken thighs into a resealable plastic bag with the soy sauce or tamari, the rice wine vinegar, the garlic, and the crushed red pepper flakes. Seal the bag and let the chicken marinate at least 1 hour in the refrigerator.
2. Preheat the air fryer to 400°F.
3. Drain the chicken and pat dry with a paper towel. Season the chicken with black pepper and liberally spray with cooking spray.
4. Place the chicken in the air fryer basket and cook for 9 minutes, turn over at 9 minutes and check for an internal temperature of 165°F, and cook another 3 minutes.

Simple Salsa Chicken Thighs

Servings:2 | Cooking Time: 35 Minutes

Ingredients:
- 1 lb boneless, skinless chicken thighs
- 1 cup mild chunky salsa
- ½ tsp taco seasoning
- 2 lime wedges for serving

Directions:
1. Preheat air fryer to 350ºF. Add chicken thighs into a baking pan and pour salsa and taco seasoning over. Place the pan in the frying basket and Air Fry for 30 minutes until golden brown. Serve with lime wedges.

Za'atar Chicken Drumsticks

Servings: 4 | Cooking Time: 45 Minutes

Ingredients:
- 2 tbsp butter, melted
- 8 chicken drumsticks
- 1 ½ tbsp Za'atar seasoning
- Salt and pepper to taste
- 1 lemon, zested
- 2 tbsp parsley, chopped

Directions:
1. Preheat air fryer to 390°F. Mix the Za'atar seasoning, lemon zest, parsley, salt, and pepper in a bowl. Add the chicken drumsticks and toss to coat. Place them in the air fryer and brush them with butter. Air Fry for 18-20 minutes, flipping once until crispy. Serve and enjoy!

Tangy Mustard Wings

Servings:4 | Cooking Time: 25 Minutes

Ingredients:
- 1 pound bone-in chicken wings, separated at joints
- ¼ cup yellow mustard
- ½ teaspoon salt
- ¼ teaspoon ground black pepper

Directions:
1. Place wings in a large bowl and toss with mustard to fully coat. Sprinkle with salt and pepper.
2. Place wings into ungreased air fryer basket. Adjust the temperature to 400°F and set the timer for 25 minutes, shaking the basket three times during cooking. Wings will be done when browned and cooked to an internal temperature of at least 165°F. Serve warm.

Hot Chicken Skin

Servings: 4 | Cooking Time: 30 Minutes

Ingredients:
- ½ teaspoon chili paste
- 8 oz chicken skin
- 1 teaspoon sesame oil
- ½ teaspoon chili powder
- ½ teaspoon salt

Directions:
1. In the shallow bowl mix up chili paste, sesame oil, chili powder, and salt. Then brush the chicken skin with chili mixture well and leave for 10 minutes to marinate. Meanwhile, preheat the air fryer to 365°F. Put the marinated chicken skin in the air fryer and cook it for 20 minutes. When the time is finished, flip the chicken skin on another side and cook it for 10 minutes more or until the chicken skin is crunchy.

Garlic Ginger Chicken

Servings:4 | Cooking Time: 12 Minutes

Ingredients:
- 1 pound boneless, skinless chicken thighs, cut into 1" pieces
- ¼ cup soy sauce
- 2 cloves garlic, peeled and finely minced
- 1 tablespoon minced ginger
- ¼ teaspoon salt

Directions:
1. Place all ingredients in a large sealable bowl or bag. Place sealed bowl or bag into refrigerator and let marinate at least 30 minutes up to overnight.
2. Remove chicken from marinade and place into ungreased air fryer basket. Adjust the temperature to 375°F and set the timer for 12 minutes, shaking the basket twice during cooking. Chicken will be golden and have an internal temperature of at least 165°F when done. Serve warm.

Jumbo Buffalo Chicken Meatballs

Servings:4 | Cooking Time: 15 Minutes

Ingredients:
- 1 pound ground chicken thighs
- 1 large egg, whisked
- ½ cup hot sauce, divided
- ½ cup crumbled blue cheese
- 2 tablespoons dry ranch seasoning

- ¼ teaspoon salt
- ¼ teaspoon ground black pepper

Directions:
1. In a large bowl, combine ground chicken, egg, ¼ cup hot sauce, blue cheese, ranch seasoning, salt, and pepper.
2. Divide mixture into eight equal sections of about ¼ cup each and form each section into a ball. Place meatballs into ungreased air fryer basket. Adjust the temperature to 370°F and set the timer for 15 minutes. Meatballs will be done when golden and have an internal temperature of at least 165°F.
3. Transfer meatballs to a large serving dish and toss with remaining hot sauce. Serve warm.

Pecan-crusted Chicken Tenders

Servings:4 | Cooking Time: 12 Minutes

Ingredients:
- 2 tablespoons mayonnaise
- 1 teaspoon Dijon mustard
- 1 pound boneless, skinless chicken tenders
- ½ teaspoon salt
- ¼ teaspoon ground black pepper
- ½ cup chopped roasted pecans, finely ground

Directions:
1. In a small bowl, whisk mayonnaise and mustard until combined. Brush mixture onto chicken tenders on both sides, then sprinkle tenders with salt and pepper.
2. Place pecans in a medium bowl and press each tender into pecans to coat each side.
3. Place tenders into ungreased air fryer basket in a single layer, working in batches if needed. Adjust the temperature to 375°F and set the timer for 12 minutes, turning tenders halfway through cooking. Tenders will be golden brown and have an internal temperature of at least 165°F when done. Serve warm.

Buffalo Chicken Meatballs

Servings:5 | Cooking Time: 12 Minutes

Ingredients:
- 1 pound ground chicken breast
- 1 packet dry ranch seasoning
- ⅓ cup plain bread crumbs
- 3 tablespoons mayonnaise
- 5 tablespoons buffalo sauce, divided

Directions:
1. Preheat the air fryer to 370°F.
2. In a large bowl, mix chicken, ranch seasoning, bread crumbs, and mayonnaise. Pour in 2 tablespoons buffalo sauce and stir to combine.
3. Roll meat mixture into balls, about 2 tablespoons for each, to make twenty meatballs.
4. Place meatballs in the air fryer basket and cook 12 minutes, shaking the basket twice during cooking, until brown and internal temperature reaches at least 165°F.
5. Toss meatballs in remaining buffalo sauce and serve.

Parmesan Chicken Tenders

Servings:4 | Cooking Time: 12 Minutes

Ingredients:
- 1 pound boneless, skinless chicken breast tenderloins
- ½ cup mayonnaise
- 1 cup grated Parmesan cheese

- 1 cup panko bread crumbs
- ½ teaspoon garlic powder
- 1 teaspoon salt
- ½ teaspoon ground black pepper
- Cooking spray

Directions:
1. Preheat the air fryer to 400°F.
2. In a large bowl, add chicken and mayonnaise and toss to coat.
3. In a medium bowl, mix Parmesan, bread crumbs, garlic powder, salt, and pepper. Press chicken into bread crumb mixture to fully coat. Spritz with cooking spray and place in the air fryer basket.
4. Cook 12 minutes, turning halfway through cooking time, until tenders are golden and crisp on the edges and internal temperature reaches at least 165°F. Serve warm.

Pickle-brined Fried Chicken

Servings:4 | Cooking Time: 20 Minutes

Ingredients:
- 4 boneless, skinless chicken thighs
- ⅓ cup dill pickle juice
- 1 large egg
- 2 ounces plain pork rinds, crushed
- ½ teaspoon salt
- ¼ teaspoon ground black pepper

Directions:
1. Place chicken thighs in a large sealable bowl or bag and pour pickle juice over them. Place sealed bowl or bag into refrigerator and allow to marinate at least 1 hour up to overnight.
2. In a small bowl, whisk egg. Place pork rinds in a separate medium bowl.
3. Remove chicken thighs from marinade. Shake off excess pickle juice and pat thighs dry with a paper towel. Sprinkle with salt and pepper.
4. Dip each thigh into egg and gently shake off excess. Press into pork rinds to coat each side. Place thighs into ungreased air fryer basket. Adjust the temperature to 400°F and set the timer for 20 minutes. When chicken thighs are done, they will be golden and crispy on the outside with an internal temperature of at least 165°F. Serve warm.

Popcorn Chicken

Servings:4 | Cooking Time: 12 Minutes

Ingredients:
- 1 ½ teaspoons salt, divided
- 1 teaspoon ground black pepper, divided
- 1 ½ teaspoons garlic powder, divided
- 1 tablespoon mayonnaise
- 1 pound boneless, skinless chicken breast, cut into 1" cubes
- 1 cup panko bread crumbs

Directions:
1. Preheat the air fryer to 350°F.
2. In a large bowl, combine 1 teaspoon salt, ½ teaspoon pepper, 1 teaspoon garlic powder, and mayonnaise. Add chicken cubes and toss to coat.
3. Place bread crumbs in a large resealable bag and add remaining ½ teaspoon salt, ½ teaspoon pepper, and ½ teaspoon garlic powder. Place chicken into the bag and toss to evenly coat.
4. Spritz chicken with cooking spray and place in the air fryer basket. Cook 12 minutes, turning halfway through cooking time, until chicken is golden brown and internal temperature reaches at

least 165°F. Serve warm.

Buttermilk-fried Drumsticks

Servings: 2 | Cooking Time: 25 Minutes

Ingredients:
- 1 egg
- ½ cup buttermilk
- ¾ cup self-rising flour
- ¾ cup seasoned panko breadcrumbs
- 1 teaspoon salt
- ¼ teaspoon ground black pepper (to mix into coating)
- 4 chicken drumsticks, skin on
- oil for misting or cooking spray

Directions:
1. Beat together egg and buttermilk in shallow dish.
2. In a second shallow dish, combine the flour, panko crumbs, salt, and pepper.
3. Sprinkle chicken legs with additional salt and pepper to taste.
4. Dip legs in buttermilk mixture, then roll in panko mixture, pressing in crumbs to make coating stick. Mist with oil or cooking spray.
5. Spray air fryer basket with cooking spray.
6. Cook drumsticks at 360°F for 10 minutes. Turn pieces over and cook an additional 10minutes.
7. Turn pieces to check for browning. If you have any white spots that haven't begun to brown, spritz them with oil or cooking spray. Continue cooking for 5 more minutes or until crust is golden brown and juices run clear. Larger, meatier drumsticks will take longer to cook than small ones.

Balsamic Duck And Cranberry Sauce

Servings: 4 | Cooking Time: 25 Minutes

Ingredients:
- 4 duck breasts, boneless, skin-on and scored
- A pinch of salt and black pepper
- 1 tablespoon olive oil
- ¼ cup balsamic vinegar
- ½ cup dried cranberries

Directions:
1. Heat up a pan that fits your air fryer with the oil over medium-high heat, add the duck breasts skin side down and cook for 5 minutes. Add the rest of the ingredients, toss, put the pan in the fryer and cook at 380°F for 20 minutes. Divide between plates and serve.

Broccoli And Cheese–stuffed Chicken

Servings:4 | Cooking Time: 20 Minutes

Ingredients:
- 2 ounces cream cheese, softened
- 1 cup chopped fresh broccoli, steamed
- ½ cup shredded sharp Cheddar cheese
- 4 boneless, skinless chicken breasts
- 2 tablespoons mayonnaise
- ¼ teaspoon salt
- ¼ teaspoon garlic powder
- ⅛ teaspoon ground black pepper

Directions:
1. In a medium bowl, combine cream cheese, broccoli, and Cheddar. Cut a 4" pocket into each chicken breast. Evenly divide mixture between chicken breasts; stuff the pocket of each chicken breast with the mixture.
2. Spread ¼ tablespoon mayonnaise per side of each chicken breast, then sprinkle both sides of breasts with salt, garlic powder, and pepper.
3. Place stuffed chicken breasts into ungreased air fryer basket so that the open seams face up. Adjust the temperature to 350°F and set the timer for 20 minutes, turning chicken halfway through cooking. When done, chicken will be golden and have an internal temperature of at least 165°F. Serve warm.

Cajun-breaded Chicken Bites

Servings:4 | Cooking Time: 12 Minutes

Ingredients:
- 1 pound boneless, skinless chicken breasts, cut into 1" cubes
- ½ cup heavy whipping cream
- ½ teaspoon salt
- ¼ teaspoon ground black pepper
- 1 ounce plain pork rinds, finely crushed
- ¼ cup unflavored whey protein powder
- ½ teaspoon Cajun seasoning

Directions:
1. Place chicken in a medium bowl and pour in cream. Stir to coat. Sprinkle with salt and pepper.
2. In a separate large bowl, combine pork rinds, protein powder, and Cajun seasoning. Remove chicken from cream, shaking off any excess, and toss in dry mix until fully coated.
3. Place bites into ungreased air fryer basket. Adjust the temperature to 400°F and set the timer for 12 minutes, shaking the basket twice during cooking. Bites will be done when golden brown and have an internal temperature of at least 165°F. Serve warm.

Butter And Bacon Chicken

Servings:6 | Cooking Time: 65 Minutes

Ingredients:
- 1 whole chicken
- 2 tablespoons salted butter, softened
- 1 teaspoon dried thyme
- ½ teaspoon garlic powder
- 1 teaspoon salt
- ½ teaspoon ground black pepper
- 6 slices sugar-free bacon

Directions:
1. Pat chicken dry with a paper towel, then rub with butter on all sides. Sprinkle thyme, garlic powder, salt, and pepper over chicken.
2. Place chicken into ungreased air fryer basket, breast side up. Lay strips of bacon over chicken and secure with toothpicks.
3. Adjust the temperature to 350°F and set the timer for 65 minutes. Halfway through cooking, remove and set aside bacon and flip chicken over. Chicken will be done when the skin is golden and crispy and the internal temperature is at least 165°F. Serve warm with bacon.

Crispy "fried" Chicken

Servings: 4 | Cooking Time: 14 Minutes

Ingredients:
- ¾ cup all-purpose flour
- ½ teaspoon paprika
- ¼ teaspoon black pepper
- ¼ teaspoon salt

- 2 large eggs
- 1½ cups panko breadcrumbs
- 1 pound boneless, skinless chicken tenders

Directions:
1. Preheat the air fryer to 400°F.
2. In a shallow bowl, mix the flour with the paprika, pepper, and salt.
3. In a separate bowl, whisk the eggs; set aside.
4. In a third bowl, place the breadcrumbs.
5. Liberally spray the air fryer basket with olive oil spray.
6. Pat the chicken tenders dry with a paper towel. Dredge the tenders one at a time in the flour, then dip them in the egg, and toss them in the breadcrumb coating. Repeat until all tenders are coated.
7. Set each tender in the air fryer, leaving room on each side of the tender to allow for flipping.
8. When the basket is full, cook 4 to 7 minutes, flip, and cook another 4 to 7 minutes.
9. Remove the tenders and let cool 5 minutes before serving. Repeat until all tenders are cooked.

Chicken Pesto Pizzas

Servings:4 | Cooking Time: 12 Minutes

Ingredients:
- 1 pound ground chicken thighs
- ¼ teaspoon salt
- ⅛ teaspoon ground black pepper
- ¼ cup basil pesto
- 1 cup shredded mozzarella cheese
- 4 grape tomatoes, sliced

Directions:
1. Cut four squares of parchment paper to fit into your air fryer basket.
2. Place ground chicken in a large bowl and mix with salt and pepper. Divide mixture into four equal sections.
3. Wet your hands with water to prevent sticking, then press each section into a 6" circle onto a piece of ungreased parchment. Place each chicken crust into air fryer basket, working in batches if needed.
4. Adjust the temperature to 350°F and set the timer for 10 minutes, turning crusts halfway through cooking.
5. When the timer beeps, spread 1 tablespoon pesto across the top of each crust, then sprinkle with ¼ cup mozzarella and top with 1 sliced tomato. Continue cooking at 350°F for 2 minutes. Cheese will be melted and brown when done. Serve warm.

Baked Chicken Nachos

Servings:4 | Cooking Time: 7 Minutes

Ingredients:
- 50 tortilla chips
- 2 cups shredded cooked chicken breast, divided
- 2 cups shredded Mexican-blend cheese, divided
- ½ cup sliced pickled jalapeño peppers, divided
- ½ cup diced red onion, divided

Directions:
1. Preheat the air fryer to 300°F.
2. Use foil to make a bowl shape that fits the shape of the air fryer basket. Place half tortilla chips in the bottom of foil bowl, then top with 1 cup chicken, 1 cup cheese, ¼ cup jalapeños, and ¼ cup onion. Repeat with remaining chips and toppings.
3. Place foil bowl in the air fryer basket and cook 7 minutes until

cheese is melted and toppings heated through. Serve warm.

Gingered Chicken Drumsticks

Servings:3 | Cooking Time:25 Minutes

Ingredients:
- ¼ cup full-fat coconut milk
- 3 chicken drumsticks
- 2 teaspoons fresh ginger, minced
- 2 teaspoons galangal, minced
- 2 teaspoons ground turmeric
- Salt, to taste

Directions:
1. Preheat the Air fryer to 375°F and grease an Air fryer basket.
2. Mix the coconut milk, galangal, ginger, and spices in a bowl.
3. Add the chicken drumsticks and coat generously with the marinade.
4. Refrigerate to marinate for at least 8 hours and transfer into the Air fryer basket.
5. Cook for about 25 minutes and dish out the chicken drumsticks onto a serving platter.

Chicken Wrapped In Bacon

Servings: 6 | Cooking Time: 25 Minutes

Ingredients:
- 6 rashers unsmoked back bacon
- 1 small chicken breast
- 1 tbsp. garlic soft cheese

Directions:
1. Cut the chicken breast into six bite-sized pieces.
2. Spread the soft cheese across one side of each slice of bacon.
3. Put the chicken on top of the cheese and wrap the bacon around it, holding it in place with a toothpick.
4. Transfer the wrapped chicken pieces to the Air Fryer and cook for 15 minutes at 350°F.

Zesty Ranch Chicken Drumsticks

Servings: 4 | Cooking Time: 20 Minutes

Ingredients:
- 8 chicken drumsticks
- 1 teaspoon salt
- ½ teaspoon ground black pepper
- ¼ cup dry ranch seasoning
- ½ cup panko bread crumbs
- ½ cup grated Parmesan cheese

Directions:
1. Preheat the air fryer to 375°F.
2. Sprinkle drumsticks with salt, pepper, and ranch seasoning.
3. In a paper lunch bag, combine bread crumbs and Parmesan. Add drumsticks to the bag and shake to coat. Spritz with cooking spray.
4. Place drumsticks in the air fryer basket and cook 20 minutes, turning halfway through cooking time, until the internal temperature reaches at least 165°F. Serve warm.

Garlic Parmesan Drumsticks

Servings:4 | Cooking Time: 25 Minutes

Ingredients:
- 8 chicken drumsticks
- ½ teaspoon salt
- ⅛ teaspoon ground black pepper
- ½ teaspoon garlic powder
- 2 tablespoons salted butter, melted
- ½ cup grated Parmesan cheese
- 1 tablespoon dried parsley

Directions:
1. Sprinkle drumsticks with salt, pepper, and garlic powder. Place drumsticks into ungreased air fryer basket.
2. Adjust the temperature to 400°F and set the timer for 25 minutes, turning drumsticks halfway through cooking. Drumsticks will be golden and have an internal temperature of at least 165°F when done.
3. Transfer drumsticks to a large serving dish. Pour butter over drumsticks, and sprinkle with Parmesan and parsley. Serve warm.

Crispy Italian Chicken Thighs

Servings:4 | Cooking Time: 25 Minutes

Ingredients:
- ½ cup mayonnaise
- 4 bone-in, skin-on chicken thighs
- 1 teaspoon salt
- ½ teaspoon ground black pepper
- 2 teaspoons Italian seasoning
- 1 cup Italian bread crumbs

Directions:
1. Preheat the air fryer to 370°F.
2. Brush mayonnaise over chicken thighs on both sides.
3. Sprinkle thighs with salt, pepper, and Italian seasoning.
4. Place bread crumbs into a resealable plastic bag and add thighs. Shake to coat.
5. Remove thighs from bag and spritz with cooking spray. Place in the air fryer basket and cook 25 minutes, turning thighs after 15 minutes, until skin is golden and crispy and internal temperature reaches at least 165°F.
6. Serve warm.

Creamy Chicken Tenders

Servings:8 | Cooking Time:20 Minutes

Ingredients:
- 2 pounds chicken tenders
- 1 cup feta cheese
- 4 tablespoons olive oil
- 1 cup cream
- Salt and black pepper, to taste

Directions:
1. Preheat the Air fryer to 340°F and grease an Air fryer basket.
2. Season the chicken tenders with salt and black pepper.
3. Arrange the chicken tenderloins in the Air fryer basket and drizzle with olive oil.
4. Cook for about 15 minutes and set the Air fryer to 390°F.
5. Cook for about 5 more minutes and dish out to serve warm.
6. Repeat with the remaining mixture and dish out to serve hot.

Crispy 'n Salted Chicken Meatballs

Servings:6 | Cooking Time: 20 Minutes

Ingredients:
- ½ cup almond flour
- ¾ pound skinless boneless chicken breasts, ground
- 1 ½ teaspoon herbs de Provence
- 1 tablespoon coconut milk
- 2 eggs, beaten
- Salt and pepper to taste

Directions:
1. Mix all ingredient in a bowl.
2. Form small balls using the palms of your hands.
3. Place in the fridge to set for at least 2 hours.
4. Preheat the air fryer for 5 minutes.
5. Place the chicken balls in the fryer basket.
6. Cook for 20 minutes at 325°F.
7. Halfway through the cooking time, give the fryer basket a shake to cook evenly on all sides.

Barbecue Chicken Drumsticks

Servings:4 | Cooking Time: 25 Minutes

Ingredients:
- 1 teaspoon salt
- 1 teaspoon chili powder
- 1 teaspoon garlic powder
- ½ teaspoon ground black pepper
- ½ teaspoon onion powder
- 8 chicken drumsticks
- 1 cup barbecue sauce, divided

Directions:
1. Preheat the air fryer to 375°F.
2. In a large bowl, combine salt, chili powder, garlic powder, pepper, and onion powder. Add drumsticks and toss to fully coat.
3. Brush drumsticks with ¾ cup barbecue sauce to coat.
4. Place in the air fryer basket and cook 25 minutes, turning three times during cooking, until drumsticks are brown and internal temperature reaches at least 165°F.
5. Before serving, brush remaining ¼ cup barbecue sauce over drumsticks. Serve warm.

Turkey-hummus Wraps

Servings: 4 | Cooking Time: 7 Minutes Per Batch

Ingredients:
- 4 large whole wheat wraps
- ½ cup hummus
- 16 thin slices deli turkey
- 8 slices provolone cheese
- 1 cup fresh baby spinach (or more to taste)

Directions:
1. To assemble, place 2 tablespoons of hummus on each wrap and spread to within about a half inch from edges. Top with 4 slices of turkey and 2 slices of provolone. Finish with ¼ cup of baby spinach—or pile on as much as you like.
2. Roll up each wrap. You don't need to fold or seal the ends.
3. Place 2 wraps in air fryer basket, seam side down.
4. Cook at 360°F for 4minutes to warm filling and melt cheese. If you like, you can continue cooking for 3 more minutes, until the wrap is slightly crispy.
5. Repeat step 4 to cook remaining wraps.

Chapter 5 Beef , pork & Lamb Recipes

Chapter 5 Beef , pork & Lamb Recipes

Sweet And Spicy Pork Ribs

Servings:4 | Cooking Time: 20 Minutes Per Batch

Ingredients:
- 1 rack pork spareribs, white membrane removed
- ¼ cup brown sugar
- 2 teaspoons salt
- 2 teaspoons ground black pepper
- 1 tablespoon chili powder
- 1 teaspoon garlic powder
- ½ teaspoon cayenne pepper

Directions:
1. Preheat the air fryer to 400°F.
2. Place ribs on a work surface and cut the rack into two pieces to fit in the air fryer basket.
3. In a medium bowl, whisk together brown sugar, salt, black pepper, chili powder, garlic powder, and cayenne to make a dry rub.
4. Massage dry rub onto both sides of ribs until well coated. Place a portion of ribs in the air fryer basket, working in batches as necessary.
5. Cook 20 minutes until internal temperature reaches at least 190°F and no pink remains. Let rest 5 minutes before cutting and serving.

Canadian-style Rib Eye Steak

Servings: 2 | Cooking Time: 15 Minutes

Ingredients:
- 2 tsp Montreal steak seasoning
- 1 ribeye steak
- 1 tbsp butter, halved
- 1 tsp chopped parsley
- ½ tsp fresh rosemary

Directions:
1. Preheat air fryer at 400ºF. Sprinkle ribeye with steak seasoning and rosemary on both sides. Place it in the basket and Bake for 10 minutes, turning once. Remove it to a cutting board and top with butter halves. Let rest for 5 minutes and scatter with parsley. Serve immediately.

Lamb Burgers

Servings: 2 | Cooking Time: 16 Minutes

Ingredients:
- 8 oz lamb, minced
- ½ teaspoon salt
- ½ teaspoon ground black pepper
- ½ teaspoon dried cilantro
- 1 tablespoon water
- Cooking spray

Directions:
1. In the mixing bowl mix up minced lamb, salt, ground black pepper, dried cilantro, and water.
2. Stir the meat mixture carefully with the help of the spoon and make 2 burgers.
3. Preheat the air fryer to 375°F.
4. Spray the air fryer basket with cooking spray and put the burg-

ers inside.
5. Cook them for 8 minutes from each side.

Spice-coated Steaks

Servings:2 | Cooking Time: 15 Minutes

Ingredients:
- ½ tsp cayenne pepper
- 1 tbsp olive oil
- ½ tsp ground paprika
- Salt and black pepper to taste

Directions:
1. Preheat air fryer to 390°F. Mix olive oil, black pepper, cayenne, paprika, and salt and rub onto steaks. Spread evenly. Put the steaks in the fryer, and cook for 6 minutes, turning them halfway through.

Crispy Pork Belly

Servings:4 | Cooking Time: 20 Minutes

Ingredients:
- 1 pound pork belly, cut into 1" cubes
- ¼ cup soy sauce
- 1 tablespoon Worcestershire sauce
- 2 teaspoons sriracha hot chili sauce
- ½ teaspoon salt
- ¼ teaspoon ground black pepper

Directions:
1. Place pork belly into a medium sealable bowl or bag and pour in soy sauce, Worcestershire sauce, and sriracha. Seal and let marinate 30 minutes in the refrigerator.
2. Remove pork from marinade, pat dry with a paper towel, and sprinkle with salt and pepper.
3. Place pork in ungreased air fryer basket. Adjust the temperature to 360°F and set the timer for 20 minutes, shaking the basket halfway through cooking. Pork belly will be done when it has an internal temperature of at least 145°F and is golden brown.
4. Let pork belly rest on a large plate 10 minutes. Serve warm.

Barbecue Country-style Pork Ribs

Servings: 3 | Cooking Time: 30 Minutes

Ingredients:
- 3 8-ounce boneless country-style pork ribs
- 1½ teaspoons Mild smoked paprika
- 1½ teaspoons Light brown sugar
- ¾ teaspoon Onion powder
- ¾ teaspoon Ground black pepper
- ¼ teaspoon Table salt
- Vegetable oil spray

Directions:
1. Preheat the air fryer to 350°F . Set the ribs in a bowl on the counter as the machine heats.
2. Mix the smoked paprika, brown sugar, onion powder, pepper, and salt in a small bowl until well combined. Rub this mixture over all the surfaces of the country-style ribs. Generously coat the country-style ribs with vegetable oil spray.
3. Set the ribs in the basket with as much air space between them

as possible. Air-fry undisturbed for 30 minutes, or until browned and sizzling and an instant-read meat thermometer inserted into one rib registers at least 145°F.
4. Use kitchen tongs to transfer the country-style ribs to a wire rack. Cool for 5 minutes before serving.

Bacon Wrapped Pork Tenderloin

Servings:4 | Cooking Time:30 Minutes

Ingredients:
• 1 pork tenderloins
• 4 bacon strips
• 2 tablespoons Dijon mustard

Directions:
1. Preheat the Air fryer to 360°F and grease an Air fryer basket.
2. Rub the tenderloin evenly with mustard and wrap the tenderloin with bacon strips.
3. Arrange the pork tenderloin in the Air fryer basket and cook for about 30 minutes, flipping once in between.
4. Dish out the steaks and cut into desired size slices to serve.

Barbecue-style Beef Cube Steak

Servings: 2 | Cooking Time: 14 Minutes

Ingredients:
• 2 4-ounce beef cube steak(s)
• 2 cups Fritos (original flavor) or a generic corn chip equivalent, crushed to crumbs
• 6 tablespoons Purchased smooth barbecue sauce, any flavor (gluten-free, if a concern)

Directions:
1. Preheat the air fryer to 375°F.
2. Spread the Fritos crumbs in a shallow soup plate or a small pie plate. Rub the barbecue sauce onto both sides of the steak(s). Dredge the steak(s) in the Fritos crumbs to coat well and thoroughly, turning several times and pressing down to get the little bits to adhere to the meat.
3. When the machine is at temperature, set the steak(s) in the basket. Leave as much air space between them as possible if you're working with more than one piece of beef. Air-fry undisturbed for 12 minutes, or until lightly brown and crunchy. If the machine is at 360°F, you may need to add 2 minutes to the cooking time.
4. Use kitchen tongs to transfer the steak(s) to a wire rack. Cool for 5 minutes before serving.

Simple Beef

Servings: 1 | Cooking Time: 25 Minutes

Ingredients:
• 1 thin beef schnitzel
• 1 egg, beaten
• ½ cup friendly bread crumbs
• 2 tbsp. olive oil
• Pepper and salt to taste

Directions:
1. Pre-heat the Air Fryer to 350°F.
2. In a shallow dish, combine the bread crumbs, oil, pepper, and salt.
3. In a second shallow dish, place the beaten egg.
4. Dredge the schnitzel in the egg before rolling it in the bread crumbs.
5. Put the coated schnitzel in the fryer basket and air fry for 12 minutes.

Hot Dogs

Servings:8 | Cooking Time: 7 Minutes

Ingredients:
• 8 beef hot dogs
• 8 hot dog buns

Directions:
1. Preheat the air fryer to 400°F.
2. Place hot dogs in the air fryer basket and cook 7 minutes. Place each hot dog in a bun. Serve warm.

Blackened Steak Nuggets

Servings:2 | Cooking Time: 7 Minutes

Ingredients:
• 1 pound rib eye steak, cut into 1" cubes
• 2 tablespoons salted butter, melted
• ½ teaspoon paprika
• ½ teaspoon salt
• ¼ teaspoon garlic powder
• ¼ teaspoon onion powder
• ¼ teaspoon ground black pepper
• ⅛ teaspoon cayenne pepper

Directions:
1. Place steak into a large bowl and pour in butter. Toss to coat. Sprinkle with remaining ingredients.
2. Place bites into ungreased air fryer basket. Adjust the temperature to 400°F and set the timer for 7 minutes, shaking the basket three times during cooking. Steak will be crispy on the outside and browned when done and internal temperature is at least 150°F for medium and 180°F for well-done. Serve warm.

Salted Porterhouse With Sage 'n Thyme Medley

Servings:2 | Cooking Time: 40 Minutes

Ingredients:
• ¼ cup fish sauce
• 2 porterhouse steaks
• 2 tablespoons marjoram
• 2 tablespoons sage
• 2 tablespoons thyme
• Salt and pepper to taste

Directions:
1. Place all ingredients in a Ziploc bag and allow to marinate in the fridge for at least 2 hours.
2. Preheat the air fryer to 390°F.
3. Place the grill pan accessory in the air fryer.
4. Grill for 20 minutes per batch.
5. Flip every 10 minutes for even grilling.

Egg Stuffed Pork Meatballs

Servings: 2 | Cooking Time: 40 Minutes

Ingredients:
• 3 soft boiled eggs, peeled
• 8 oz ground pork
• 2 tsp dried tarragon
• ½ tsp hot paprika
• 2 tsp garlic powder
• Salt and pepper to taste

Directions:

1. Preheat air fryer to 350°F. Combine the pork, tarragon, hot paprika, garlic powder, salt, and pepper in a bowl and stir until all spices are evenly spread throughout the meat. Divide the meat mixture into three equal portions in the mixing bowl, and shape each into balls.

2. Flatten one of the meatballs on top to make a wide, flat meat circle. Place an egg in the middle. Use your hands to mold the mixture up and around to enclose the egg. Repeat with the remaining eggs. Place the stuffed balls in the air fryer. Air Fry for 18-20 minutes, shaking the basket once until the meat is crispy and golden brown. Serve.

Cheddar Bacon Ranch Pinwheels

Servings:5 | Cooking Time: 12 Minutes Per Batch

Ingredients:
- 4 ounces full-fat cream cheese, softened
- 1 tablespoon dry ranch seasoning
- ½ cup shredded Cheddar cheese
- 1 sheet frozen puff pastry dough, thawed
- 6 slices bacon, cooked and crumbled

Directions:
1. Preheat the air fryer to 320°F. Cut parchment paper to fit the air fryer basket.
2. In a medium bowl, mix cream cheese, ranch seasoning, and Cheddar. Unfold puff pastry and gently spread cheese mixture over pastry.
3. Sprinkle crumbled bacon on top. Starting from a long side, roll dough into a log, pressing in the edges to seal.
4. Cut log into ten pieces, then place on parchment in the air fryer basket, working in batches as necessary.
5. Cook 12 minutes, turning each piece after 7 minutes. Let cool 5 minutes before serving.

Basil Pork

Servings: 4 | Cooking Time: 25 Minutes

Ingredients:
- 4 pork chops
- A pinch of salt and black pepper
- 2 teaspoons basil, dried
- 2 tablespoons olive oil
- ½ teaspoon chili powder

Directions:
1. In a pan that fits your air fryer, mix all the ingredients, toss, introduce in the fryer and cook at 400°F for 25 minutes. Divide everything between plates and serve.

Corn Dogs

Servings:4 | Cooking Time: 8 Minutes

Ingredients:
- 1½ cups shredded mozzarella cheese
- 1 ounce cream cheese
- ½ cup blanched finely ground almond flour
- 4 beef hot dogs

Directions:
1. Place mozzarella, cream cheese, and flour in a large microwave-safe bowl. Microwave on high 45 seconds, then stir with a fork until a soft ball of dough forms.
2. Press dough out into a 12" × 6" rectangle, then use a knife to separate into four smaller rectangles.
3. Wrap each hot dog in one rectangle of dough and place into

ungreased air fryer basket. Adjust the temperature to 400°F and set the timer for 8 minutes, turning corn dogs halfway through cooking. Corn dogs will be golden brown when done. Serve warm.

Simple Pork Chops

Servings: 4 | Cooking Time: 20 Minutes

Ingredients:
- 4 pork chops, boneless
- 1 1/2 tbsp Mr. Dash seasoning
- Pepper
- Salt

Directions:
1. Coat pork chops with Mr. dash seasoning, pepper, and salt.
2. Place pork chops in the air fryer and cook at 360°F for 10 minutes.
3. Turn pork chops to another side and cook for 10 minutes more.
4. Serve and enjoy.

Bacon With Shallot And Greens

Servings: 2 | Cooking Time: 10 Minutes

Ingredients:
- 7 ounces mixed greens
- 8 thick slices pork bacon
- 2 shallots, peeled and diced
- Nonstick cooking spray

Directions:
1. Begin by preheating the air fryer to 345°F.
2. Now, add the shallot and bacon to the Air Fryer cooking basket; set the timer for 2 minutes. Spritz with a nonstick cooking spray.
3. After that, pause the Air Fryer; throw in the mixed greens; give it a good stir and cook an additional 5 minutes. Serve warm.

Jerk Pork

Servings: 4 | Cooking Time: 20 Minutes

Ingredients:
- 1 1/2 lbs pork butt, chopped into pieces
- 3 tbsp jerk paste

Directions:
1. Add meat and jerk paste into the bowl and coat well. Place in the fridge for overnight.
2. Spray air fryer basket with cooking spray.
3. Preheat the air fryer to 390°F.
4. Add marinated meat into the air fryer and cook for 20 minutes. Turn halfway through.
5. Serve and enjoy.

Friday Night Cheeseburgers

Servings: 4 | Cooking Time: 20 Minutes

Ingredients:
- 1 lb ground beef
- 1 tsp Worcestershire sauce
- 1 tbsp allspice
- Salt and pepper to taste
- 4 cheddar cheese slices
- 4 buns

Directions:
1. Preheat air fryer to 360°F. Combine beef, Worcestershire

sauce, allspice, salt and pepper in a large bowl. Divide into 4 equal portions and shape into patties. Place the burgers in the greased frying basket and Air Fry for 8 minutes. Flip and cook for another 3-4 minutes. Top each burger with cheddar cheese and cook for another minute so the cheese melts. Transfer to a bun and serve.

Pork Spare Ribs

Servings:4 | Cooking Time: 30 Minutes

Ingredients:
- 1 rack pork spare ribs
- 1 teaspoon ground cumin
- 2 teaspoons salt
- 1 teaspoon ground black pepper
- 1 teaspoon garlic powder
- ½ teaspoon dry ground mustard
- ½ cup low-carb barbecue sauce

Directions:
1. Place ribs on ungreased aluminum foil sheet. Carefully use a knife to remove membrane and sprinkle meat evenly on both sides with cumin, salt, pepper, garlic powder, and ground mustard.
2. Cut rack into portions that will fit in your air fryer, and wrap each portion in one layer of aluminum foil, working in batches if needed.
3. Place ribs into ungreased air fryer basket. Adjust the temperature to 400°F and set the timer for 25 minutes.
4. When the timer beeps, carefully remove ribs from foil and brush with barbecue sauce. Return to air fryer and cook at 400°F for an additional 5 minutes to brown. Ribs will be done when no pink remains and internal temperature is at least 180°F. Serve warm.

Quick & Easy Meatballs

Servings: 4 | Cooking Time: 12 Minutes

Ingredients:
- 4 oz lamb meat, minced
- 1 tbsp oregano, chopped
- ½ tbsp lemon zest
- 1 egg, lightly beaten
- Pepper
- Salt

Directions:
1. Add all ingredients into the bowl and mix until well combined.
2. Spray air fryer basket with cooking spray.
3. Make balls from bowl mixture and place into the air fryer basket and cook at 400°F for 12 minutes.
4. Serve and enjoy.

Air Fried Thyme Garlic Lamb Chops

Servings: 4 | Cooking Time: 12 Minutes

Ingredients:
- 4 lamb chops
- 4 garlic cloves, minced
- 3 tbsp olive oil
- 1 tbsp dried thyme
- Pepper
- Salt

Directions:
1. Preheat the air fryer to 390°F.

2. Season lamb chops with pepper and salt.
3. In a small bowl, mix together thyme, oil, and garlic and rub over lamb chops.
4. Place lamb chops into the air fryer and cook for 12 minutes. Turn halfway through.
5. Serve and enjoy.

Easy-peasy Beef Sliders

Servings:4 | Cooking Time: 25 Minutes

Ingredients:
- 1 lb ground beef
- ¼ tsp cumin
- ¼ tsp mustard power
- 1/3 cup grated yellow onion
- ½ tsp smoked paprika
- Salt and pepper to taste

Directions:
1. Preheat air fryer to 350ºF. Combine the ground beef, cumin, mustard, onion, paprika, salt, and black pepper in a bowl. Form mixture into 8 patties and make a slight indentation in the middle of each. Place beef patties in the greased frying basket and Air Fry for 8-10 minutes, flipping once. Serve right away and enjoy!

Mccornick Pork Chops

Servings: 2 | Cooking Time: 15 Minutes

Ingredients:
- 2 pork chops
- 1/2 tsp McCormick Montreal chicken seasoning
- 2 tbsp arrowroot flour
- 1 1/2 tbsp coconut milk
- Salt

Directions:
1. Season pork chops with pepper and salt.
2. Drizzle milk over the pork chops.
3. Place pork chops in a zip-lock bag with flour and shake well to coat. Marinate pork chops for 30 minutes.
4. Place marinated pork chops into the air fryer basket and cook at 380°F for 15 minutes. Turn halfway through.
5. Serve and enjoy.

Crispy Pork Pork Escalopes

Servings: 4 | Cooking Time: 20 Minutes

Ingredients:
- 4 pork loin steaks
- Salt and pepper to taste
- ¼ cup flour
- 2 tbsp bread crumbs
- Cooking spray

Directions:
1. Preheat air fryer to 380°F. Season pork with salt and pepper. In one shallow bowl, add flour. In another, add bread crumbs. Dip the steaks first in the flour, then in the crumbs. Place them in the fryer and spray with oil. Bake for 12-14 minutes, flipping once until crisp. Serve.

Flatiron Steak Grill On Parsley Salad

Servings:4 | Cooking Time: 45 Minutes

Ingredients:
- ½ cup parmesan cheese, grated
- 1 ½ pounds flatiron steak
- 1 tablespoon fresh lemon juice
- 2 cups parsley leaves
- 3 tablespoons olive oil
- Salt and pepper to taste

Directions:
1. Preheat the air fryer to 390°F.
2. Place the grill pan accessory in the air fryer.
3. Mix together the steak, oil, salt and pepper.
4. Grill for 15 minutes per batch and make sure to flip the meat halfway through the cooking time.
5. Meanwhile, prepare the salad by combining in a bowl the parsley leaves, parmesan cheese and lemon juice. Season with salt and pepper.

Tasty Filet Mignon

Servings:2 | Cooking Time: 30 Minutes

Ingredients:
- 2 filet mignon steaks
- ¼ tsp garlic powder
- Salt and pepper to taste
- 1 tbsp butter, melted

Directions:
1. Preheat air fryer to 370ºF. Sprinkle the steaks with salt, garlic and pepper on both sides. Place them in the greased frying basket and Air Fry for 12 minutes to yield a medium-rare steak, turning twice. Transfer steaks to a cutting board, brush them with butter and let rest 5 minutes before serving.

Crunchy Fried Pork Loin Chops

Servings: 3 | Cooking Time: 12 Minutes

Ingredients:
- 1 cup All-purpose flour or tapioca flour
- 1 Large egg(s), well beaten
- 1½ cups Seasoned Italian-style dried bread crumbs (gluten-free, if a concern)
- 3 4- to 5-ounce boneless center-cut pork loin chops
- Vegetable oil spray

Directions:
1. Preheat the air fryer to 350°F .
2. Set up and fill three shallow soup plates or small pie plates on your counter: one for the flour, one for the beaten egg(s), and one for the bread crumbs.
3. Dredge a pork chop in the flour, coating both sides as well as around the edge. Gently shake off any excess, then dip the chop in the egg(s), again coating both sides and the edge. Let any excess egg slip back into the rest, then set the chop in the bread crumbs, turning it and pressing gently to coat well on both sides and the edge. Coat the pork chop all over with vegetable oil spray and set aside so you can dredge, coat, and spray the additional chop(s).
4. Set the chops in the basket with as much air space between them as possible. Air-fry undisturbed for 12 minutes, or until brown and crunchy and an instant-read meat thermometer inserted into the center of a chop registers 145°F.
5. Use kitchen tongs to transfer the chops to a wire rack. Cool for 5 minutes before serving.

Pesto-rubbed Veal Chops

Servings: 2 | Cooking Time: 12-15 Minutes

Ingredients:
- ¼ cup Purchased pesto
- 2 10-ounce bone-in veal loin or rib chop(s)
- ½ teaspoon Ground black pepper

Directions:
1. Preheat the air fryer to 400°F.
2. Rub the pesto onto both sides of the veal chop(s). Sprinkle one side of the chop(s) with the ground black pepper. Set aside at room temperature as the machine comes up to temperature.
3. Set the chop(s) in the basket. If you're cooking more than one chop, leave as much air space between them as possible. Air-fry undisturbed for 12 minutes for medium-rare, or until an instant-read meat thermometer inserted into the center of a chop registers 135°F. Or air-fry undisturbed for 15 minutes for medium-well, or until an instant-read meat thermometer registers 145°F.
4. Use kitchen tongs to transfer the chops to a cutting board or a wire rack. Cool for 5 minutes before serving.

Honey-sriracha Pork Ribs

Servings:4 | Cooking Time: 25 Minutes

Ingredients:
- 3 pounds pork back ribs, white membrane removed
- 2 teaspoons salt
- 1 teaspoon ground black pepper
- ½ cup sriracha
- ⅓ cup honey
- 1 tablespoon lemon juice

Directions:
1. Preheat the air fryer to 400°F.
2. Place ribs on a work surface and cut the rack into two pieces to fit in the air fryer basket.
3. Sprinkle ribs with salt and pepper and place in the air fryer basket meat side down. Cook 15 minutes.
4. In a small bowl, combine the sriracha, honey, and lemon juice to make a sauce.
5. Remove ribs from the air fryer basket and pour sauce over both sides. Return them to the air fryer basket meat side up and cook an additional 10 minutes until brown and the internal temperature reaches at least 190°F. Serve warm.

Venison Backstrap

Servings: 4 | Cooking Time: 10 Minutes

Ingredients:
- 2 eggs
- ¼ cup milk
- 1 cup whole wheat flour
- ½ teaspoon salt
- ¼ teaspoon pepper
- 1 pound venison backstrap, sliced
- salt and pepper
- oil for misting or cooking spray

Directions:
1. Beat together eggs and milk in a shallow dish.
2. In another shallow dish, combine the flour, salt, and pepper. Stir to mix well.
3. Sprinkle venison steaks with additional salt and pepper to taste. Dip in flour, egg wash, then in flour again, pressing in coat-

ing.

4. Spray steaks with oil or cooking spray on both sides.

5. Cooking in 2 batches, place steaks in the air fryer basket in a single layer. Cook at 360°F for 8minutes. Spray with oil, turn over, and spray other side. Cook for 2 minutes longer, until coating is crispy brown and meat is done to your liking.

6. Repeat to cook remaining venison.

7. Spray both sides with oil and cook for 5minutes. If needed, mist with oil and continue cooking for 3 minutes longer. This second batch will cook a little faster than the first because your air fryer is already hot.

8. Serve with marinara sauce on the side for dipping.

Wasabi-coated Pork Loin Chops

Servings: 3 | Cooking Time: 14 Minutes

Ingredients:
- 1½ cups Wasabi peas
- ¼ cup Plain panko bread crumbs
- 1 Large egg white(s)
- 2 tablespoons Water
- 3 5- to 6-ounce boneless center-cut pork loin chops (about ½ inch thick)

Directions:
1. Preheat the air fryer to 375°F.

2. Put the wasabi peas in a food processor. Cover and process until finely ground, about like panko bread crumbs. Add the bread crumbs and pulse a few times to blend.

3. Set up and fill two shallow soup plates or small pie plates on your counter: one for the egg white(s), whisked with the water until uniform; and one for the wasabi pea mixture.

4. Dip a pork chop in the egg white mixture, coating the chop on both sides as well as around the edge. Allow any excess egg white mixture to slip back into the rest, then set the chop in the wasabi pea mixture. Press gently and turn it several times to coat evenly on both sides and around the edge. Set aside, then dip and coat the remaining chop(s).

5. Set the chops in the basket with as much air space between them as possible. Air-fry, turning once at the 6-minute mark, for 12 minutes, or until the chops are crisp and browned and an instant-read meat thermometer inserted into the center of a chop registers 145°F. If the machine is at 360°F, you may need to add 2 minutes to the cooking time.

6. Use kitchen tongs to transfer the chops to a wire rack. Cool for a couple of minutes before serving.

Delicious Cheeseburgers

Servings: 4 | Cooking Time: 12 Minutes

Ingredients:
- 1 lb ground beef
- 4 cheddar cheese slices
- 1/2 tsp Italian seasoning
- Pepper
- Salt
- Cooking spray

Directions:
1. Spray air fryer basket with cooking spray.

2. In a bowl, mix together ground beef, Italian seasoning, pepper, and salt.

3. Make four equal shapes of patties from meat mixture and place into the air fryer basket.

4. Cook at 375°F for 5 minutes. Turn patties to another side and

cook for 5 minutes more.

5. Place cheese slices on top of each patty and cook for 2 minutes more.

6. Serve and enjoy.

Marinated Rib Eye

Servings:4 | Cooking Time: 10 Minutes

Ingredients:
- 1 pound rib eye steak
- ¼ cup soy sauce
- 1 tablespoon Worcestershire sauce
- 1 tablespoon granular brown erythritol
- 2 tablespoons olive oil
- ½ teaspoon salt
- ¼ teaspoon ground black pepper

Directions:
1. Place rib eye in a large sealable bowl or bag and pour in soy sauce, Worcestershire sauce, erythritol, and olive oil. Seal and let marinate 30 minutes in the refrigerator.

2. Remove rib eye from marinade, pat dry, and sprinkle on all sides with salt and pepper. Place rib eye into ungreased air fryer basket. Adjust the temperature to 400°F and set the timer for 10 minutes. Steak will be done when browned at the edges and has an internal temperature of 150°F for medium or 180°F for well-done. Serve warm.

Spinach And Mushroom Steak Rolls

Servings:4 | Cooking Time: 19 Minutes

Ingredients:
- ½ medium yellow onion, peeled and chopped
- ½ cup chopped baby bella mushrooms
- 1 cup chopped fresh spinach
- 1 pound flank steak
- 8 slices provolone cheese
- 1 teaspoon salt
- ½ teaspoon ground black pepper
- Cooking spray

Directions:
1. In a medium skillet over medium heat, sauté onion 2 minutes until fragrant and beginning to soften. Add mushrooms and spinach and continue cooking 5 more minutes until spinach is wilted and mushrooms are soft.

2. Preheat the air fryer to 400°F.

3. Carefully butterfly steak, leaving the two halves connected. Place slices of cheese on top of steak, then top with cooked vegetables.

4. Place steak so that the grain runs horizontally. Tightly roll up steak and secure it closed with eight evenly placed toothpicks or eight sections of butcher's twine.

5. Slice steak into four rolls. Spritz with cooking spray, then sprinkle with salt and pepper. Place in the air fryer basket and cook 12 minutes until steak is brown on the edges and internal temperature reaches at least 160°F for well-done. Serve.

Bacon Blue Cheese Burger

Servings:4 | Cooking Time: 15 Minutes

Ingredients:
- 1 pound ground sirloin
- ½ cup crumbled blue cheese
- 8 slices bacon, cooked and crumbled
- 1 teaspoon Worcestershire sauce
- 1 teaspoon salt
- ½ teaspoon ground black pepper
- 4 pretzel buns
- Cooking spray

Directions:
1. Preheat the air fryer to 370°F.
2. In a large bowl, mix sirloin, cheese, bacon, and Worcestershire until well combined.
3. Form into four patties and sprinkle each side with salt and pepper. Spritz with cooking spray and place in the air fryer basket.
4. Cook 15 minutes, turning halfway through cooking time, until internal temperature reaches at least 160°F for well-done. Place on pretzel buns to serve.

Perfect Pork Chops

Servings: 3 | Cooking Time: 10 Minutes

Ingredients:
- ¾ teaspoon Mild paprika
- ¾ teaspoon Dried thyme
- ¾ teaspoon Onion powder
- ¼ teaspoon Garlic powder
- ¼ teaspoon Table salt
- ¼ teaspoon Ground black pepper
- 3 6-ounce boneless center-cut pork loin chops
- Vegetable oil spray

Directions:
1. Preheat the air fryer to 400°F.
2. Mix the paprika, thyme, onion powder, garlic powder, salt, and pepper in a small bowl until well combined. Massage this mixture into both sides of the chops. Generously coat both sides of the chops with vegetable oil spray.
3. When the machine is at temperature, set the chops in the basket with as much air space between them as possible. Air-fry undisturbed for 10 minutes, or until an instant-read meat thermometer inserted into the thickest part of a chop registers 145°F.
4. Use kitchen tongs to transfer the chops to a cutting board or serving plates. Cool for 5 minutes before serving.

Cheese-stuffed Steak Burgers

Servings:4 | Cooking Time: 10 Minutes

Ingredients:
- 1 pound 80/20 ground sirloin
- 4 ounces mild Cheddar cheese, cubed
- ½ teaspoon salt
- ¼ teaspoon ground black pepper

Directions:
1. Form ground sirloin into four equal balls, then separate each ball in half and flatten into two thin patties, for eight total patties. Place 1 ounce Cheddar into center of one patty, then top with a second patty and press edges to seal burger closed. Repeat with remaining patties and Cheddar to create four burgers.
2. Sprinkle salt and pepper over both sides of burgers and carefully place burgers into ungreased air fryer basket. Adjust the temperature to 350°F and set the timer for 10 minutes. Burgers will be done when browned on the edges and top. Serve warm.

Mustard Herb Pork Tenderloin

Servings:6 | Cooking Time: 20 Minutes

Ingredients:
- ¼ cup mayonnaise
- 2 tablespoons Dijon mustard
- ½ teaspoon dried thyme
- ¼ teaspoon dried rosemary
- 1 pork tenderloin
- ½ teaspoon salt
- ¼ teaspoon ground black pepper

Directions:
1. In a small bowl, mix mayonnaise, mustard, thyme, and rosemary. Brush tenderloin with mixture on all sides, then sprinkle with salt and pepper on all sides.
2. Place tenderloin into ungreased air fryer basket. Adjust the temperature to 400°F and set the timer for 20 minutes, turning tenderloin halfway through cooking. Tenderloin will be golden and have an internal temperature of at least 145°F when done. Serve warm.

Marinated Steak Kebabs

Servings:4 | Cooking Time: 5 Minutes

Ingredients:
- 1 pound strip steak, fat trimmed, cut into 1" cubes
- ½ cup soy sauce
- ¼ cup olive oil
- 1 tablespoon granular brown erythritol
- ½ teaspoon salt
- ¼ teaspoon ground black pepper
- 1 medium green bell pepper, seeded and chopped into 1" cubes

Directions:
1. Place steak into a large sealable bowl or bag and pour in soy sauce and olive oil. Add erythritol, then stir to coat steak. Marinate at room temperature 30 minutes.
2. Remove streak from marinade and sprinkle with salt and black pepper.
3. Place meat and vegetables onto 6" skewer sticks, alternating between steak and bell pepper.
4. Place kebabs into ungreased air fryer basket. Adjust the temperature to 400°F and set the timer for 5 minutes. Steak will be done when crispy at the edges and peppers are tender. Serve warm.

Lamb Chops

Servings: 2 | Cooking Time: 20 Minutes

Ingredients:
- 2 teaspoons oil
- ½ teaspoon ground rosemary
- ½ teaspoon lemon juice
- 1 pound lamb chops, approximately 1-inch thick
- salt and pepper
- cooking spray

Directions:
1. Mix the oil, rosemary, and lemon juice together and rub into all sides of the lamb chops. Season to taste with salt and pepper.
2. For best flavor, cover lamb chops and allow them to rest in the fridge for 20 minutes.

3. Spray air fryer basket with nonstick spray and place lamb chops in it.
4. Cook at 360°F for approximately 20minutes. This will cook chops to medium. The meat will be juicy but have no remaining pink. Cook for a minute or two longer for well done chops. For rare chops, stop cooking after about 12minutes and check for doneness.

Garlic And Oregano Lamb Chops

Servings: 4 | Cooking Time: 17 Minutes

Ingredients:
- 1½ tablespoons Olive oil
- 1 tablespoon Minced garlic
- 1 teaspoon Dried oregano
- 1 teaspoon Finely minced orange zest
- ¾ teaspoon Fennel seeds
- ¾ teaspoon Table salt
- ¾ teaspoon Ground black pepper
- 6 4-ounce, 1-inch-thick lamb loin chops

Directions:
1. Mix the olive oil, garlic, oregano, orange zest, fennel seeds, salt, and pepper in a large bowl. Add the chops and toss well to coat. Set aside as the air fryer heats, tossing one more time.
2. Preheat the air fryer to 400°F.
3. Set the chops bone side down in the basket with as much air space between them as possible. Air-fry undisturbed for 14 minutes for medium-rare, or until an instant-read meat thermometer inserted into the thickest part of a chop registers 132°F. Or air-fry undisturbed for 17 minutes for well done, or until an instant-read meat thermometer registers 145°F.
4. Use kitchen tongs to transfer the chops to a wire rack. Cool for 5 minutes before serving.

Honey Mesquite Pork Chops

Servings: 2 | Cooking Time: 10 Minutes

Ingredients:
- 2 tablespoons mesquite seasoning
- ¼ cup honey
- 1 tablespoon olive oil
- 1 tablespoon water
- freshly ground black pepper
- 2 bone-in center cut pork chops

Directions:
1. Whisk the mesquite seasoning, honey, olive oil, water and freshly ground black pepper together in a shallow glass dish. Pierce the chops all over and on both sides with a fork or meat tenderizer. Add the pork chops to the marinade and massage the marinade into the chops. Cover and marinate for 30 minutes.
2. Preheat the air fryer to 330°F.
3. Transfer the pork chops to the air fryer basket and pour half of the marinade over the chops, reserving the remaining marinade. Air-fry the pork chops for 6 minutes. Flip the pork chops over and pour the remaining marinade on top. Air-fry for an additional 3 minutes at 330°F. Then, increase the air fryer temperature to 400°F and air-fry the pork chops for an additional minute.
4. Transfer the pork chops to a serving plate, and let them rest for 5 minutes before serving. If you'd like a sauce for these chops, pour the cooked marinade from the bottom of the air fryer over the top.

Kielbasa Chunks With Pineapple & Peppers

Servings: 2 | Cooking Time: 10 Minutes

Ingredients:
- ¾ pound kielbasa sausage
- 1 cup bell pepper chunks (any color)
- 1 8-ounce can pineapple chunks in juice, drained
- 1 tablespoon barbeque seasoning
- 1 tablespoon soy sauce
- cooking spray

Directions:
1. Cut sausage into ½-inch slices.
2. In a medium bowl, toss all ingredients together.
3. Spray air fryer basket with nonstick cooking spray.
4. Pour sausage mixture into the basket.
5. Cook at 390°F for approximately 5 minutes. Shake basket and cook an additional 5 minutes.

Mozzarella-stuffed Meatloaf

Servings:6 | Cooking Time: 30 Minutes

Ingredients:
- 1 pound 80/20 ground beef
- ½ medium green bell pepper, seeded and chopped
- ¼ medium yellow onion, peeled and chopped
- ½ teaspoon salt
- ¼ teaspoon ground black pepper
- 2 ounces mozzarella cheese, sliced into ¼"-thick slices
- ¼ cup low-carb ketchup

Directions:
1. In a large bowl, combine ground beef, bell pepper, onion, salt, and black pepper. Cut a piece of parchment to fit air fryer basket. Place half beef mixture on ungreased parchment and form a 9" × 4" loaf, about ½" thick.
2. Center mozzarella slices on beef loaf, leaving at least ¼" around each edge.
3. Press remaining beef into a second 9" × 4" loaf and place on top of mozzarella, pressing edges of loaves together to seal.
4. Place parchment with meatloaf into air fryer basket. Adjust the temperature to 350°F and set the timer for 30 minutes, carefully turning loaf and brushing top with ketchup halfway through cooking. Loaf will be browned and have an internal temperature of at least 180°F when done. Slice and serve warm.

Simple Lamb Chops

Servings:2 | Cooking Time:6 Minutes

Ingredients:
- 4 lamb chops
- Salt and black pepper, to taste
- 1 tablespoon olive oil

Directions:
1. Preheat the Air fryer to 390°F and grease an Air fryer basket.
2. Mix the olive oil, salt, and black pepper in a large bowl and add chops.
3. Arrange the chops in the Air fryer basket and cook for about 6 minutes.
4. Dish out the lamb chops and serve hot.

Beef Short Ribs

Servings: 4 | Cooking Time: 25 Minutes

Ingredients:
- 3 pounds beef short ribs
- 2 tablespoons olive oil
- 3 teaspoons salt
- 3 teaspoons ground black pepper
- ½ cup barbecue sauce

Directions:
1. Preheat the air fryer to 375°F.
2. Place short ribs in a large bowl. Drizzle with oil and sprinkle both sides with salt and pepper.
3. Place in the air fryer basket and cook 20 minutes. Remove from basket and brush with barbecue sauce. Return to the air fryer basket and cook 5 additional minutes until sauce is dark brown and internal temperature reaches at least 160°F. Serve warm.

Buttery Pork Chops

Servings: 4 | Cooking Time: 12 Minutes

Ingredients:
- 4 boneless pork chops
- 1 teaspoon salt
- ½ teaspoon ground black pepper
- 4 tablespoons salted butter, sliced into 8 (½-tablespoon) pats, divided

Directions:
1. Preheat the air fryer to 400°F.
2. Sprinkle pork chops with salt and pepper. Top each pork chop with a ½-tablespoon butter pat.
3. Place chops in the air fryer basket and cook 12 minutes, turning halfway through cooking time, until tops and edges are golden brown and internal temperature reaches at least 145°F.
4. Use remaining butter pats to top each pork chop while hot, then let cool 5 minutes before serving warm.

Almond And Sun-dried Tomato Crusted Pork Chops

Servings: 4 | Cooking Time: 10 Minutes

Ingredients:
- ½ cup oil-packed sun-dried tomatoes
- ½ cup toasted almonds
- ¼ cup grated Parmesan cheese
- ½ cup olive oil
- 2 tablespoons water
- ½ teaspoon salt
- freshly ground black pepper
- 4 center-cut boneless pork chops

Directions:
1. Place the sun-dried tomatoes into a food processor and pulse them until they are coarsely chopped. Add the almonds, Parmesan cheese, olive oil, water, salt and pepper. Process all the ingredients into a smooth paste. Spread most of the paste onto both sides of the pork chops and then pierce the meat several times with a needle-style meat tenderizer or a fork. Let the pork chops sit and marinate for at least 1 hour.
2. Preheat the air fryer to 370°F.
3. Brush a little olive oil on the bottom of the air fryer basket. Transfer the pork chops into the air fryer basket, spooning a little more of the sun-dried tomato paste onto the pork chops if there are any gaps where the paste may have been rubbed off. Air-fry the pork chops at 370°F for 10 minutes, turning the chops over halfway through the cooking process.
4. When the pork chops have finished cooking, transfer them to a serving plate and serve with mashed potatoes and vegetables for a hearty meal.

Crispy Pierogi With Kielbasa And Onions

Servings: 3 | Cooking Time: 20 Minutes

Ingredients:
- 6 Frozen potato and cheese pierogi, thawed
- ½ pound Smoked kielbasa, sliced into ½-inch-thick rounds
- ¾ cup Very roughly chopped sweet onion, preferably Vidalia
- Vegetable oil spray

Directions:
1. Preheat the air fryer to 375°F .
2. Put the pierogi, kielbasa rounds, and onion in a large bowl. Coat them with vegetable oil spray, toss well, spray again, and toss until everything is glistening.
3. When the machine is at temperature, dump the contents of the bowl it into the basket. Air-fry, tossing and rearranging everything twice so that all covered surfaces get exposed, for 20 minutes, or until the sausages have begun to brown and the pierogi are crisp.
4. Pour the contents of the basket onto a serving platter. Wait a minute or two just to take make sure nothing's searing hot before serving.

Boneless Ribeyes

Servings: 2 | Cooking Time: 10-15 Minutes

Ingredients:
- 2 8-ounce boneless ribeye steaks
- 4 teaspoons Worcestershire sauce
- ½ teaspoon garlic powder
- pepper
- 4 teaspoons extra virgin olive oil
- salt

Directions:
1. Season steaks on both sides with Worcestershire sauce. Use the back of a spoon to spread evenly.
2. Sprinkle both sides of steaks with garlic powder and coarsely ground black pepper to taste.
3. Drizzle both sides of steaks with olive oil, again using the back of a spoon to spread evenly over surfaces.
4. Allow steaks to marinate for 30minutes.
5. Place both steaks in air fryer basket and cook at 390°F for 5minutes.
6. Turn steaks over and cook until done: medium rare: additional 5 minutes, medium: additional 7 minutes, well done: additional 10 minutes.
7. Remove steaks from air fryer basket and let sit 5minutes. Salt to taste and serve.

London Broil

Servings:4 | Cooking Time: 12 Minutes

Ingredients:
- 1 pound top round steak
- 1 tablespoon Worcestershire sauce
- ¼ cup soy sauce
- 2 cloves garlic, peeled and finely minced
- ½ teaspoon ground black pepper
- ½ teaspoon salt
- 2 tablespoons salted butter, melted

Directions:
1. Place steak in a large sealable bowl or bag. Pour in Worcestershire sauce and soy sauce, then add garlic, pepper, and salt. Toss to coat. Seal and place into refrigerator to let marinate 2 hours.
2. Remove steak from marinade and pat dry. Drizzle top side with butter, then place into ungreased air fryer basket. Adjust the temperature to 375°F and set the timer for 12 minutes, turning steak halfway through cooking. Steak will be done when browned at the edges and it has an internal temperature of 150°F for medium or 180°F for well-done.
3. Let steak rest on a large plate 10 minutes before slicing into thin pieces. Serve warm.

Extra Crispy Country-style Pork Riblets

Servings: 3 | Cooking Time: 30 Minutes

Ingredients:
- ⅓ cup Tapioca flour
- 2½ tablespoons Chile powder
- ¾ teaspoon Table salt (optional)
- 1¼ pounds Boneless country-style pork ribs, cut into 1½-inch chunks
- Vegetable oil spray

Directions:
1. Preheat the air fryer to 375°F.
2. Mix the tapioca flour, chile powder, and salt in a large bowl until well combined. Add the country-style rib chunks and toss well to coat thoroughly.
3. When the machine is at temperature, gently shake off any excess tapioca coating from the chunks. Generously coat them on all sides with vegetable oil spray. Arrange the chunks in the basket in one layer. The pieces may touch. Air-fry for 30 minutes, rearranging the pieces at the 10- and 20-minute marks to expose any touching bits, until very crisp and well browned.
4. Gently pour the contents of the basket onto a wire rack. Cool for 5 minutes before serving.

Lamb Koftas Meatballs

Servings: 3 | Cooking Time: 8 Minutes

Ingredients:
- 1 pound ground lamb
- 1 teaspoon ground cumin
- 1 teaspoon ground coriander
- 2 tablespoons chopped fresh mint
- 1 egg, beaten
- ½ teaspoon salt
- freshly ground black pepper

Directions:
1. Combine all ingredients in a bowl and mix together well. Divide the mixture into 10 portions. Roll each portion into a ball and then by cupping the meatball in your hand, shape it into an oval.
2. Preheat the air fryer to 400°F.
3. Air-fry the koftas for 8 minutes.
4. Serve warm with the cucumber-yogurt dip.

Chapter 6 Fish And Seafood Recipes

Chapter 6 Fish And Seafood Recipes

Nacho Chips Crusted Prawns

Servings:2 | Cooking Time: 8 Minutes

Ingredients:
- ¾ pound prawns, peeled and deveined
- 1 large egg
- 5 ounces Nacho flavored chips, finely crushed

Directions:
1. In a shallow bowl, beat the egg.
2. In another bowl, place the nacho chips
3. Dip each prawn into the beaten egg and then, coat with the crushed nacho chips.
4. Set the temperature of air fryer to 350°F. Grease an air fryer basket.
5. Arrange prawns into the prepared air fryer basket.
6. Air fry for about 8 minutes.
7. Remove from air fryer and transfer the prawns onto serving plates.
8. Serve hot.

Smoked Halibut And Eggs In Brioche

Servings: 4 | Cooking Time: 25 Minutes

Ingredients:
- 4 brioche rolls
- 1 pound smoked halibut, chopped
- 4 eggs
- 1 teaspoon dried thyme
- 1 teaspoon dried basil
- Salt and black pepper, to taste
- Cooking spray

Directions:
1. Cut off the top of each brioche; then, scoop out the insides to make the shells.
2. Lay the prepared brioche shells in the lightly greased cooking basket.
3. Spritz with cooking oil; add the halibut. Crack an egg into each brioche shell; sprinkle with thyme, basil, salt, and black pepper.
4. Bake in the preheated Air Fryer at 325°F for 20 minutes. Bon appétit!

Crab-stuffed Avocado Boats

Servings:4 | Cooking Time: 7 Minutes

Ingredients:
- 2 medium avocados, halved and pitted
- 8 ounces cooked crabmeat
- ¼ teaspoon Old Bay Seasoning
- 2 tablespoons peeled and diced yellow onion
- 2 tablespoons mayonnaise

Directions:
1. Scoop out avocado flesh in each avocado half, leaving ½" around edges to form a shell. Chop scooped-out avocado.
2. In a medium bowl, combine crabmeat, Old Bay Seasoning, onion, mayonnaise, and chopped avocado. Place ¼ mixture into each avocado shell.
3. Place avocado boats into ungreased air fryer basket. Adjust the temperature to 350°F and set the timer for 7 minutes. Avocado will be browned on the top and mixture will be bubbling when done. Serve warm.

Buttery Lobster Tails

Servings:4 | Cooking Time: 6 Minutes

Ingredients:
- 4 6- to 8-ounce shell-on raw lobster tails
- 2 tablespoons Butter, melted and cooled
- 1 teaspoon Lemon juice
- ½ teaspoon Finely grated lemon zest
- ½ teaspoon Garlic powder
- ½ teaspoon Table salt
- ½ teaspoon Ground black pepper

Directions:
1. Preheat the air fryer to 375°F .
2. To give the tails that restaurant look, you need to butterfly the meat. To do so, place a tail on a cutting board so that the shell is convex. Use kitchen shears to cut a line down the middle of the shell from the larger end to the smaller, cutting only the shell and not the meat below, and stopping before the back fins. Pry open the shell, leaving it intact. Use your clean fingers to separate the meat from the shell's sides and bottom, keeping it attached to the shell at the back near the fins. Pull the meat up and out of the shell through the cut line, laying the meat on top of the shell and closing the shell under the meat. Make two equidistant cuts down the meat from the larger end to near the smaller end, each about ¼ inch deep, for the classic restaurant look on the plate. Repeat this procedure with the remaining tail(s).
3. Stir the butter, lemon juice, zest, garlic powder, salt, and pepper in a small bowl until well combined. Brush this mixture over the lobster meat set atop the shells.
4. When the machine is at temperature, place the tails shell side down in the basket with as much air space between them as possible. Air-fry undistubed for 6 minutes, or until the lobster meat has pink streaks over it and is firm.
5. Use kitchen tongs to transfer the tails to a wire rack. Cool for only a minute or two before serving.

Timeless Garlic-lemon Scallops

Servings:2 | Cooking Time: 15 Minutes

Ingredients:
- 2 tbsp butter, melted
- 1 garlic clove, minced
- 1 tbsp lemon juice
- 1 lb jumbo sea scallops

Directions:
1. Preheat air fryer to 400ºF. Whisk butter, garlic, and lemon juice in a bowl. Roll scallops in the mixture to coat all sides. Place scallops in the frying basket and Air Fry for 4 minutes, flipping once. Brush the tops of each scallop with butter mixture and cook for 4 more minutes, flipping once. Serve and enjoy!

Perfect Soft-shelled Crabs

Servings:2 | Cooking Time: 12 Minutes

Ingredients:
- ½ cup All-purpose flour
- 1 tablespoon Old Bay seasoning
- 1 Large egg(s), well beaten
- 1 cup Ground oyster crackers
- 2 2½-ounce cleaned soft-shelled crab(s), about 4 inches across
- Vegetable oil spray

Directions:
1. Preheat the air fryer to 375°F.
2. Set up and fill three shallow soup plates or small pie plates on your counter: one for the flour, whisked with the Old Bay until well combined; one for the beaten egg(s); and one for the cracker crumbs.
3. Set a soft-shelled crab in the flour mixture and turn to coat evenly and well on all sides, even inside the legs. Dip the crab into the egg(s) and coat well, turning at least once, again getting some of the egg between the legs. Let any excess egg slip back into the rest, then set the crab in the cracker crumbs. Turn several times, pressing very gently to get the crab evenly coated with crumbs, even between the legs. Generously coat the crab on all sides with vegetable oil spray. Set it aside if you're making more than one and coat these in the same way.
4. Set the crab(s) in the basket with as much air space between them as possible. They may overlap slightly, particularly at the ends of their legs, depending on the basket's size. Air-fry undisturbed for 12 minutes, or until very crisp and golden brown. If the machine is at 390°F, the crabs may be done in only 10 minutes.
5. Use kitchen tongs to gently transfer the crab(s) to a wire rack. Cool for a couple of minutes before serving.

Garlic-lemon Scallops

Servings:4 | Cooking Time: 12 Minutes

Ingredients:
- ¼ teaspoon salt
- ¼ teaspoon ground black pepper
- 8 sea scallops, rinsed and patted dry
- 4 tablespoons salted butter, melted
- 4 teaspoons finely minced garlic
- Zest and juice of ½ small lemon

Directions:
1. Preheat the air fryer to 375°F.
2. Sprinkle salt and pepper evenly over scallops. Spritz scallops lightly with cooking spray. Place in the air fryer basket in a single layer and cook 12 minutes, turning halfway through cooking time, until scallops are opaque and firm and internal temperature reaches at least 130°F.
3. While scallops are cooking, in a small bowl, mix butter, garlic, lemon zest, and juice. Set aside.
4. When scallops are done, drizzle with garlic–lemon butter. Serve warm.

Better Fish Sticks

Servings:3 | Cooking Time: 8 Minutes

Ingredients:
- ¾ cup Seasoned Italian-style dried bread crumbs (gluten-free, if a concern)
- 3 tablespoons (about ½ ounce) Finely grated Parmesan cheese
- 10 ounces Skinless cod fillets, cut lengthwise into 1-inch-wide pieces
- 3 tablespoons Regular or low-fat mayonnaise (not fat-free; gluten-free, if a concern)
- Vegetable oil spray

Directions:
1. Preheat the air fryer to 400°F.
2. Mix the bread crumbs and grated Parmesan in a shallow soup bowl or a small pie plate.
3. Smear the fish fillet sticks completely with the mayonnaise, then dip them one by one in the bread-crumb mixture, turning and pressing gently to make an even and thorough coating. Coat each stick on all sides with vegetable oil spray.
4. Set the fish sticks in the basket with at least ¼ inch between them. Air-fry undisturbed for 8 minutes, or until golden brown and crisp.
5. Use a nonstick-safe spatula to gently transfer them from the basket to a wire rack. Cool for only a minute or two before serving.

Shrimp "scampi"

Servings:4 | Cooking Time: 5 Minutes

Ingredients:
- 1½ pounds Large shrimp, peeled and deveined
- ¼ cup Olive oil
- 2 tablespoons Minced garlic
- 1 teaspoon Dried oregano
- Up to 1 teaspoon Red pepper flakes
- ½ teaspoon Table salt
- 2 tablespoons White balsamic vinegar

Directions:
1. Preheat the air fryer to 400°F.
2. Stir the shrimp, olive oil, garlic, oregano, red pepper flakes, and salt in a large bowl until the shrimp are well coated.
3. When the machine is at temperature, transfer the shrimp to the basket. They will overlap and even sit on top of each other. Air-fry for 5 minutes, tossing and rearranging the shrimp twice to make sure the covered surfaces are exposed, until pink and firm.
4. Pour the contents of the basket into a serving bowl. Pour the vinegar over the shrimp while hot and toss to coat.

Fish Fillet Sandwich

Servings:4 | Cooking Time: 18 Minutes

Ingredients:
- 4 cod fillets
- ½ teaspoon salt
- ¼ teaspoon ground black pepper
- 2 cups unsweetened cornflakes, crushed
- 1 cup Italian bread crumbs
- 2 large eggs
- 4 sandwich buns

Directions:
1. Preheat the air fryer to 375°F.
2. Sprinkle cod with salt and pepper on both sides.
3. In a large bowl, combine cornflakes and bread crumbs.
4. In a medium bowl, whisk eggs. Press each piece of cod into eggs to coat, shaking off excess, then into cornflake mixture to coat evenly on both sides. Spritz with cooking spray.
5. Place in the air fryer basket and cook 18 minutes, turning halfway through cooking time, until fillets are brown and internal temperature reaches at least 145°F. Place on buns to serve.

Sea Scallops

Servings: 4 | Cooking Time: 8 Minutes

Ingredients:
- 1½ pounds sea scallops
- salt and pepper
- 2 eggs
- ½ cup flour
- ½ cup plain breadcrumbs
- oil for misting or cooking spray

Directions:
1. Rinse scallops and remove the tough side muscle. Sprinkle to taste with salt and pepper.
2. Beat eggs together in a shallow dish. Place flour in a second shallow dish and breadcrumbs in a third.
3. Preheat air fryer to 390°F.
4. Dip scallops in flour, then eggs, and then roll in breadcrumbs. Mist with oil or cooking spray.
5. Place scallops in air fryer basket in a single layer, leaving some space between. You should be able to cook about a dozen at a time.
6. Cook at 390°F for 8 minutes, watching carefully so as not to overcook. Scallops are done when they turn opaque all the way through. They will feel slightly firm when pressed with tines of a fork.
7. Repeat step 6 to cook remaining scallops.

Teriyaki Salmon

Servings:4 | Cooking Time: 27 Minutes

Ingredients:
- ½ cup teriyaki sauce
- ¼ teaspoon salt
- 1 teaspoon ground ginger
- ½ teaspoon garlic powder
- 4 boneless, skinless salmon fillets
- 2 tablespoons toasted sesame seeds

Directions:
1. In a large bowl, whisk teriyaki sauce, salt, ginger, and garlic powder. Add salmon to the bowl, being sure to coat each side with marinade. Cover and let marinate in refrigerator 15 minutes.
2. Preheat the air fryer to 375°F.
3. Spritz fillets with cooking spray and place in the air fryer basket. Cook 12 minutes, turning halfway through cooking time, until glaze has caramelized to a dark brown color, salmon flakes easily, and internal temperature reaches at least 145°F. Sprinkle sesame seeds on salmon and serve warm.

Tuna-stuffed Tomatoes

Servings:2 | Cooking Time: 5 Minutes

Ingredients:
- 2 medium beefsteak tomatoes, tops removed, seeded, membranes removed
- 2 pouches tuna packed in water, drained
- 1 medium stalk celery, trimmed and chopped
- 2 tablespoons mayonnaise
- ¼ teaspoon salt
- ¼ teaspoon ground black pepper
- 2 teaspoons coconut oil
- ¼ cup shredded mild Cheddar cheese

Directions:
1. Scoop pulp out of each tomato, leaving ½" shell.

2. In a medium bowl, mix tuna, celery, mayonnaise, salt, and pepper. Drizzle with coconut oil. Spoon ½ mixture into each tomato and top each with 2 tablespoons Cheddar.
3. Place tomatoes into ungreased air fryer basket. Adjust the temperature to 320°F and set the timer for 5 minutes. Cheese will be melted when done. Serve warm.

Bacon-wrapped Cajun Scallops

Servings:4 | Cooking Time: 13 Minutes

Ingredients:
- 8 slices bacon
- 8 sea scallops, rinsed and patted dry
- 1 teaspoon Cajun seasoning
- 4 tablespoons salted butter, melted

Directions:
1. Preheat the air fryer to 375°F.
2. Place bacon in the air fryer basket and cook 3 minutes. Remove bacon and wrap each scallop in one slice bacon before securing with a toothpick.
3. Sprinkle Cajun seasoning evenly over scallops. Spritz scallops lightly with cooking spray and place in the air fryer basket in a single layer. Cook 10 minutes, turning halfway through cooking time, until scallops are opaque and firm and internal temperature reaches at least 130°F. Drizzle with butter. Serve warm.

Lemon Shrimp And Zucchinis

Servings: 4 | Cooking Time: 15 Minutes

Ingredients:
- 1 pound shrimp, peeled and deveined
- A pinch of salt and black pepper
- 2 zucchinis, cut into medium cubes
- 1 tablespoon lemon juice
- 1 tablespoon olive oil
- 1 tablespoon garlic, minced

Directions:
1. In a pan that fits the air fryer, combine all the ingredients, toss, put the pan in the machine and cook at 370°F for 15 minutes. Divide between plates and serve right away.

Outrageous Crispy Fried Salmon Skin

Servings:4 | Cooking Time: 10 Minutes

Ingredients:
- ½ pound salmon skin, patted dry
- 4 tablespoons coconut oil
- Salt and pepper to taste

Directions:
1. Preheat the air fryer for 5 minutes.
2. In a large bowl, combine everything and mix well.
3. Place in the fryer basket and close.
4. Cook for 10 minutes at 400°F.
5. Halfway through the cooking time, give a good shake to evenly cook the skin.

Lemon Pepper–breaded Tilapia

Servings:4 | Cooking Time: 10 Minutes

Ingredients:
- 1 large egg
- ⅓ cup all-purpose flour
- ¼ cup grated Parmesan cheese
- ½ tablespoon lemon pepper seasoning
- 4 boneless, skinless tilapia fillets

Directions:
1. Preheat the air fryer to 375°F.
2. In a medium bowl, whisk egg. On a large plate, mix flour, Parmesan, and lemon pepper seasoning.
3. Pat tilapia dry. Dip each fillet into egg, gently shaking off excess. Press into flour mixture, then spritz both sides with cooking spray.
4. Place in the air fryer basket and cook 10 minutes, turning halfway through cooking, until fillets are golden and crispy and internal temperature reaches at least 145°F. Serve warm.

Shrimp Burgers

Servings:4 | Cooking Time: 10 Minutes

Ingredients:
- 10 ounces medium shrimp, peeled and deveined
- ¼ cup mayonnaise
- ½ cup panko bread crumbs
- ½ teaspoon Old Bay Seasoning
- ¼ teaspoon salt
- ⅛ teaspoon ground black pepper
- 4 hamburger buns

Directions:
1. Preheat the air fryer to 400°F.
2. In a food processor, add shrimp and pulse four times until broken down.
3. Scoop shrimp into a large bowl and mix with mayonnaise, bread crumbs, Old Bay, salt, and pepper until well combined.
4. Separate mixture into four portions and form into patties. They will feel wet but should be able to hold their shape.
5. Place in the air fryer basket and cook 10 minutes, turning halfway through cooking time, until burgers are brown and internal temperature reaches at least 145°F. Serve warm on buns.

Lemon Butter Scallops

Servings: 1 | Cooking Time: 30 Minutes

Ingredients:
- 1 lemon
- 1 lb. scallops
- ½ cup butter
- ¼ cup parsley, chopped

Directions:
1. Juice the lemon into a Ziploc bag.
2. Wash your scallops, dry them, and season to taste. Put them in the bag with the lemon juice. Refrigerate for an hour.
3. Remove the bag from the refrigerator and leave for about twenty minutes until it returns to room temperature. Transfer the scallops into a foil pan that is small enough to be placed inside the fryer.
4. Pre-heat the fryer at 400°F and put the rack inside.
5. Place the foil pan on the rack and cook for five minutes.
6. In the meantime, melt the butter in a saucepan over a medium heat. Zest the lemon over the saucepan, then add in the chopped

parsley. Mix well.
7. Take care when removing the pan from the fryer. Transfer the contents to a plate and drizzle with the lemon-butter mixture. Serve hot.

Simple Salmon

Servings:2 | Cooking Time:10 Minutes

Ingredients:
- 2 salmon fillets
- Salt and black pepper, as required
- 1 tablespoon olive oil

Directions:
1. Preheat the Air fryer to 390°F and grease an Air fryer basket.
2. Season each salmon fillet with salt and black pepper and drizzle with olive oil.
3. Arrange salmon fillets into the Air fryer basket and cook for about 10 minutes.
4. Remove from the Air fryer and dish out the salmon fillets onto the serving plates.

Lime Bay Scallops

Servings:4 | Cooking Time: 10 Minutes

Ingredients:
- 2 tbsp butter, melted
- 1 lime, juiced
- ¼ tsp salt
- 1 lb bay scallops
- 2 tbsp chopped cilantro

Directions:
1. Preheat air fryer to 350ºF. Combine all ingredients in a bowl, except for the cilantro. Place scallops in the frying basket and Air Fry for 5 minutes, tossing once. Serve immediately topped with cilantro.

Fish-in-chips

Servings:4 | Cooking Time: 11 Minutes

Ingredients:
- 1 cup All-purpose flour or potato starch
- 2 Large egg(s), well beaten
- 1½ cups Crushed plain potato chips, preferably thick-cut or ruffled (gluten-free, if a concern)
- 4 4-ounce skinless cod fillets

Directions:
1. Preheat the air fryer to 400°F.
2. Set up and fill three shallow soup plates or small pie plates on your counter: one for the flour, one for the beaten egg(s), and one for the crushed potato chips.
3. Dip a piece of cod in the flour, turning it to coat on all sides, even the ends and sides. Gently shake off any excess flour, then dip it in the beaten egg(s). Gently turn to coat it on all sides, then let any excess egg slip back into the rest. Set the fillet in the crushed potato chips and turn several times and onto all sides, pressing gently to coat the fish. Dip it back in the egg(s), coating all sides but taking care that the coating doesn't slip off; then dip it back in the potato chips for a thick, even coating. Set it aside and coat more fillets in the same way.
4. When the machine is at temperature, set the fillets in the basket with as much air space between them as possible. Air-fry undisturbed for 11 minutes, until golden brown and firm but not hard.
5. Use kitchen tongs to transfer the fillets to a wire rack. Cool for just a minute or two before serving.

Sesame Tuna Steak

Servings: 2 | Cooking Time: 12 Minutes

Ingredients:
- 1 tbsp. coconut oil, melted
- 2 x 6-oz. tuna steaks
- ½ tsp. garlic powder
- 2 tsp. black sesame seeds
- 2 tsp. white sesame seeds

Directions:
1. Apply the coconut oil to the tuna steaks with a brunch, then season with garlic powder.
2. Combine the black and white sesame seeds. Embed them in the tuna steaks, covering the fish all over. Place the tuna into your air fryer.
3. Cook for eight minutes at 400°F, turning the fish halfway through.
4. The tuna steaks are ready when they have reached a temperature of 145°F. Serve straightaway.

Crunchy And Buttery Cod With Ritz Cracker Crust

Servings: 2 | Cooking Time: 10 Minutes

Ingredients:
- 4 tablespoons butter, melted
- 8 to 10 RITZ crackers, crushed into crumbs
- 2 cod fillets
- salt and freshly ground black pepper
- 1 lemon

Directions:
1. Preheat the air fryer to 380°F.
2. Melt the butter in a small saucepan on the stovetop or in a microwavable dish in the microwave, and then transfer the butter to a shallow dish. Place the crushed RITZ crackers into a second shallow dish.
3. Season the fish fillets with salt and freshly ground black pepper. Dip them into the butter and then coat both sides with the RITZ crackers.
4. Place the fish into the air fryer basket and air-fry at 380°F for 10 minutes, flipping the fish over halfway through the cooking time.
5. Serve with a wedge of lemon to squeeze over the top.

Fried Oysters

Servings:12 | Cooking Time: 8 Minutes

Ingredients:
- 1½ cups All-purpose flour
- 1½ cups Yellow cornmeal
- 1½ tablespoons Cajun dried seasoning blend
- 1¼ cups, plus more if needed Amber beer, pale ale, or IPA
- 12 Large shucked oysters, any liquid drained off
- Vegetable oil spray

Directions:
1. Preheat the air fryer to 400°F.
2. Whisk ⅔ cup of the flour, ½ cup of the cornmeal, and the seasoning blend in a bowl until uniform. Set aside.
3. Whisk the remaining ⅓ cup flour and the remaining ½ cup cornmeal with the beer in a second bowl, adding more beer in dribs and drabs until the mixture is the consistency of pancake batter.

4. Using a fork, dip a shucked oyster in the beer batter, coating it thoroughly. Gently shake off any excess batter, then set the oyster in the dry mixture and turn gently to coat well and evenly. Set the coated oyster on a cutting board and continue dipping and coating the remainder of the oysters.
5. Coat the oysters with vegetable oil spray, then set them in the basket with as much air space between them as possible. Air-fry undisturbed for 8 minutes, or until lightly browned and crisp.
6. Use a nonstick-safe spatula to transfer the oysters to a wire rack. Cool for a couple of minutes before serving.

Lemon-roasted Salmon Fillets

Servings:3 | Cooking Time: 7 Minutes

Ingredients:
- 3 6-ounce skin-on salmon fillets
- Olive oil spray
- 9 Very thin lemon slices
- ¾ teaspoon Ground black pepper
- ¼ teaspoon Table salt

Directions:
1. Preheat the air fryer to 400°F.
2. Generously coat the skin of each of the fillets with olive oil spray. Set the fillets skin side down on your work surface. Place three overlapping lemon slices down the length of each salmon fillet. Sprinkle them with the pepper and salt. Coat lightly with olive oil spray.
3. Use a nonstick-safe spatula to transfer the fillets one by one to the basket, leaving as much air space between them as possible. Air-fry undisturbed for 7 minutes, or until cooked through.
4. Use a nonstick-safe spatula to transfer the fillets to serving plates. Cool for only a minute or two before serving.

Curried Sweet-and-spicy Scallops

Servings:3 | Cooking Time: 5 Minutes

Ingredients:
- 6 tablespoons Thai sweet chili sauce
- 2 cups Crushed Rice Krispies or other rice-puff cereal
- 2 teaspoons Yellow curry powder, purchased or homemade
- 1 pound Sea scallops
- Vegetable oil spray

Directions:
1. Preheat the air fryer to 400°F.
2. Set up and fill two shallow soup plates or small pie plates on your counter: one for the chili sauce and one for crumbs, mixed with the curry powder.
3. Dip a scallop into the chili sauce, coating it on all sides. Set it in the cereal mixture and turn several times to coat evenly. Gently shake off any excess and set the scallop on a cutting board. Continue dipping and coating the remaining scallops. Coat them all on all sides with the vegetable oil spray.
4. Set the scallops in the basket with as much air space between them as possible. Air-fry undisturbed for 5 minutes, or until lightly browned and crunchy.
5. Remove the basket. Set aside for 2 minutes to let the coating set up. Then gently pour the contents of the basket onto a platter and serve at once.

Snapper Fillets With Thai Sauce

Servings: 2 | Cooking Time: 30 Minutes + Marinating Time

Ingredients:
- 1/2 cup full-fat coconut milk
- 2 tablespoons lemon juice
- 1 teaspoon fresh ginger, grated
- 2 snapper fillets
- 1 tablespoon olive oil
- Salt and white pepper, to taste

Directions:
1. Place the milk, lemon juice, and ginger in a glass bowl; add fish and let it marinate for 1 hour.
2. Removed the fish from the milk mixture and place in the Air Fryer basket. Drizzle olive oil all over the fish fillets.
3. Cook in the preheated Air Fryer at 390°F for 15 minutes.
4. Meanwhile, heat the milk mixture over medium-high heat; bring to a rapid boil, stirring continuously. Reduce to simmer and add the salt, and pepper; continue to cook 12 minutes more.
5. Spoon the sauce over the warm snapper fillets and serve immediately. Bon appétit!

Lobster Tails

Servings:4 | Cooking Time: 10 Minutes

Ingredients:
- 4 lobster tails
- 2 tablespoons salted butter, melted
- 1 tablespoon finely minced garlic
- ¼ teaspoon salt
- ¼ teaspoon ground black pepper
- 2 tablespoons lemon juice

Directions:
1. Preheat the air fryer to 400°F.
2. Carefully cut open lobster tails with kitchen scissors and pull back the shell a little to expose the meat. Drizzle butter over each tail, then sprinkle with garlic, salt, and pepper.
3. Place tails in the air fryer basket and cook 10 minutes until lobster is firm and opaque and internal temperature reaches at least 145°F.
4. Drizzle lemon juice over lobster meat. Serve warm.

Beer-battered Cod

Servings:3 | Cooking Time: 12 Minutes

Ingredients:
- 1½ cups All-purpose flour
- 3 tablespoons Old Bay seasoning
- 1 Large egg(s)
- ¼ cup Amber beer, pale ale, or IPA
- 3 4-ounce skinless cod fillets
- Vegetable oil spray

Directions:
1. Preheat the air fryer to 400°F.
2. Set up and fill two shallow soup plates or small pie plates on your counter: one with the flour, whisked with the Old Bay until well combined; and one with the egg(s), whisked with the beer until foamy and uniform.
3. Dip a piece of cod in the flour mixture, turning it to coat on all sides. Gently shake off any excess flour and dip the fish in the egg mixture, turning it to coat. Let any excess egg mixture slip back into the rest, then set the fish back in the flour mixture and coat it again, then back in the egg mixture for a second wash, then back in the flour mixture for a third time. Coat the fish on all sides with vegetable oil spray and set it aside. "Batter" the remaining piece(s) of cod in the same way.
4. Set the coated cod fillets in the basket with as much space between them as possible. They should not touch. Air-fry undisturbed for 12 minutes, or until brown and crisp.
5. Use kitchen tongs to gently transfer the fish to a wire rack. Cool for only a couple of minutes before serving.

Salmon Patties

Servings:4 | Cooking Time: 12 Minutes

Ingredients:
- 1 pouch cooked salmon
- 6 tablespoons panko bread crumbs
- ½ cup mayonnaise
- 2 teaspoons Old Bay Seasoning

Directions:
1. Preheat the air fryer to 350°F.
2. In a large bowl, combine all ingredients.
3. Divide mixture into four equal portions. Using your hands, form into patties and spritz with cooking spray.
4. Place in the air fryer basket and cook 12 minutes, turning halfway through cooking time, until brown and firm. Serve warm.

Crispy Sweet-and-sour Cod Fillets

Servings:3 | Cooking Time: 12 Minutes

Ingredients:
- 1½ cups Plain panko bread crumbs (gluten-free, if a concern)
- 2 tablespoons Regular or low-fat mayonnaise (not fat-free; gluten-free, if a concern)
- ¼ cup Sweet pickle relish
- 3 4- to 5-ounce skinless cod fillets

Directions:
1. Preheat the air fryer to 400°F.
2. Pour the bread crumbs into a shallow soup plate or a small pie plate. Mix the mayonnaise and relish in a small bowl until well combined. Smear this mixture all over the cod fillets. Set them in the crumbs and turn until evenly coated on all sides, even on the ends.
3. Set the coated cod fillets in the basket with as much air space between them as possible. They should not touch. Air-fry undisturbed for 12 minutes, or until browned and crisp.
4. Use a nonstick-safe spatula to transfer the cod pieces to a wire rack. Cool for only a minute or two before serving hot.

Spicy Mackerel

Servings: 2 | Cooking Time: 20 Minutes

Ingredients:
- 2 mackerel fillets
- 2 tbsp. red chili flakes
- 2 tsp. garlic, minced
- 1 tsp. lemon juice

Directions:
1. Season the mackerel fillets with the red pepper flakes, minced garlic, and a drizzle of lemon juice. Allow to sit for five minutes.
2. Preheat your fryer at 350°F.
3. Cook the mackerel for five minutes, before opening the drawer, flipping the fillets, and allowing to cook on the other side for another five minutes.
4. Plate the fillets, making sure to spoon any remaining juice over them before serving.

Great Cat Fish

Servings:4 | Cooking Time: 25 Minutes

Ingredients:
- ¼ cup seasoned fish fry
- 1 tbsp olive oil
- 1 tbsp parsley, chopped

Directions:
1. Preheat your air fryer to 400°F, and add seasoned fish fry, and fillets in a large Ziploc bag; massage well to coat. Place the fillets in your air fryer's cooking basket and cook for 10 minutes. Flip the fish and cook for 2-3 more minutes. Top with parsley and serve.

Very Easy Lime-garlic Shrimps

Servings:1 | Cooking Time: 6 Minutes

Ingredients:
- 1 clove of garlic, minced
- 1 cup raw shrimps
- 1 lime, juiced and zested
- Salt and pepper to taste

Directions:
1. In a mixing bowl, combine all Ingredients and give a good stir.
2. Preheat the air fryer to 390°F.
3. Skewer the shrimps onto the metal skewers that come with the double layer rack accessory.
4. Place on the rack and cook for 6 minutes.

Italian Tuna Roast

Servings: 8 | Cooking Time: 21 Minutes

Ingredients:
- cooking spray
- 1 tablespoon Italian seasoning
- ⅛ teaspoon ground black pepper
- 1 tablespoon extra-light olive oil
- 1 teaspoon lemon juice
- 1 tuna loin

Directions:
1. Spray baking dish with cooking spray and place in air fryer basket. Preheat air fryer to 390°F.
2. Mix together the Italian seasoning, pepper, oil, and lemon juice.
3. Using a dull table knife or butter knife, pierce top of tuna about every half inch: Insert knife into top of tuna roast and pierce almost all the way to the bottom.
4. Spoon oil mixture into each of the holes and use the knife to push seasonings into the tuna as deeply as possible.
5. Spread any remaining oil mixture on all outer surfaces of tuna.
6. Place tuna roast in baking dish and cook at 390°F for 20 minutes. Check temperature with a meat thermometer. Cook for an additional 1 minutes or until temperature reaches 145°F.
7. Remove basket from fryer and let tuna sit in basket for 10 minutes.

Crispy Smelts

Servings:3 | Cooking Time: 20 Minutes

Ingredients:
- 1 pound Cleaned smelts
- 3 tablespoons Tapioca flour
- Vegetable oil spray
- To taste Coarse sea salt or kosher salt

Directions:
1. Preheat the air fryer to 400°F.
2. Toss the smelts and tapioca flour in a large bowl until the little fish are evenly coated.
3. Lay the smelts out on a large cutting board. Lightly coat both sides of each fish with vegetable oil spray.
4. When the machine is at temperature, set the smelts close together in the basket, with a few even overlapping on top. Air-fry undisturbed for 20 minutes, until lightly browned and crisp.
5. Remove the basket from the machine and turn out the fish onto a wire rack. The smelts will most likely come out as one large block, or maybe in a couple of large pieces. Cool for a minute or two, then sprinkle the smelts with salt and break the block(s) into much smaller sections or individual fish to serve.

Mediterranean-style Cod

Servings:4 | Cooking Time: 12 Minutes

Ingredients:
- 4 cod fillets
- 3 tablespoons fresh lemon juice
- 1 tablespoon olive oil
- ¼ teaspoon salt
- 6 cherry tomatoes, halved
- ¼ cup pitted and sliced kalamata olives

Directions:
1. Place cod into an ungreased 6" round nonstick baking dish. Pour lemon juice into dish and drizzle cod with olive oil. Sprinkle with salt. Place tomatoes and olives around baking dish in between fillets.
2. Place dish into air fryer basket. Adjust the temperature to 350°F and set the timer for 12 minutes, carefully turning cod halfway through cooking. Fillets will be lightly browned, easily flake, and have an internal temperature of at least 145°F when done. Serve warm.

Herbed Haddock

Servings:2 | Cooking Time:8 Minutes

Ingredients:
- 2 haddock fillets
- 2 tablespoons pine nuts
- 3 tablespoons fresh basil, chopped
- 1 tablespoon Parmesan cheese, grated
- ½ cup extra-virgin olive oil
- Salt and black pepper, to taste

Directions:
1. Preheat the Air fryer to 355°F and grease an Air fryer basket.
2. Coat the haddock fillets evenly with olive oil and season with salt and black pepper.
3. Place the haddock fillets in the Air fryer basket and cook for about 8 minutes.
4. Dish out the haddock fillets in serving plates.
5. Meanwhile, put remaining ingredients in a food processor and pulse until smooth.
6. Top this cheese sauce over the haddock fillets and serve hot.

Lemon Butter Cod

Servings:4 | Cooking Time: 12 Minutes

Ingredients:
- 4 cod fillets
- 2 tablespoons salted butter, melted
- 1 teaspoon Old Bay Seasoning
- ½ medium lemon, cut into 4 slices

Directions:
1. Place cod fillets into an ungreased 6" round nonstick baking dish. Brush tops of fillets with butter and sprinkle with Old Bay Seasoning. Lay 1 lemon slice on each fillet.
2. Cover dish with aluminum foil and place into air fryer basket. Adjust the temperature to 350°F and set the timer for 12 minutes, turning fillets halfway through cooking. Fish will be opaque and have an internal temperature of at least 145°F when done. Serve warm.

Chili-lime Shrimp

Servings:4 | Cooking Time: 10 Minutes

Ingredients:
- 1 pound medium shrimp, peeled and deveined
- ½ cup lime juice
- 2 tablespoons olive oil
- 2 tablespoons sriracha
- 1 teaspoon salt
- ¼ teaspoon ground black pepper

Directions:
1. Preheat the air fryer to 375°F.
2. In an 6" round cake pan, combine all ingredients.
3. Place pan in the air fryer and cook 10 minutes, stirring halfway through cooking time, until the inside of shrimp are pearly white and opaque and internal temperature reaches at least 145°F. Serve warm.

Sardinas Fritas

Servings: 2 | Cooking Time: 15 Minutes

Ingredients:
- 2 cans boneless, skinless sardines in mustard sauce
- Salt and pepper to taste
- ½ cup bread crumbs
- 2 lemon wedges
- 1 tsp chopped parsley

Directions:
1. Preheat air fryer at 350ºF. Add breadcrumbs, salt and black pepper to a bowl. Roll sardines in the breadcrumbs to coat. Place them in the greased frying basket and Air Fry for 6 minutes, flipping once. Transfer them to a serving dish. Serve topped with parsley and lemon wedges.

Tortilla-crusted With Lemon Filets

Servings:4 | Cooking Time: 15 Minutes

Ingredients:
- 1 cup tortilla chips, pulverized
- 1 egg, beaten
- 1 tablespoon lemon juice
- 4 fillets of white fish fillet
- Salt and pepper to taste

Directions:
1. Preheat the air fryer to 390°F.

2. Place a grill pan in the air fryer.
3. Season the fish fillet with salt, pepper, and lemon juice.
4. Soak in beaten eggs and dredge in tortilla chips.
5. Place on the grill pan.
6. Cook for 15 minutes.
7. Make sure to flip the fish halfway through the cooking time.

Cod Nuggets

Servings:4 | Cooking Time: 12 Minutes

Ingredients:
- 2 boneless, skinless cod fillets
- 1 ½ teaspoons salt, divided
- ¾ teaspoon ground black pepper, divided
- 2 large eggs
- 1 cup plain bread crumbs

Directions:
1. Preheat the air fryer to 350°F.
2. Cut cod fillets into sixteen even-sized pieces. In a large bowl, add cod nuggets and sprinkle with 1 teaspoon salt and ½ teaspoon pepper.
3. In a small bowl, whisk eggs. In another small bowl, mix bread crumbs with remaining ½ teaspoon salt and ¼ teaspoon pepper.
4. One by one, dip nuggets in the eggs, shaking off excess before rolling in the bread crumb mixture. Repeat to make sixteen nuggets.
5. Place nuggets in the air fryer basket and spritz with cooking spray. Cook 12 minutes, turning halfway through cooking time. Nuggets will be done when golden brown and have an internal temperature of at least 145°F. Serve warm.

Lemon Butter–dill Salmon

Servings: 4 | Cooking Time: 10 Minutes

Ingredients:
- 4 skin-on salmon fillets
- ¾ teaspoon salt
- ½ teaspoon ground black pepper
- 1 medium lemon, halved
- 2 tablespoons salted butter, melted
- 1 teaspoon dried dill

Directions:
1. Preheat the air fryer to 375°F.
2. Sprinkle salmon with salt and pepper.
3. Juice half the lemon and slice the other half into ¼"-thick pieces. In a small bowl, combine juice with butter. Brush mixture over salmon.
4. Sprinkle dill evenly over salmon. Place lemon slices on top of salmon.
5. Place salmon in the air fryer basket and cook 10 minutes until salmon flakes easily and internal temperature reaches at least 145°F. Remove lemon slices before serving.

Crispy Parmesan Lobster Tails

Servings:4 | Cooking Time: 7 Minutes

Ingredients:
- 4 lobster tails
- 2 tablespoons salted butter, melted
- 1½ teaspoons Cajun seasoning, divided
- ¼ teaspoon salt
- ¼ teaspoon ground black pepper
- ¼ cup grated Parmesan cheese

- ½ ounce plain pork rinds, finely crushed

Directions:
1. Cut lobster tails open carefully with a pair of scissors and gently pull meat away from shells, resting meat on top of shells.
2. Brush lobster meat with butter and sprinkle with 1 teaspoon Cajun seasoning, ¼ teaspoon per tail.
3. In a small bowl, mix remaining Cajun seasoning, salt, pepper, Parmesan, and pork rinds. Gently press ¼ mixture onto meat on each lobster tail.
4. Carefully place tails into ungreased air fryer basket. Adjust the temperature to 400°F and set the timer for 7 minutes. Lobster tails will be crispy and golden on top and have an internal temperature of at least 145°F when done. Serve warm.

Simple Salmon Fillets

Servings: 2 | Cooking Time: 7 Minutes

Ingredients:
- 2 salmon fillets
- 2 tsp olive oil
- 2 tsp paprika
- Pepper
- Salt

Directions:
1. Rub salmon fillet with oil, paprika, pepper, and salt.
2. Place salmon fillets in the air fryer basket and cook at 390°F for 7 minutes.
3. Serve and enjoy.

Cajun Flounder Fillets

Servings:2 | Cooking Time: 5 Minutes

Ingredients:
- 2 4-ounce skinless flounder fillet(s)
- 2 teaspoons Peanut oil
- 1 teaspoon Purchased or homemade Cajun dried seasoning blend

Directions:
1. Preheat the air fryer to 400°F.
2. Oil the fillet(s) by drizzling on the peanut oil, then gently rubbing in the oil with your clean, dry fingers. Sprinkle the seasoning blend evenly over both sides of the fillet(s).
3. When the machine is at temperature, set the fillet(s) in the basket. If working with more than one fillet, they should not touch, although they may be quite close together, depending on the basket's size. Air-fry undisturbed for 5 minutes, or until lightly browned and cooked through.
4. Use a nonstick-safe spatula to transfer the fillets to a serving platter or plate(s). Serve at once.

Tilapia Fish Fillets

Servings: 2 | Cooking Time: 7 Minutes

Ingredients:
- 2 tilapia fillets
- 1 tsp old bay seasoning
- 1/2 tsp butter
- 1/4 tsp lemon pepper
- Pepper
- Salt

Directions:
1. Spray air fryer basket with cooking spray.
2. Place fish fillets into the air fryer basket and season with lemon pepper, old bay seasoning, pepper, and salt.
3. Spray fish fillets with cooking spray and cook at 400°F for 7 minutes.
4. Serve and enjoy.

Spicy Prawns

Servings: 2 | Cooking Time: 8 Minutes

Ingredients:
- 6 prawns
- 1/4 tsp pepper
- 1/2 tsp chili powder
- 1 tsp chili flakes
- 1/4 tsp salt

Directions:
1. Preheat the air fryer to 350°F.
2. In a bowl, mix together spices add prawns.
3. Spray air fryer basket with cooking spray.
4. Transfer prawns into the air fryer basket and cook for 8 minutes.
5. Serve and enjoy.

Catfish Nuggets

Servings: 4 | Cooking Time: 7 Minutes Per Batch

Ingredients:
- 2 medium catfish fillets, cut in chunks
- salt and pepper
- 2 eggs
- 2 tablespoons skim milk
- ½ cup cornstarch
- 1 cup panko breadcrumbs, crushed
- oil for misting or cooking spray

Directions:
1. Season catfish chunks with salt and pepper to your liking.
2. Beat together eggs and milk in a small bowl.
3. Place cornstarch in a second small bowl.
4. Place breadcrumbs in a third small bowl.
5. Dip catfish chunks in cornstarch, dip in egg wash, shake off excess, then roll in breadcrumbs.
6. Spray all sides of catfish chunks with oil or cooking spray.
7. Place chunks in air fryer basket in a single layer, leaving space between for air circulation.
8. Cook at 390°F for 4minutes, turn, and cook an additional 3 minutes, until fish flakes easily and outside is crispy brown.
9. Repeat steps 7 and 8 to cook remaining catfish nuggets.

Air Fried Calamari

Servings:3 | Cooking Time: 30 Minutes

Ingredients:
- ½ cup cornmeal or cornstarch
- 2 large eggs, beaten
- 2 mashed garlic cloves
- 1 cup breadcrumbs
- lemon juice

Directions:
1. Coat calamari with the cornmeal. The first mixture is prepared by mixing the eggs and garlic. Dip the calamari in the eggs' mixture. Then dip them in the breadcrumbs. Put the rings in the fridge for 2 hours.
2. Then, line them in the air fryer and add oil generously. Fry for 10 to 13 minutes at 390°F, shaking once halfway through. Serve with garlic mayonnaise and top with lemon juice.

Chili Lime Shrimp

Servings:4 | Cooking Time: 5 Minutes

Ingredients:
- 1 pound medium shrimp, peeled and deveined
- 1 tablespoon salted butter, melted
- 2 teaspoons chili powder
- ¼ teaspoon garlic powder
- ¼ teaspoon salt
- ¼ teaspoon ground black pepper
- ½ small lime, zested and juiced, divided

Directions:
1. In a medium bowl, toss shrimp with butter, then sprinkle with chili powder, garlic powder, salt, pepper, and lime zest.
2. Place shrimp into ungreased air fryer basket. Adjust the temperature to 400°F and set the timer for 5 minutes. Shrimp will be firm and form a "C" shape when done.
3. Transfer shrimp to a large serving dish and drizzle with lime juice. Serve warm.

Miso-rubbed Salmon Fillets

Servings:3 | Cooking Time: 5 Minutes

Ingredients:
- ¼ cup White (shiro) miso paste (usually made from rice and soy beans)
- 1½ tablespoons Mirin or a substitute
- 2½ teaspoons Unseasoned rice vinegar
- Vegetable oil spray
- 3 6-ounce skin-on salmon fillets

Directions:
1. Preheat the air fryer to 400°F.
2. Mix the miso, mirin, and vinegar in a small bowl until uniform.
3. Remove the basket from the machine. Generously spray the skin side of each fillet. Pick them up one by one with a non-stick-safe spatula and set them in the basket skin side down with as much air space between them as possible. Coat the top of each fillet with the miso mixture, dividing it evenly between them.
4. Return the basket to the machine. Air-fry undisturbed for 5 minutes, or until lightly browned and firm.
5. Use a nonstick-safe spatula to transfer the fillets to serving plates. Cool for only a minute or so before serving.

Garlic And Dill Salmon

Servings: 2 | Cooking Time: 8 Minutes

Ingredients:
- 12 ounces salmon filets with skin
- 2 tablespoons melted butter
- 1 tablespoon extra-virgin olive oil
- 2 garlic cloves, minced
- 1 tablespoon fresh dill
- ½ teaspoon sea salt
- ½ lemon

Directions:
1. Pat the salmon dry with paper towels.
2. In a small bowl, mix together the melted butter, olive oil, garlic, and dill.
3. Sprinkle the top of the salmon with sea salt. Brush all sides of the salmon with the garlic and dill butter.
4. Preheat the air fryer to 350°F.
5. Place the salmon, skin side down, in the air fryer basket. Cook for 6 to 8 minutes, or until the fish flakes in the center.
6. Remove the salmon and plate on a serving platter. Squeeze fresh lemon over the top of the salmon. Serve immediately.

Chapter 7 Vegetarians Recipes

Chapter 7 Vegetarians Recipes

Cauliflower Rice–stuffed Peppers

Servings:4 | Cooking Time: 15 Minutes

Ingredients:
- 2 cups uncooked cauliflower rice
- ¾ cup drained canned petite diced tomatoes
- 2 tablespoons olive oil
- 1 cup shredded mozzarella cheese
- ¼ teaspoon salt
- ¼ teaspoon ground black pepper
- 4 medium green bell peppers, tops removed, seeded

Directions:
1. In a large bowl, mix all ingredients except bell peppers. Scoop mixture evenly into peppers.
2. Place peppers into ungreased air fryer basket. Adjust the temperature to 350°F and set the timer for 15 minutes. Peppers will be tender and cheese will be melted when done. Serve warm.

Crispy Apple Fries With Caramel Sauce

Servings: 4 | Cooking Time: 15 Minutes

Ingredients:
- 4 medium apples, cored
- ¼ tsp cinnamon
- ¼ tsp nutmeg
- 1 cup caramel sauce

Directions:
1. Preheat air fryer to 350°F. Slice the apples to a 1/3-inch thickness for a crunchy chip. Place in a large bowl and sprinkle with cinnamon and nutmeg. Place the slices in the air fryer basket. Bake for 6 minutes. Shake the basket, then cook for another 4 minutes or until crunchy. Serve drizzled with caramel sauce and enjoy!

Lemon Caper Cauliflower Steaks

Servings:4 | Cooking Time: 15 Minutes

Ingredients:
- 1 small head cauliflower, leaves and core removed, cut into 4 (½"-thick) "steaks"
- 4 tablespoons olive oil, divided
- 1 medium lemon, zested and juiced, divided
- ¼ teaspoon salt
- ⅛ teaspoon ground black pepper
- 1 tablespoon salted butter, melted
- 1 tablespoon capers, rinsed

Directions:
1. Brush each cauliflower "steak" with ½ tablespoon olive oil on both sides and sprinkle with lemon zest, salt, and pepper on both sides.
2. Place cauliflower into ungreased air fryer basket. Adjust the temperature to 400°F and set the timer for 15 minutes, turning cauliflower halfway through cooking. Steaks will be golden at the edges and browned when done.
3. Transfer steaks to four medium plates. In a small bowl, whisk remaining olive oil, butter, lemon juice, and capers, and pour evenly over steaks. Serve warm.

Zucchini Gratin

Servings: 2 | Cooking Time: 15 Minutes

Ingredients:
- 5 oz. parmesan cheese, shredded
- 1 tbsp. coconut flour
- 1 tbsp. dried parsley
- 2 zucchinis
- 1 tsp. butter, melted

Directions:
1. Mix the parmesan and coconut flour together in a bowl, seasoning with parsley to taste.
2. Cut the zucchini in half lengthwise and chop the halves into four slices.
3. Pre-heat the fryer at 400°F.
4. Pour the melted butter over the zucchini and then dip the zucchini into the parmesan-flour mixture, coating it all over. Cook the zucchini in the fryer for thirteen minutes.

Caribbean-style Fried Plantains

Servings: 2 | Cooking Time: 20 Minutes

Ingredients:
- 2 plantains, peeled and cut into slices
- 2 tablespoons avocado oil
- 2 teaspoons Caribbean Sorrel Rum Spice Mix

Directions:
1. Toss the plantains with the avocado oil and spice mix.
2. Cook in the preheated Air Fryer at 400°F for 10 minutes, shaking the cooking basket halfway through the cooking time.
3. Adjust the seasonings to taste and enjoy!

Broccoli Salad

Servings: 2 | Cooking Time: 15 Minutes

Ingredients:
- 3 cups fresh broccoli florets
- 2 tbsp. coconut oil, melted
- ¼ cup sliced s
- ½ medium lemon, juiced

Directions:
1. Take a six-inch baking dish and fill with the broccoli florets. Pour the melted coconut oil over the broccoli and add in the sliced s. Toss together. Put the dish in the air fryer.
2. Cook at 380°F for seven minutes, stirring at the halfway point.
3. Place the broccoli in a bowl and drizzle the lemon juice over it.

Breadcrumbs Stuffed Mushrooms

Servings:4 | Cooking Time:10 Minutes

Ingredients:
- 1½ spelt bread slices
- 1 tablespoon flat-leaf parsley, finely chopped
- 16 small button mushrooms, stemmed and gills removed
- 1½ tablespoons olive oil
- 1 garlic clove, crushed
- Salt and black pepper, to taste

Directions:
1. Preheat the Air fryer to 390°F and grease an Air fryer basket.
2. Put the bread slices in a food processor and pulse until fine crumbs form.
3. Transfer the crumbs into a bowl and stir in the olive oil, garlic, parsley, salt, and black pepper.
4. Stuff the breadcrumbs mixture in each mushroom cap and arrange the mushrooms in the Air fryer basket.
5. Cook for about 10 minutes and dish out in a bowl to serve warm.

Brussels Sprouts With Balsamic Oil

Servings:4 | Cooking Time: 15 Minutes

Ingredients:
• ¼ teaspoon salt
• 1 tablespoon balsamic vinegar
• 2 cups Brussels sprouts, halved
• 2 tablespoons olive oil

Directions:
1. Preheat the air fryer for 5 minutes.
2. Mix all ingredients in a bowl until the zucchini fries are well coated.
3. Place in the air fryer basket.
4. Close and cook for 15 minutes for 350°F.

Easy Glazed Carrots

Servings:4 | Cooking Time:12 Minutes

Ingredients:
• 3 cups carrots, peeled and cut into large chunks
• 1 tablespoon olive oil
• 1 tablespoon honey
• Salt and black pepper, to taste

Directions:
1. Preheat the Air fryer to 390°F and grease an Air fryer basket.
2. Mix all the ingredients in a bowl and toss to coat well.
3. Transfer into the Air fryer basket and cook for about 12 minutes.
4. Dish out and serve hot.

Grilled 'n Glazed Strawberries

Servings:2 | Cooking Time: 20 Minutes

Ingredients:
• 1 tbsp honey
• 1 tsp lemon zest
• 1-lb large strawberries
• 3 tbsp melted butter
• Lemon wedges
• Pinch kosher salt

Directions:
1. Thread strawberries in 4 skewers.
2. In a small bowl, mix well remaining ingredients except for lemon wedges. Brush all over strawberries.
3. Place skewer on air fryer skewer rack.
4. For 10 minutes, cook on 360°F. Halfway through cooking time, brush with honey mixture and turnover skewer.
5. Serve and enjoy with a squeeze of lemon.

Cheesy Brussel Sprouts

Servings:3 | Cooking Time:10 Minutes

Ingredients:
• 1 pound Brussels sprouts, trimmed and halved
• ¼ cup whole wheat breadcrumbs
• ¼ cup Parmesan cheese, shredded
• 1 tablespoon balsamic vinegar
• 1 tablespoon extra-virgin olive oil
• Salt and black pepper, to taste

Directions:
1. Preheat the Air fryer to 400°F and grease an Air fryer basket.
2. Mix Brussel sprouts, vinegar, oil, salt, and black pepper in a bowl and toss to coat well.
3. Arrange the Brussel sprouts in the Air fryer basket and cook for about 5 minutes.
4. Sprinkle with breadcrumbs and cheese and cook for about 5 more minutes.
5. Dish out and serve hot.

Sweet Roasted Carrots

Servings: 4 | Cooking Time: 25 Minutes

Ingredients:
• 6 carrots, cut into ½-inch pieces
• 2 tbsp butter, melted
• 2 tbsp parsley, chopped
• 1 tsp honey

Directions:
1. Preheat air fryer to 390°F. Add carrots to a baking pan and pour over butter, honey, and 2-3 tbsp of water. Mix well. Transfer the carrots to the greased frying basket and Roast for 12 minutes, shaking the basket once. Sprinkle with parsley and serve warm.

Tortilla Pizza Margherita

Servings: 1 | Cooking Time: 15 Minutes

Ingredients:
• 1 flour tortilla
• ¼ cup tomato sauce
• 1/3 cup grated mozzarella
• 3 basil leaves

Directions:
1. Preheat air fryer to 350°F. Put the tortilla in the greased basket and pour the sauce in the center. Spread across the whole tortilla. Sprinkle with cheese and Bake for 8-10 minutes or until crisp. Remove carefully and top with basil leaves. Serve hot.

Avocado Rolls

Servings:5 | Cooking Time: 15 Minutes

Ingredients:
• 10 egg roll wrappers
• 1 tomato, diced
• ¼ tsp pepper
• ½ tsp salt

Directions:
1. Place all filling ingredients in a bowl; mash with a fork until somewhat smooth. There should be chunks left. Divide the feeling between the egg wrappers. Wet your finger and brush along the edges, so the wrappers can seal well. Roll and seal the wrappers.
2. Arrange them on a baking sheet lined dish, and place in the air fryer. Cook at 350°F for 5 minutes. Serve with sweet chili dipping and enjoy.

Italian Seasoned Easy Pasta Chips

Servings:2 | Cooking Time:10 Minutes

Ingredients:
- ½ teaspoon salt
- 1 ½ teaspoon Italian seasoning blend
- 1 tablespoon nutritional yeast
- 1 tablespoon olive oil
- 2 cups whole wheat bowtie pasta

Directions:
1. Place the baking dish accessory in the air fryer.
2. Give a good stir.
3. Close the air fryer and cook for 10 minutes at 390°F.

Cheese And Bean Enchiladas

Servings:4 | Cooking Time: 9 Minutes

Ingredients:
- 1 can pinto beans, drained and rinsed
- 1 ½ tablespoons taco seasoning
- 1 cup red enchilada sauce, divided
- 1 ½ cups shredded Mexican-blend cheese, divided
- 4 fajita-size flour tortillas

Directions:
1. Preheat the air fryer to 320°F.
2. In a large microwave-safe bowl, microwave beans for 1 minute. Mash half the beans and fold into whole beans. Mix in taco seasoning, ¼ cup enchilada sauce, and 1 cup cheese until well combined.
3. Place ¼ cup bean mixture onto each tortilla. Fold up one end about 1", then roll to close.
4. Place enchiladas into a 3-quart baking pan, pushing together as needed to make them fit. Pour remaining ¾ cup enchilada sauce over enchiladas and top with remaining ½ cup cheese.
5. Place pan in the air fryer basket and cook 8 minutes until cheese is brown and bubbling and the edges of tortillas are brown. Serve warm.

Cheese & Bean Burgers

Servings: 2 | Cooking Time: 35 Minutes

Ingredients:
- 1 cup cooked black beans
- ½ cup shredded cheddar
- 1 egg, beaten
- Salt and pepper to taste
- 1 cup bread crumbs
- ½ cup grated carrots

Directions:
1. Preheat air fryer to 350°F. Mash the beans with a fork in a bowl. Mix in the cheese, salt, and pepper until evenly combined. Stir in half of the bread crumbs and egg. Shape the mixture into 2 patties. Coat each patty with the remaining bread crumbs and spray with cooking oil. Air Fry for 14-16 minutes, turning once. When ready, remove to a plate. Top with grated carrots and serve.

Vegetable Nuggets

Servings:6 | Cooking Time: 10 Minutes Per Batch

Ingredients:
- 1 cup shredded carrots
- 2 cups broccoli florets
- 2 large eggs
- 1 cup shredded Cheddar cheese
- 1 cup Italian bread crumbs
- 1 teaspoon salt
- ½ teaspoon ground black pepper

Directions:
1. Preheat the air fryer to 400°F.
2. In a food processor, combine carrots and broccoli and pulse five times. Add eggs, Cheddar, bread crumbs, salt, and pepper, and pulse ten times.
3. Carefully scoop twenty-four balls, about 1 heaping tablespoon each, out of the mixture. Spritz balls with cooking spray.
4. Place balls in the air fryer basket, working in batches as necessary, and cook 10 minutes, shaking the basket twice during cooking to ensure even browning. Serve warm.

Cauliflower Pizza Crust

Servings:2 | Cooking Time: 7 Minutes

Ingredients:
- 1 steamer bag cauliflower, cooked according to package instructions
- ½ cup shredded sharp Cheddar cheese
- 1 large egg
- 2 tablespoons blanched finely ground almond flour
- 1 teaspoon Italian seasoning

Directions:
1. Let cooked cauliflower cool for 10 minutes. Using a kitchen towel, wring out excess moisture from cauliflower and place into food processor.
2. Add Cheddar, egg, flour, and Italian seasoning to processor and pulse ten times until cauliflower is smooth and all ingredients are combined.
3. Cut two pieces of parchment paper to fit air fryer basket. Divide cauliflower mixture into two equal portions and press each into a 6" round on ungreased parchment.
4. Place crusts on parchment into air fryer basket. Adjust the temperature to 360°F and set the timer for 7 minutes, gently turning crusts halfway through cooking.
5. Store crusts in refrigerator in an airtight container up to 4 days or freeze between sheets of parchment in a sealable storage bag for up to 2 months.

Cheesy Cauliflower Crust Pizza

Servings:2 | Cooking Time: 12 Minutes Per Batch

Ingredients:
- 2 steamer bags cauliflower florets
- 1 large egg
- 1 cup grated vegetarian Parmesan cheese
- 3 cups shredded mozzarella cheese, divided
- 1 cup pizza sauce

Directions:
1. Preheat the air fryer to 375°F. Cut two pieces of parchment paper to fit the air fryer basket, one for each crust.
2. Cook cauliflower in the microwave according to package instructions, then drain in a colander. Run under cold water until

cool to the touch. Use a cheesecloth to squeeze the excess water from cauliflower, removing as much as possible.
3. In a food processor, combine cauliflower, egg, Parmesan, and 1 cup mozzarella. Process on low about 15 seconds until a sticky ball forms.
4. Separate dough into two pieces. Working with damp hands to prevent dough from sticking, press each dough ball into a 6" round.
5. Place crust on parchment in the air fryer basket, working in batches as necessary. Cook 6 minutes, then flip over with a spatula and top the crust with ½ cup pizza sauce and 1 cup mozzarella. Cook an additional 6 minutes until edges are dark brown and cheese is brown and bubbling. Let cool at least 5 minutes before serving. The crust firms up as it cools.

Twice-baked Broccoli-cheddar Potatoes

Servings:4 | Cooking Time: 35 Minutes

Ingredients:
• 4 large russet potatoes
• 2 tablespoons plus 2 teaspoons ranch dressing
• 1 teaspoon salt
• ½ teaspoon ground black pepper
• ¼ cup chopped cooked broccoli florets
• 1 cup shredded sharp Cheddar cheese

Directions:
1. Preheat the air fryer to 400°F.
2. Using a fork, poke several holes in potatoes. Place in the air fryer basket and cook 30 minutes until fork-tender.
3. Once potatoes are cool enough to handle, slice lengthwise and scoop out the cooked potato into a large bowl, being careful to maintain the structural integrity of potato skins. Add ranch dressing, salt, pepper, broccoli, and Cheddar to potato flesh and stir until well combined.
4. Scoop potato mixture back into potato skins and return to the air fryer basket. Cook an additional 5 minutes until cheese is melted. Serve warm.

Spicy Roasted Cashew Nuts

Servings: 4 | Cooking Time: 20 Minutes

Ingredients:
• 1 cup whole cashews
• 1 teaspoon olive oil
• Salt and ground black pepper, to taste
• 1/2 teaspoon smoked paprika
• 1/2 teaspoon ancho chili powder

Directions:
1. Toss all ingredients in the mixing bowl.
2. Line the Air Fryer basket with baking parchment. Spread out the spiced cashews in a single layer in the basket.
3. Roast at 350°F for 6 to 8 minutes, shaking the basket once or twice. Work in batches. Enjoy!

Caramelized Carrots

Servings:3 | Cooking Time:15 Minutes

Ingredients:
• 1 small bag baby carrots
• ½ cup butter, melted
• ½ cup brown sugar

Directions:
1. Preheat the Air fryer to 400°F and grease an Air fryer basket.

2. Mix the butter and brown sugar in a bowl.
3. Add the carrots and toss to coat well.
4. Arrange the carrots in the Air fryer basket and cook for about 15 minutes.
5. Dish out and serve warm.

Parmesan Artichokes

Servings: 4 | Cooking Time: 35 Minutes

Ingredients:
• 2 medium artichokes, trimmed and quartered, with the centers removed
• 2 tbsp. coconut oil, melted
• 1 egg, beaten
• ½ cup parmesan cheese, grated
• ¼ cup blanched, finely ground flour

Directions:
1. Place the artichokes in a bowl with the coconut oil and toss to coat, then dip the artichokes into a bowl of beaten egg.
2. In a separate bowl, mix together the parmesan cheese and the flour. Combine with the pieces of artichoke, making sure to coat each piece well. Transfer the artichoke to the fryer.
3. Cook at 400°F for ten minutes, shaking occasionally throughout the cooking time. Serve hot.

Pesto Vegetable Skewers

Servings:8 | Cooking Time: 8 Minutes

Ingredients:
• 1 medium zucchini, trimmed and cut into ½" slices
• ½ medium yellow onion, peeled and cut into 1» squares
• 1 medium red bell pepper, seeded and cut into 1" squares
• 16 whole cremini mushrooms
• ⅓ cup basil pesto
• ½ teaspoon salt
• ¼ teaspoon ground black pepper

Directions:
1. Divide zucchini slices, onion, and bell pepper into eight even portions. Place on 6" skewers for a total of eight kebabs. Add 2 mushrooms to each skewer and brush kebabs generously with pesto.
2. Sprinkle each kebab with salt and black pepper on all sides, then place into ungreased air fryer basket. Adjust the temperature to 375°F and set the timer for 8 minutes, turning kebabs halfway through cooking. Vegetables will be browned at the edges and tender-crisp when done. Serve warm.

Caramelized Brussels Sprout

Servings:4 | Cooking Time:35 Minutes

Ingredients:
• 1 pound Brussels sprouts, trimmed and halved
• 4 teaspoons butter, melted
• Salt and black pepper, to taste

Directions:
1. Preheat the Air fryer to 400°F and grease an Air fryer basket.
2. Mix all the ingredients in a bowl and toss to coat well.
3. Arrange the Brussels sprouts in the Air fryer basket and cook for about 35 minutes.
4. Dish out and serve warm.

Zucchini Fritters

Servings:4 | Cooking Time: 12 Minutes

Ingredients:
- 1½ medium zucchini, trimmed and grated
- ½ teaspoon salt, divided
- 1 large egg, whisked
- ¼ teaspoon garlic powder
- ¼ cup grated Parmesan cheese

Directions:
1. Place grated zucchini on a kitchen towel and sprinkle with ¼ teaspoon salt. Wrap in towel and let sit 30 minutes, then wring out as much excess moisture as possible.
2. Place zucchini into a large bowl and mix with egg, remaining salt, garlic powder, and Parmesan. Cut a piece of parchment to fit air fryer basket. Divide mixture into four mounds, about ⅓ cup each, and press out into 4" rounds on ungreased parchment.
3. Place parchment with rounds into air fryer basket. Adjust the temperature to 400°F and set the timer for 12 minutes, turning fritters halfway through cooking. Fritters will be crispy on the edges and tender but firm in the center when done. Serve warm.

Toasted Ravioli

Servings:4 | Cooking Time: 8 Minutes

Ingredients:
- 1 cup Italian bread crumbs
- 2 tablespoons grated vegetarian Parmesan cheese
- 1 large egg
- ¼ cup whole milk
- 1 package fresh cheese ravioli
- Cooking spray

Directions:
1. Preheat the air fryer to 400°F.
2. In a large bowl, whisk together bread crumbs and Parmesan.
3. In a medium bowl, whisk together egg and milk.
4. Dip each ravioli into egg mixture, shaking off the excess, then press into bread crumb mixture until well coated. Spritz each side with cooking spray.
5. Place in the air fryer basket and cook 8 minutes, turning halfway through cooking time, until ravioli is brown at the edges and crispy. Serve warm.

Portobello Mini Pizzas

Servings:4 | Cooking Time: 10 Minutes

Ingredients:
- 4 large portobello mushrooms, stems removed
- 2 cups shredded mozzarella cheese, divided
- ½ cup full-fat ricotta cheese
- 1 teaspoon salt, divided
- ½ teaspoon ground black pepper
- 1 teaspoon Italian seasoning
- 1 cup pizza sauce

Directions:
1. Preheat the air fryer to 350°F.
2. Use a spoon to hollow out mushroom caps. Spritz mushrooms with cooking spray. Place ¼ cup mozzarella into each mushroom cap.
3. In a small bowl, mix ricotta, ½ teaspoon salt, pepper, and Italian seasoning. Divide mixture evenly and spoon into mushroom caps.
4. Pour ¼ cup pizza sauce into each mushroom cap, then top each with ¼ cup mozzarella. Sprinkle tops of pizzas with remaining salt.
5. Place mushrooms in the air fryer basket and cook 10 minutes until cheese is brown and bubbling. Serve warm.

Crispy Eggplant Rounds

Servings:4 | Cooking Time: 10 Minutes

Ingredients:
- 1 large eggplant, ends trimmed, cut into ½" slices
- ½ teaspoon salt
- 2 ounces Parmesan 100% cheese crisps, finely ground
- ½ teaspoon paprika
- ¼ teaspoon garlic powder
- 1 large egg

Directions:
1. Sprinkle eggplant rounds with salt. Place rounds on a kitchen towel for 30 minutes to draw out excess water. Pat rounds dry.
2. In a medium bowl, mix cheese crisps, paprika, and garlic powder. In a separate medium bowl, whisk egg. Dip each eggplant round in egg, then gently press into cheese crisps to coat both sides.
3. Place eggplant rounds into ungreased air fryer basket. Adjust the temperature to 400°F and set the timer for 10 minutes, turning rounds halfway through cooking. Eggplant will be golden and crispy when done. Serve warm.

Eggplant Parmesan

Servings:4 | Cooking Time: 17 Minutes

Ingredients:
- 1 medium eggplant, ends trimmed, sliced into ½" rounds
- ¼ teaspoon salt
- 2 tablespoons coconut oil
- ½ cup grated Parmesan cheese
- 1 ounce 100% cheese crisps, finely crushed
- ½ cup low-carb marinara sauce
- ½ cup shredded mozzarella cheese

Directions:
1. Sprinkle eggplant rounds with salt on both sides and wrap in a kitchen towel for 30 minutes. Press to remove excess water, then drizzle rounds with coconut oil on both sides.
2. In a medium bowl, mix Parmesan and cheese crisps. Press each eggplant slice into mixture to coat both sides.
3. Place rounds into ungreased air fryer basket. Adjust the temperature to 350°F and set the timer for 15 minutes, turning rounds halfway through cooking. They will be crispy around the edges when done.
4. When timer beeps, spoon marinara over rounds and sprinkle with mozzarella. Continue cooking an additional 2 minutes at 350°F until cheese is melted. Serve warm.

Honey Pear Chips

Servings: 4 | Cooking Time: 30 Minutes

Ingredients:
- 2 firm pears, thinly sliced
- 1 tbsp lemon juice
- ½ tsp ground cinnamon
- 1 tsp honey

Directions:
1. Preheat air fryer to 380°F. Arrange the pear slices on the parchment-lined cooking basket. Drizzle with lemon juice and honey

and sprinkle with cinnamon. Air Fry for 6-8 minutes, shaking the basket once, until golden. Leave to cool. Serve immediately or save for later in an airtight container. Good for 2 days.

Stuffed Mushrooms

Servings:4 | Cooking Time: 10 Minutes

Ingredients:
- 12 baby bella mushrooms, stems removed
- 4 ounces full-fat cream cheese, softened
- ¼ cup grated vegetarian Parmesan cheese
- ¼ cup Italian bread crumbs
- 1 teaspoon crushed red pepper flakes

Directions:
1. Preheat the air fryer to 400°F.
2. Use a spoon to hollow out mushroom caps.
3. In a medium bowl, combine cream cheese, Parmesan, bread crumbs, and red pepper flakes. Scoop approximately 1 tablespoon mixture into each mushroom cap.
4. Place stuffed mushrooms in the air fryer basket and cook 10 minutes until stuffing is brown. Let cool 5 minutes before serving.

Thyme Lentil Patties

Servings: 2 | Cooking Time: 35 Minutes

Ingredients:
- ½ cup grated American cheese
- 1 cup cooked lentils
- ¼ tsp dried thyme
- 2 eggs, beaten
- Salt and pepper to taste
- 1 cup bread crumbs

Directions:
1. Preheat air fryer to 350°F. Put the eggs, lentils, and cheese in a bowl and mix to combine. Stir in half the bread crumbs, thyme, salt, and pepper. Form the mixture into 2 patties and coat them in the remaining bread crumbs. Transfer to the greased frying basket. Air Fry for 14-16 minutes until brown, flipping once. Serve.

Buttered Broccoli

Servings:4 | Cooking Time:7 Minutes

Ingredients:
- 4 cups fresh broccoli florets
- 2 tablespoons butter, melted
- ¼ cup water
- Salt and black pepper, to taste

Directions:
1. Preheat the Air fryer to 400°F and grease an Air fryer basket.
2. Mix broccoli, butter, salt, and black pepper in a bowl and toss to coat well.
3. Place water at the bottom of Air fryer pan and arrange the broccoli florets into the Air fryer basket.
4. Cook for about 7 minutes and dish out in a bowl to serve hot.

Colorful Vegetable Medley

Servings: 4 | Cooking Time: 20 Minutes

Ingredients:
- 1 lb green beans, chopped
- 2 carrots, cubed
- Salt and pepper to taste
- 1 zucchini, cut into chunks
- 1 red bell pepper, sliced
- Cooking spray

Directions:
1. Preheat air fryer to 390°F. Combine green beans, carrots, salt and pepper in a large bowl. Spray with cooking oil and transfer to the frying basket. Roast for 6 minutes.
2. Combine zucchini and red pepper in a bowl. Season to taste and spray with cooking oil; set aside. When the cooking time is up, add the zucchini and red pepper to the basket. Cook for another 6 minutes. Serve and enjoy.

Sautéed Spinach

Servings:2 | Cooking Time:9 Minutes

Ingredients:
- 1 small onion, chopped
- 6 ounces fresh spinach
- 2 tablespoons olive oil
- 1 teaspoon ginger, minced
- Salt and black pepper, to taste

Directions:
1. Preheat the Air fryer to 360°F and grease an Air fryer pan.
2. Put olive oil, onions and ginger in the Air fryer pan and place in the Air fryer basket.
3. Cook for about 4 minutes and add spinach, salt, and black pepper.
4. Cook for about 4 more minutes and dish out in a bowl to serve.

Wine Infused Mushrooms

Servings:6 | Cooking Time: 32 Minutes

Ingredients:
- 1 tablespoon butter
- 2 teaspoons Herbs de Provence
- ½ teaspoon garlic powder
- 2 pounds fresh mushrooms, quartered
- 2 tablespoons white vermouth

Directions:
1. Set the temperature of air fryer to 320°F.
2. In an air fryer pan, mix together the butter, Herbs de Provence, and garlic powder and air fry for about 2 minutes.
3. Stir in the mushrooms and air fry for about 25 minutes.
4. Stir in the vermouth and air fry for 5 more minutes.
5. Remove from air fryer and transfer the mushrooms onto serving plates.
6. Serve hot.

Almond Asparagus

Servings:3 | Cooking Time:6 Minutes

Ingredients:
- 1 pound asparagus
- 1/3 cup almonds, sliced
- 2 tablespoons olive oil
- 2 tablespoons balsamic vinegar
- Salt and black pepper, to taste

Directions:
1. Preheat the Air fryer to 400°F and grease an Air fryer basket.
2. Mix asparagus, oil, vinegar, salt, and black pepper in a bowl and toss to coat well.
3. Arrange asparagus into the Air fryer basket and sprinkle with the almond slices.
4. Cook for about 6 minutes and dish out to serve hot.

Spaghetti Squash

Servings:4 | Cooking Time: 45 Minutes

Ingredients:
- 1 large spaghetti squash, halved lengthwise and seeded
- 1 teaspoon salt
- ½ teaspoon ground black pepper
- 1 teaspoon garlic powder
- 1 teaspoon dried parsley
- 2 tablespoons salted butter, melted

Directions:
1. Preheat the air fryer to 350°F.
2. Sprinkle squash with salt, pepper, garlic powder, and parsley. Spritz with cooking spray.
3. Place skin side down in the air fryer basket and cook 30 minutes.
4. Turn squash skin side up and cook an additional 15 minutes until fork-tender. You should be able to easily use a fork to scrape across the surface to separate the strands.
5. Place strands in a medium bowl, top with butter, and toss. Serve warm.

Crispy Wings With Lemony Old Bay Spice

Servings:4 | Cooking Time: 25 Minutes

Ingredients:
- ½ cup butter
- ¾ cup almond flour
- 1 tablespoon old bay spices
- 1 teaspoon lemon juice, freshly squeezed
- 3 pounds chicken wings
- Salt and pepper to taste

Directions:
1. Preheat the air fryer for 5 minutes.
2. In a mixing bowl, combine all ingredients except for the butter.
3. Place in the air fryer basket.
4. Cook for 25 minutes at 350°F.
5. Halfway through the cooking time, shake the fryer basket for even cooking.
6. Once cooked, drizzle with melted butter.

Pizza Dough

Servings:4 | Cooking Time: 1 Hour 10 Minutes, Plus 10 Minutes For Additional Batches

Ingredients:
- 2 cups all-purpose flour
- 1 tablespoon granulated sugar
- 1 tablespoon quick-rise yeast
- 4 tablespoons olive oil, divided
- ¾ cup warm water

Directions:
1. In a large bowl, mix flour, sugar, and yeast until combined. Add 2 tablespoons oil and warm water and mix until dough becomes smooth.
2. On a lightly floured surface, knead dough 10 minutes, then form into a smooth ball. Drizzle with remaining 2 tablespoons oil, then cover with plastic. Let dough rise 1 hour until doubled in size.
3. Preheat the air fryer to 320°F.
4. Separate dough into four pieces and press each into a 6" pan or air fryer pizza tray that has been spritzed with cooking oil.
5. Add any desired toppings. Place in the air fryer basket, working in batches as necessary, and cook 10 minutes until crust is brown at the edges and toppings are heated through. Serve warm.

Pepper-pineapple With Butter-sugar Glaze

Servings:2 | Cooking Time: 10 Minutes

Ingredients:
- 1 medium-sized pineapple, peeled and sliced
- 1 red bell pepper, seeded and julienned
- 1 teaspoon brown sugar
- 2 teaspoons melted butter
- Salt to taste

Directions:
1. Preheat the air fryer to 390°F.
2. Place the grill pan accessory in the air fryer.
3. Mix all ingredients in a Ziploc bag and give a good shake.
4. Dump onto the grill pan and cook for 10 minutes making sure that you flip the pineapples every 5 minutes.

Cauliflower Steak With Thick Sauce

Servings:2 | Cooking Time: 15 Minutes

Ingredients:
- ¼ cup almond milk
- ¼ teaspoon vegetable stock powder
- 1 cauliflower, sliced into two
- 1 tablespoon olive oil
- 2 tablespoons onion, chopped
- salt and pepper to taste

Directions:
1. Soak the cauliflower in salted water or brine for at least 2 hours.
2. Preheat the air fryer to 400°F.
3. Rinse the cauliflower and place inside the air fryer and cook for 15 minutes.
4. Meanwhile, heat oil in a skillet over medium flame. Sauté the onions and stir until translucent. Add the vegetable stock powder and milk.
5. Bring to boil and adjust the heat to low.
6. Allow the sauce to reduce and season with salt and pepper.
7. Place cauliflower steak on a plate and pour over sauce.

Broccoli & Parmesan Dish

Servings:4 | Cooking Time: 25 Minutes

Ingredients:
- 1 tbsp olive oil
- 1 lemon, Juiced
- Salt and pepper to taste
- 1-ounce Parmesan cheese, grated

Directions:
1. In a bowl, mix all ingredients. Add the mixture to your air fryer and cook for 20 minutes at 360°F. Serve.

Sesame Seeds Bok Choy

Servings:4 | Cooking Time: 6 Minutes

Ingredients:
- 4 bunches baby bok choy, bottoms removed and leaves separated
- Olive oil cooking spray
- 1 teaspoon garlic powder
- 1 teaspoon sesame seeds

Directions:
1. Set the temperature of air fryer to 325°F.
2. Arrange bok choy leaves into the air fryer basket in a single layer.
3. Spray with the cooking spray and sprinkle with garlic powder.
4. Air fry for about 5-6 minutes, shaking after every 2 minutes.
5. Remove from air fryer and transfer the bok choy onto serving plates.
6. Garnish with sesame seeds and serve hot.

White Cheddar And Mushroom Soufflés

Servings:4 | Cooking Time: 12 Minutes

Ingredients:
- 3 large eggs, whites and yolks separated
- ½ cup sharp white Cheddar cheese
- 3 ounces cream cheese, softened
- ¼ teaspoon cream of tartar
- ¼ teaspoon salt
- ¼ teaspoon ground black pepper
- ½ cup cremini mushrooms, sliced

Directions:
1. In a large bowl, whip egg whites until stiff peaks form, about 2 minutes. In a separate large bowl, beat Cheddar, egg yolks, cream cheese, cream of tartar, salt, and pepper together until combined.
2. Fold egg whites into cheese mixture, being careful not to stir. Fold in mushrooms, then pour mixture evenly into four ungreased 4" ramekins.
3. Place ramekins into air fryer basket. Adjust the temperature to 350°F and set the timer for 12 minutes. Eggs will be browned on the top and firm in the center when done. Serve warm.

Sweet Pepper Nachos

Servings:2 | Cooking Time: 5 Minutes

Ingredients:
- 6 mini sweet peppers, seeded and sliced in half
- ¾ cup shredded Colby jack cheese
- ¼ cup sliced pickled jalapeños
- ½ medium avocado, peeled, pitted, and diced
- 2 tablespoons sour cream

Directions:

1. Place peppers into an ungreased 6" round nonstick baking dish. Sprinkle with Colby and top with jalapeños.
2. Place dish into air fryer basket. Adjust the temperature to 350°F and set the timer for 5 minutes. Cheese will be melted and bubbly when done.
3. Remove dish from air fryer and top with avocado. Drizzle with sour cream. Serve warm.

Pesto Spinach Flatbread

Servings:4 | Cooking Time: 8 Minutes

Ingredients:
- 1 cup blanched finely ground almond flour
- 2 ounces cream cheese
- 2 cups shredded mozzarella cheese
- 1 cup chopped fresh spinach leaves
- 2 tablespoons basil pesto

Directions:
1. Place flour, cream cheese, and mozzarella in a large microwave-safe bowl and microwave on high 45 seconds, then stir.
2. Fold in spinach and microwave an additional 15 seconds. Stir until a soft dough ball forms.
3. Cut two pieces of parchment paper to fit air fryer basket. Separate dough into two sections and press each out on ungreased parchment to create 6" rounds.
4. Spread 1 tablespoon pesto over each flatbread and place rounds on parchment into ungreased air fryer basket. Adjust the temperature to 350°F and set the timer for 8 minutes, turning crusts halfway through cooking. Flatbread will be golden when done.
5. Let cool 5 minutes before slicing and serving.

Spinach And Artichoke–stuffed Peppers

Servings:4 | Cooking Time: 15 Minutes

Ingredients:
- 2 ounces cream cheese, softened
- ½ cup shredded mozzarella cheese
- ½ cup chopped fresh spinach leaves
- ¼ cup chopped canned artichoke hearts
- 2 medium green bell peppers, halved and seeded

Directions:
1. In a medium bowl, mix cream cheese, mozzarella, spinach, and artichokes. Spoon ¼ cheese mixture into each pepper half.
2. Place peppers into ungreased air fryer basket. Adjust the temperature to 320°F and set the timer for 15 minutes. Peppers will be tender and cheese will be bubbling and brown when done. Serve warm.

Baked Polenta With Chili-cheese

Servings:3 | Cooking Time: 10 Minutes

Ingredients:
- 1 commercial polenta roll, sliced
- 1 cup cheddar cheese sauce
- 1 tablespoon chili powder

Directions:
1. Place the baking dish accessory in the air fryer.
2. Arrange the polenta slices in the baking dish.
3. Add the chili powder and cheddar cheese sauce.
4. Close the air fryer and cook for 10 minutes at 390°F.

Roasted Vegetable Grilled Cheese

Servings:4 | Cooking Time: 6 Minutes

Ingredients:
- 8 slices sourdough bread
- 4 slices provolone cheese
- ½ cup chopped roasted red peppers
- ¼ cup chopped yellow onion
- 4 slices white American cheese

Directions:
1. Preheat the air fryer to 300°F.
2. Place a slice of bread on a work surface. Top with a slice of provolone, then with 2 tablespoons roasted red peppers and 1 tablespoon onion. Repeat with three more bread slices and remaining provolone and vegetables.
3. Place loaded bread slices in the air fryer basket and cook 1 minute until cheese is melted and onion is softened.
4. Remove the air fryer basket and carefully place 1 slice of American cheese on top of each slice of bread, finishing each with a second slice of bread to complete each sandwich.
5. Spritz the top with cooking spray. Increase the air fryer temperature to 400°F and cook 5 minutes, turning carefully after 3 minutes, until bread is golden and cheese is melted. Serve warm.

Spinach And Feta Pinwheels

Servings:4 | Cooking Time: 15 Minutes

Ingredients:
- 1 sheet frozen puff pastry, thawed
- 3 ounces full-fat cream cheese, softened
- 1 bag frozen spinach, thawed and drained
- ¼ teaspoon salt
- ⅓ cup crumbled feta cheese
- 1 large egg, whisked

Directions:
1. Preheat the air fryer to 320°F. Unroll puff pastry into a flat rectangle.
2. In a medium bowl, mix cream cheese, spinach, and salt until well combined.
3. Spoon cream cheese mixture onto pastry in an even layer, leaving a ½" border around the edges.
4. Sprinkle feta evenly across dough and gently press into filling to secure. Roll lengthwise to form a log shape.
5. Cut the roll into twelve 1" pieces. Brush with egg. Place in the air fryer basket and cook 15 minutes, turning halfway through cooking time.
6. Let cool 5 minutes before serving.

Garlic Okra Chips

Servings: 4 | Cooking Time: 20 Minutes

Ingredients:
- 2 cups okra, cut into rounds
- 1 ½ tbsp. melted butter
- 1 garlic clove, minced
- 1 tsp powdered paprika
- Salt and pepper to taste

Directions:
1. Preheat air fryer to 350°F. Toss okra, melted butter, paprika, garlic, salt and pepper in a medium bowl until okra is coated. Place okra in the frying basket and Air Fry for 5 minutes. Shake the basket and Air Fry for another 5 minutes. Shake one more time and Air Fry for 2 minutes until crispy. Serve warm and enjoy.

Broccoli With Cauliflower

Servings:4 | Cooking Time:20 Minutes

Ingredients:
- 1½ cups broccoli, cut into 1-inch pieces
- 1½ cups cauliflower, cut into 1-inch pieces
- 1 tablespoon olive oil
- Salt, as required

Directions:
1. Preheat the Air fryer to 375°F and grease an Air fryer basket.
2. Mix the vegetables, olive oil, and salt in a bowl and toss to coat well.
3. Arrange the veggie mixture in the Air fryer basket and cook for about 20 minutes, tossing once in between.
4. Dish out in a bowl and serve hot.

Chapter 8 Vegetable Side Dishes Recipes

Chapter 8 Vegetable Side Dishes Recipes

Fried Corn On The Cob

Servings: 2 | Cooking Time: 10 Minutes

Ingredients:
- 1½ tablespoons Regular or low-fat mayonnaise (not fat-free; gluten-free, if a concern)
- 1½ teaspoons Minced garlic
- ¼ teaspoon Table salt
- ¾ cup Plain panko bread crumbs (gluten-free, if a concern)
- 3 4-inch lengths husked and de-silked corn on the cob
- Vegetable oil spray

Directions:
1. Preheat the air fryer to 400°F.
2. Stir the mayonnaise, garlic, and salt in a small bowl until well combined. Spread the panko on a dinner plate.
3. Brush the mayonnaise mixture over the kernels of a piece of corn on the cob. Set the corn in the bread crumbs, then roll, pressing gently, to coat it. Lightly coat with vegetable oil spray. Set it aside, then coat the remaining piece(s) of corn in the same way.
4. Set the coated corn on the cob in the basket with as much air space between the pieces as possible. Air-fry undisturbed for 10 minutes, or until brown and crisp along the coating.
5. Use kitchen tongs to gently transfer the pieces of corn to a wire rack. Cool for 5 minutes before serving.

Almond Green Beans

Servings: 4 | Cooking Time: 20 Minutes

Ingredients:
- 2 cups green beans, trimmed
- ¼ cup slivered almonds
- 2 tbsp butter, melted
- Salt and pepper to taste
- 2 tsp lemon juice
- Lemon zest and slices

Directions:
1. Preheat air fryer at 375ºF. Add almonds to the frying basket and Air Fry for 2 minutes, tossing once. Set aside in a small bowl. Combine the remaining ingredients, except 1 tbsp of butter, in a bowl.
2. Place green beans in the frying basket and Air Fry for 10 minutes, tossing once. Then, transfer them to a large serving dish. Scatter with the melted butter, lemon juice and roasted almonds and toss. Serve immediately garnished with lemon zest and lemon slices.

Sweet Roasted Pumpkin Rounds

Servings: 4 | Cooking Time: 35 Minutes

Ingredients:
- 1 pumpkin
- 1 tbsp honey
- 1 tbsp melted butter
- ¼ tsp cardamom
- ¼ tsp sea salt

Directions:
1. Preheat the air fryer to 370°F. Cut the pumpkin in half lengthwise and remove the seeds. Slice each half crosswise into 1-inch-wide half-circles, then cut each half-circle in half again to make quarter rounds. Combine the honey, butter, cardamom, and salt in a bowl and mix well. Toss the pumpkin in the mixture until coated, then put into the frying basket. Bake for 15-20 minutes, shaking once during cooking until the edges start to brown and the squash is tender.

Green Beans And Tomatoes Recipe

Servings: 4 | Cooking Time:25 Minutes

Ingredients:
- 1-pint cherry tomatoes
- 2 tbsp. olive oil
- 1 lb. green beans
- Salt and black pepper to the taste

Directions:
1. In a bowl; mix cherry tomatoes with green beans, olive oil, salt and pepper, toss, transfer to your air fryer and cook at 400 °F, for 15 minutes. Divide among plates and serve right away

Roasted Garlic

Servings: 20 | Cooking Time: 40 Minutes

Ingredients:
- 20 Peeled medium garlic cloves
- 2 tablespoons, plus more Olive oil

Directions:
1. Preheat the air fryer to 400°F.
2. Set a 10-inch sheet of aluminum foil on your work surface for a small batch, a 14-inch sheet for a medium batch, or a 16-inch sheet for a large batch. Put the garlic cloves in its center in one layer without bunching the cloves together. Drizzle the small batch with 1 tablespoon oil, the medium batch with 2 tablespoons, or the large one with 3 tablespoons. Fold up the sides and seal the foil into a packet.
3. When the machine is at temperature, put the packet in the basket. Air-fry for 40 minutes, or until very fragrant. The cloves inside should be golden and soft.
4. Transfer the packet to a cutting board. Cool for 5 minutes, then open and use the cloves hot. Or cool them to room temperature, set them in a small container or jar, pour in enough olive oil to cover them, seal or cover the container, and refrigerate for up to 2 weeks.

Cheesy Texas Toast

Servings: 2 | Cooking Time: 4 Minutes

Ingredients:
- 2 1-inch-thick slice(s) Italian bread
- 4 teaspoons Softened butter
- 2 teaspoons Minced garlic
- ¼ cup (about ¾ ounce) Finely grated Parmesan cheese

Directions:
1. Preheat the air fryer to 400°F.
2. Spread one side of a slice of bread with 2 teaspoons butter. Sprinkle with 1 teaspoon minced garlic, followed by 2 tablespoons grated cheese. Repeat this process if you're making one or more additional toasts.

3. When the machine is at temperature, put the bread slice(s) cheese side up in the basket (with as much air space between them as possible if you're making more than one). Air-fry undisturbed for 4 minutes, or until browned and crunchy.
4. Use a nonstick-safe spatula to transfer the toasts cheese side up to a wire rack. Cool for 5 minutes before serving.

Rich Baked Sweet Potatoes

Servings: 2 | Cooking Time: 55 Minutes

Ingredients:
- 1 lb sweet potatoes, scrubbed and perforated with a fork
- 2 tsp olive oil
- Salt and pepper to taste
- 2 tbsp butter
- 3 tbsp honey

Directions:
1. Preheat air fryer at 400ºF. Mix olive oil, salt, black pepper, and honey. Brush with the prepared mix over both sweet potatoes. Place them in the frying basket and Bake for 45 minutes, turning at 30 minutes mark. Let cool on a cutting board for 10 minutes until cool enough to handle. Slice each potato lengthwise. Press ends of one potato together to open up the slices. Top with butter to serve.

Polenta

Servings: 4 | Cooking Time: 15 Minutes

Ingredients:
- 1 pound polenta
- ¼ cup flour
- oil for misting or cooking spray

Directions:
1. Cut polenta into ½-inch slices.
2. Dip slices in flour to coat well. Spray both sides with oil or cooking spray.
3. Cook at 390°F for 5minutes. Turn polenta and spray both sides again with oil.
4. Cook 10 more minutes or until brown and crispy.

Roasted Heirloom Carrots With Orange And Thyme

Servings: 2 | Cooking Time: 12 Minutes

Ingredients:
- 10 to 12 heirloom or rainbow carrots, scrubbed but not peeled
- 1 teaspoon olive oil
- salt and freshly ground black pepper
- 1 tablespoon butter
- 1 teaspoon fresh orange zest
- 1 teaspoon chopped fresh thyme

Directions:
1. Preheat the air fryer to 400°F.
2. Scrub the carrots and halve them lengthwise. Toss them in the olive oil, season with salt and freshly ground black pepper and transfer to the air fryer.
3. Air-fry at 400°F for 12 minutes, shaking the basket every once in a while to rotate the carrots as they cook.
4. As soon as the carrots have finished cooking, add the butter, orange zest and thyme and toss all the ingredients together in the air fryer basket to melt the butter and coat evenly. Serve warm.

Roasted Broccoli

Servings:4 | Cooking Time: 8 Minutes

Ingredients:
- 12 ounces broccoli florets
- 2 tablespoons olive oil
- ½ teaspoon salt
- ¼ teaspoon ground black pepper

Directions:
1. Preheat the air fryer to 360°F.
2. In a medium bowl, place broccoli and drizzle with oil. Sprinkle with salt and pepper.
3. Place in the air fryer basket and cook 8 minutes, shaking the basket twice during cooking, until the edges are brown and the center is tender. Serve warm.

Roasted Brussels Sprouts

Servings:6 | Cooking Time: 10 Minutes

Ingredients:
- 1 pound fresh Brussels sprouts, trimmed and halved
- 2 tablespoons coconut oil
- ½ teaspoon salt
- ¼ teaspoon ground black pepper
- ½ teaspoon garlic powder
- 1 tablespoon salted butter, melted

Directions:
1. Place Brussels sprouts into a large bowl. Drizzle with coconut oil and sprinkle with salt, pepper, and garlic powder.
2. Place Brussels sprouts into ungreased air fryer basket. Adjust the temperature to 350°F and set the timer for 10 minutes, shaking the basket three times during cooking. Brussels sprouts will be dark golden and tender when done.
3. Place cooked sprouts in a large serving dish and drizzle with butter. Serve warm.

Roman Artichokes

Servings: 4 | Cooking Time: 12 Minutes

Ingredients:
- 2 9-ounce box(es) frozen artichoke heart quarters, thawed
- 1½ tablespoons Olive oil
- 2 teaspoons Minced garlic
- 1 teaspoon Table salt
- Up to ½ teaspoon Red pepper flakes

Directions:
1. Preheat the air fryer to 400°F.
2. Gently toss the artichoke heart quarters, oil, garlic, salt, and red pepper flakes in a bowl until the quarters are well coated.
3. When the machine is at temperature, scrape the contents of the bowl into the basket. Spread the artichoke heart quarters out into as close to one layer as possible. Air-fry undisturbed for 8 minutes. Gently toss and rearrange the quarters so that any covered or touching parts are now exposed to the air currents, then air-fry undisturbed for 4 minutes more, until very crisp.
4. Gently pour the contents of the basket onto a wire rack. Cool for a few minutes before serving.

Pop Corn Broccoli

Servings: 1 | Cooking Time: 10 Minutes

Ingredients:
- 4 egg yolks
- ¼ cup butter, melted
- 2 cups coconut flower
- Salt and pepper
- 2 cups broccoli florets

Directions:
1. In a bowl, whisk the egg yolks and melted butter together. Throw in the coconut flour, salt and pepper, then stir again to combine well.
2. Pre-heat the fryer at 400°F.
3. Dip each broccoli floret into the mixture and place in the fryer. Cook for six minutes, in multiple batches if necessary. Take care when removing them from the fryer and enjoy!

Fried Pearl Onions With Balsamic Vinegar And Basil

Servings: 2 | Cooking Time: 10 Minutes

Ingredients:
- 1 pound fresh pearl onions
- 1 tablespoon olive oil
- salt and freshly ground black pepper
- 1 teaspoon high quality aged balsamic vinegar
- 1 tablespoon chopped fresh basil leaves (or mint)

Directions:
1. Preheat the air fryer to 400°F.
2. Decide whether you want to peel the onions before or after they cook. Peeling them ahead of time is a little more laborious. Peeling after they cook is easier, but a little messier since the onions are hot and you may discard more of the onion than you'd like to. If you opt to peel them first, trim the tiny root of the onions off and pinch off any loose papery skins. Toss the pearl onions with the olive oil, salt and freshly ground black pepper.
3. Air-fry for 10 minutes, shaking the basket a couple of times during the cooking process.
4. Let the onions cool slightly and then slip off any remaining skins.
5. Toss the onions with the balsamic vinegar and basil and serve.

Turmeric Cabbage Mix

Servings: 4 | Cooking Time: 12 Minutes

Ingredients:
- 1 tablespoon olive oil
- 1 big green cabbage head, shredded
- ½ cup yellow onion, chopped
- 2 teaspoons turmeric powder
- Salt and black pepper to taste
- 4 tablespoons tomato sauce

Directions:
1. Take the oil and grease a pan that fits your air fryer.
2. Add all of the other ingredients and toss.
3. Place the pan in the fryer and cook at 365ºF for 12 minutes.
4. Divide between plates and serve as a side dish.

Roasted Herbed Shiitake Mushrooms

Servings: 4 | Cooking Time: 5 Minutes

Ingredients:
- 8 ounces shiitake mushrooms, stems removed and caps roughly chopped
- 1 tablespoon olive oil
- ½ teaspoon salt
- freshly ground black pepper
- 1 teaspoon chopped fresh thyme leaves
- 1 teaspoon chopped fresh oregano
- 1 tablespoon chopped fresh parsley

Directions:
1. Preheat the air fryer to 400°F.
2. Toss the mushrooms with the olive oil, salt, pepper, thyme and oregano. Air-fry for 5 minutes, shaking the basket once or twice during the cooking process. The mushrooms will still be somewhat chewy with a meaty texture. If you'd like them a little more tender, add a couple of minutes to this cooking time.
3. Once cooked, add the parsley to the mushrooms and toss. Season again to taste and serve.

Grilled Cheese

Servings: 2 | Cooking Time: 25 Minutes

Ingredients:
- 4 slices bread
- ½ cup sharp cheddar cheese
- ¼ cup butter, melted

Directions:
1. Pre-heat the Air Fryer at 360°F.
2. Put cheese and butter in separate bowls.
3. Apply the butter to each side of the bread slices with a brush.
4. Spread the cheese across two of the slices of bread and make two sandwiches. Transfer both to the fryer.
5. Cook for 5 – 7 minutes or until a golden brown color is achieved and the cheese is melted.

Pancetta Mushroom & Onion Sautée

Servings:4 | Cooking Time: 20 Minutes

Ingredients:
- 16 oz white button mushrooms, stems trimmed, halved
- 1 onion, cut into half-moons
- 4 pancetta slices, diced
- 1 clove garlic, minced

Directions:
1. Preheat air fryer to 350ºF. Add all ingredients, except for the garlic, to the frying basket and Air Fry for 8 minutes, tossing once. Stir in the garlic and cook for 1 more minute. Serve right away.

Green Peas With Mint

Servings: 4 | Cooking Time: 5 Minutes

Ingredients:
- 1 cup shredded lettuce
- 1 10-ounce package frozen green peas, thawed
- 1 tablespoon fresh mint, shredded
- 1 teaspoon melted butter

Directions:
1. Lay the shredded lettuce in the air fryer basket.
2. Toss together the peas, mint, and melted butter and spoon over the lettuce.
3. Cook at 360°F for 5minutes, until peas are warm and lettuce wilts.

Grits Again

Servings: 2 | Cooking Time: 10 Minutes

Ingredients:
- cooked grits
- plain breadcrumbs
- oil for misting or cooking spray
- honey or maple syrup for serving (optional)

Directions:
1. While grits are still warm, spread them into a square or rectangular baking pan, about ½-inch thick. If your grits are thicker than that, scoop some out into another pan.
2. Chill several hours or overnight, until grits are cold and firm.
3. When ready to cook, pour off any water that has collected in pan and cut grits into 2- to 3-inch squares.
4. Dip grits squares in breadcrumbs and place in air fryer basket in single layer, close but not touching.
5. Cook at 390°F for 10 minutes, until heated through and crispy brown on the outside.
6. Serve while hot either plain or with a drizzle of honey or maple syrup.

Spicy Kale

Servings: 4 | Cooking Time: 10 Minutes

Ingredients:
- 1 pound kale, torn
- 1 tablespoon olive oil
- 1 teaspoon hot paprika
- A pinch of salt and black pepper
- 2 tablespoons oregano, chopped

Directions:
1. In a pan that fits the air fryer, combine all the ingredients and toss. Put the pan in the air fryer and cook at 380ºF for 10 minutes. Divide between plates and serve.

Zucchini Bites

Servings: 4 | Cooking Time: 15 Minutes

Ingredients:
- 4 zucchinis
- 1 egg
- ½ cup parmesan cheese, grated
- 1 tbsp. Italian herbs
- 1 cup coconut, grated

Directions:
1. Thinly grate the zucchini and dry with a cheesecloth, ensuring to remove all of the moisture.

2. In a bowl, combine the zucchini with the egg, parmesan, Italian herbs, and grated coconut, mixing well to incorporate everything. Using your hands, mold the mixture into balls.
3. Pre-heat the fryer at 400°F and place a rack inside. Lay the zucchini balls on the rack and cook for ten minutes. Serve hot.

Bacon-jalapeño Cheesy "breadsticks"

Servings:8 | Cooking Time: 15 Minutes

Ingredients:
- 2 cups shredded mozzarella cheese
- ¼ cup grated Parmesan cheese
- ¼ cup chopped pickled jalapeños
- 2 large eggs, whisked
- 4 slices cooked sugar-free bacon, chopped

Directions:
1. Mix all ingredients together in a large bowl. Cut a piece of parchment paper to fit inside air fryer basket.
2. Dampen your hands with a bit of water and press out mixture into a circle to fit on ungreased parchment. You may need to separate into two smaller circles, depending on the size of air fryer.
3. Place parchment with cheese mixture into air fryer basket. Adjust the temperature to 320°F and set the timer for 15 minutes. Carefully flip when 5 minutes remain on timer. The top will be golden brown when done. Slice into eight sticks. Serve warm.

Sweet Potato Fries

Servings: 3 | Cooking Time: 20 Minutes

Ingredients:
- 2 10-ounce sweet potato(es)
- Vegetable oil spray
- To taste Coarse sea salt or kosher salt

Directions:
1. Preheat the air fryer to 400°F.
2. Peel the sweet potato(es), then cut lengthwise into ¼-inch-thick slices. Cut these slices lengthwise into ¼-inch-thick matchsticks. Place these matchsticks in a bowl and coat them with vegetable oil spray. Toss well, spray them again, and toss several times to make sure they're all evenly coated.
3. When the machine is at temperature, pour the sweet potato matchsticks into the basket, spreading them out in as close to an even layer as possible. Air-fry for 20 minutes, tossing and rearranging the matchsticks every 5 minutes, until lightly browned and crisp.
4. Pour the contents of the basket into a bowl, add some salt to taste, and toss well to coat.

Basic Corn On The Cob

Servings: 4 | Cooking Time: 15 Minutes

Ingredients:
- 3 ears of corn, shucked and halved
- 2 tbsp butter, melted
- Salt and pepper to taste
- 1 tsp minced garlic
- 1 tsp paprika

Directions:
1. Preheat air fryer at 400ºF. Toss all ingredients in a bowl. Place corn in the frying basket and Bake for 7 minutes, turning once. Serve immediately.

Dinner Rolls

Servings:6 | Cooking Time: 12 Minutes

Ingredients:
- 1 cup shredded mozzarella cheese
- 1 ounce cream cheese, broken into small pieces
- 1 cup blanched finely ground almond flour
- ¼ cup ground flaxseed
- ½ teaspoon baking powder
- 1 large egg, whisked

Directions:
1. Place mozzarella, cream cheese, and flour in a large microwave-safe bowl. Microwave on high 1 minute. Mix until smooth.
2. Add flaxseed, baking powder, and egg to mixture until fully combined and smooth. Microwave an additional 15 seconds if dough becomes too firm.
3. Separate dough into six equal pieces and roll each into a ball. Place rolls into ungreased air fryer basket. Adjust the temperature to 320°F and set the timer for 12 minutes, turning rolls halfway through cooking. Allow rolls to cool completely before serving, about 5 minutes.

Flaky Biscuits

Servings:8 | Cooking Time: 15 Minutes Per Batch

Ingredients:
- ¼ cup salted butter
- 2 cups self-rising flour
- ¼ teaspoon salt
- ⅔ cup whole milk

Directions:
1. Preheat the air fryer to 320°F. Cut parchment paper to fit the air fryer basket.
2. Place butter in the freezer 10 minutes. In a large bowl, mix flour and salt.
3. Grate butter into bowl and use a wooden spoon to evenly distribute. Add milk and stir until a soft dough forms.
4. Turn dough onto a lightly floured surface. Gently press and flatten dough until mostly smooth and uniform. Gently roll into an 8" × 10" rectangle. Use a sharp knife dusted in flour to cut dough into eight squares.
5. Place biscuits on parchment paper in the air fryer basket, working in batches as necessary, and cook 15 minutes until golden brown on the top and edges and feel firm to the touch. Let cool 5 minutes before serving.

Cheesy Baked Asparagus

Servings:4 | Cooking Time: 18 Minutes

Ingredients:
- ½ cup heavy whipping cream
- ½ cup grated Parmesan cheese
- 2 ounces cream cheese, softened
- 1 pound asparagus, ends trimmed, chopped into 1" pieces
- ¼ teaspoon salt
- ¼ teaspoon ground black pepper

Directions:
1. In a medium bowl, whisk together heavy cream, Parmesan, and cream cheese until combined.
2. Place asparagus into an ungreased 6" round nonstick baking dish. Pour cheese mixture over top and sprinkle with salt and pepper.
3. Place dish into air fryer basket. Adjust the temperature to 350°F and set the timer for 18 minutes. Asparagus will be tender when done. Serve warm.

Caraway Seed Pretzel Sticks

Servings: 4 | Cooking Time: 30 Minutes

Ingredients:
- ½ pizza dough
- 1 tsp baking soda
- 2 tbsp caraway seeds
- 1 cup of hot water
- Cooking spray

Directions:
1. Preheat air fryer to 400°F. Roll out the dough, on parchment paper, into a rectangle, then cut it into 8 strips. Whisk the baking soda and 1 cup of hot water until well dissolved in a bowl. Submerge each strip, shake off any excess, and stretch another 1 to 2 inches. Scatter with caraway seeds and let rise for 10 minutes in the frying basket. Grease with cooking spray and Air Fry for 8 minutes until golden brown, turning once. Serve.

Tasty Brussels Sprouts With Guanciale

Servings: 4 | Cooking Time: 50 Minutes

Ingredients:
- 3 guanciale slices, halved
- 1 lb Brussels sprouts, halved
- 2 tbsp olive oil
- ¼ tsp salt
- ¼ tsp dried thyme

Directions:
1. Preheat air fryer to 350°F. Air Fry Lay the guanciale in the air fryer, until crispy, 10 minutes. Remove and drain on a paper towel. Give the guanciale a rough chop and Set aside. Coat Brussels sprouts with olive oil in a large bowl. Add salt and thyme, then toss. Place the sprouts in the frying basket. Air Fry for about 12-15 minutes, shake the basket once until the sprouts are golden and tender. Top with guanciale and serve.

Acorn Squash Halves With Maple Butter Glaze

Servings: 2 | Cooking Time: 33 Minutes

Ingredients:
- 1 medium Acorn squash
- Vegetable oil spray
- ¼ teaspoon Table salt
- 1½ tablespoons Butter, melted
- 1½ tablespoons Maple syrup

Directions:
1. Preheat the air fryer to 325°F.
2. Cut a squash in half through the stem end. Use a flatware spoon to scrape out and discard the seeds and membranes in each half. Use a paring knife to make a crisscross pattern of cuts about ½ inch apart and ¼ inch deep across the "meat" of the squash. If working with a second squash, repeat this step for that one.
3. Generously coat the cut side of the squash halves with vegetable oil spray. Sprinkle the halves with the salt. Set them in the basket cut side up with at least ¼ inch between them. Air-fry undisturbed for 30 minutes.
4. Increase the machine's temperature to 400°F. Mix the melted butter and syrup in a small bowl until uniform. Brush this mixture

over the cut sides of the squash(es), letting it pool in the center. Air-fry undisturbed for 3 minutes, or until the glaze is bubbling.
5. Use a nonstick-safe spatula and kitchen tongs to transfer the squash halves cut side up to a wire rack. Cool for 5 to 10 minutes before serving.

Easy Green Bean Casserole

Servings:4 | Cooking Time: 20 Minutes

Ingredients:
- 1 can condensed cream of mushroom soup
- ¼ cup heavy cream
- 2 cans cut green beans, drained
- 1 teaspoon minced garlic
- ½ teaspoon salt
- ¼ teaspoon ground black pepper
- 1 cup packaged French fried onions

Directions:
1. Preheat the air fryer to 320°F.
2. In a 4-quart baking dish, pour soup and cream over green beans and mix to combine.
3. Stir in garlic, salt, and pepper until combined. Top with French fried onions.
4. Place in the air fryer basket and cook 20 minutes until top is lightly brown and dish is heated through. Serve warm.

Southwest-style Corn Cobs

Servings: 6 | Cooking Time: 15 Minutes

Ingredients:
- ½ cup sour cream
- 1 ½ teaspoons chili powder
- Juice and zest of 1 medium lime
- ¼ teaspoon salt
- 6 mini corn cobs
- ½ cup crumbled cotija cheese

Directions:
1. Preheat the air fryer to 350°F.
2. In a medium bowl, mix sour cream, chili powder, lime zest and juice, and salt.
3. Brush mixture all over corn cobs and place them in the air fryer basket. Cook 15 minutes until corn is tender.
4. Sprinkle with cotija and serve.

Roasted Cauliflower With Garlic And Capers

Servings: 3 | Cooking Time: 10 Minutes

Ingredients:
- 3 cups 1-inch cauliflower florets
- 2 tablespoons Olive oil
- 1½ tablespoons Drained and rinsed capers, chopped
- 2 teaspoons Minced garlic
- ¼ teaspoon Table salt
- Up to ¼ teaspoon Red pepper flakes

Directions:
1. Preheat the air fryer to 375°F .
2. Stir the cauliflower florets, olive oil, capers, garlic, salt, and red pepper flakes in a large bowl until the florets are evenly coated.
3. When the machine is at temperature, put the florets in the basket, spreading them out to as close to one layer as you can. Air-fry

for 10 minutes, tossing once to get any covered pieces exposed to the air currents, until tender and lightly browned.
4. Dump the contents of the basket into a serving bowl or onto a serving platter. Cool for a minute or two before serving.

Blistered Tomatoes

Servings: 20 | Cooking Time: 15 Minutes

Ingredients:
- 1½ pounds Cherry or grape tomatoes
- Olive oil spray
- 1½ teaspoons Balsamic vinegar
- ¼ teaspoon Table salt
- ¼ teaspoon Ground black pepper

Directions:
1. Put the basket in a drawer-style air fryer, or a baking tray in the lower third of a toaster oven–style air fryer. Place a 6-inch round cake pan in the basket or on the tray for a small batch, a 7-inch round cake pan for a medium batch, or an 8-inch round cake pan for a large one. Heat the air fryer to 400°F with the pan in the basket. When the machine is at temperature, keep heating the pan for 5 minutes more.
2. Place the tomatoes in a large bowl, coat them with the olive oil spray, toss gently, then spritz a couple of times more, tossing after each spritz, until the tomatoes are glistening.
3. Pour the tomatoes into the cake pan and air-fry undisturbed for 10 minutes, or until they split and begin to brown.
4. Use kitchen tongs and a nonstick-safe spatula, or silicone baking mitts, to remove the cake pan from the basket. Toss the hot tomatoes with the vinegar, salt, and pepper. Cool in the pan for a few minutes before serving.

Simple Zucchini Ribbons

Servings:4 | Cooking Time: 15 Minutes

Ingredients:
- 2 zucchini
- 2 tsp butter, melted
- ¼ tsp garlic powder
- ¼ tsp chili flakes
- 8 cherry tomatoes, halved
- Salt and pepper to taste

Directions:
1. Preheat air fryer to 275ºF. Cut the zucchini into ribbons with a vegetable peeler. Mix them with butter, garlic, chili flakes, salt, and pepper in a bowl. Transfer to the frying basket and Air Fry for 2 minutes. Toss and add the cherry tomatoes. Cook for another 2 minutes. Serve.

Blistered Green Beans

Servings: 3 | Cooking Time: 10 Minutes

Ingredients:
- ¾ pound Green beans, trimmed on both ends
- 1½ tablespoons Olive oil
- 3 tablespoons Pine nuts
- 1½ tablespoons Balsamic vinegar
- 1½ teaspoons Minced garlic
- ¾ teaspoon Table salt
- ¾ teaspoon Ground black pepper

Directions:
1. Preheat the air fryer to 400°F.
2. Toss the green beans and oil in a large bowl until all the green

beans are glistening.

3. When the machine is at temperature, pile the green beans into the basket. Air-fry for 10 minutes, tossing often to rearrange the green beans in the basket, or until blistered and tender.

4. Dump the contents of the basket into a serving bowl. Add the pine nuts, vinegar, garlic, salt, and pepper. Toss well to coat and combine. Serve warm or at room temperature.

Baked Jalapeño And Cheese Cauliflower Mash

Servings:6 | Cooking Time: 15 Minutes

Ingredients:
- 1 steamer bag cauliflower florets, cooked according to package instructions
- 2 tablespoons salted butter, softened
- 2 ounces cream cheese, softened
- ½ cup shredded sharp Cheddar cheese
- ¼ cup pickled jalapeños
- ½ teaspoon salt
- ¼ teaspoon ground black pepper

Directions:
1. Place cooked cauliflower into a food processor with remaining ingredients. Pulse twenty times until cauliflower is smooth and all ingredients are combined.
2. Spoon mash into an ungreased 6" round nonstick baking dish. Place dish into air fryer basket. Adjust the temperature to 380°F and set the timer for 15 minutes. The top will be golden brown when done. Serve warm.

Onions

Servings: 4 | Cooking Time: 18 Minutes

Ingredients:
- 2 yellow onions
- salt and pepper
- ¼ teaspoon ground thyme
- ¼ teaspoon smoked paprika
- 2 teaspoons olive oil
- 1 ounce Gruyère cheese, grated

Directions:
1. Peel onions and halve lengthwise.
2. Sprinkle cut sides of onions with salt, pepper, thyme, and paprika.
3. Place each onion half, cut-surface up, on a large square of aluminum foil. Pull sides of foil up to cup around onion. Drizzle cut surface of onions with oil.
4. Crimp foil at top to seal closed.
5. Place wrapped onions in air fryer basket and cook at 390°F for 18 minutes. When done, onions should be soft enough to pierce with fork but still slightly firm.
6. Open foil just enough to sprinkle each onion with grated cheese.
7. Cook for 30 seconds to 1 minute to melt cheese.

Simple Peppared Carrot Chips

Servings: 4 | Cooking Time: 15 Minutes

Ingredients:
- 3 carrots, cut into coins
- 1 tbsp sesame oil
- Salt and pepper to taste

Directions:
1. Preheat air fryer at 375ºF. Combine all ingredients in a bowl. Place carrots in the frying basket and Roast for 10 minutes, tossing once. Serve right away.

Bacon-wrapped Asparagus

Servings: 4 | Cooking Time: 10 Minutes

Ingredients:
- 1 tablespoon extra-virgin olive oil
- ½ teaspoon sea salt
- ¼ cup grated Parmesan cheese
- 1 pound asparagus, ends trimmed
- 8 slices bacon

Directions:
1. Preheat the air fryer to 380°F.
2. In large bowl, mix together the olive oil, sea salt, and Parmesan cheese. Toss the asparagus in the olive oil mixture.
3. Evenly divide the asparagus into 8 bundles. Wrap 1 piece of bacon around each bundle, not overlapping the bacon but spreading it across the bundle.
4. Place the asparagus bundles into the air fryer basket, not touching. Work in batches as needed.
5. Cook for 8 minutes; check for doneness, and cook another 2 minutes.

Hasselbacks

Servings: 4 | Cooking Time: 41 Minutes

Ingredients:
- 2 large potatoes
- oil for misting or cooking spray
- salt, pepper, and garlic powder
- 1½ ounces sharp Cheddar cheese, sliced very thin
- ¼ cup chopped green onions
- 2 strips turkey bacon, cooked and crumbled
- light sour cream for serving (optional)

Directions:
1. Preheat air fryer to 390°F.
2. Scrub potatoes. Cut thin vertical slices ¼-inch thick crosswise about three-quarters of the way down so that bottom of potato remains intact.
3. Fan potatoes slightly to separate slices. Mist with oil and sprinkle with salt, pepper, and garlic powder to taste. Potatoes will be very stiff, but try to get some of the oil and seasoning between the slices.
4. Place potatoes in air fryer basket and cook for 40 minutes or until centers test done when pierced with a fork.
5. Top potatoes with cheese slices and cook for 30 seconds to 1 minute to melt cheese.
6. Cut each potato in half crosswise, and sprinkle with green onions and crumbled bacon. If you like, add a dollop of sour cream before serving.

Brussels Sprouts

Servings: 3 | Cooking Time: 5 Minutes

Ingredients:
- 1 10-ounce package frozen brussels sprouts, thawed and halved
- 2 teaspoons olive oil
- salt and pepper

Directions:
1. Toss the brussels sprouts and olive oil together.
2. Place them in the air fryer basket and season to taste with salt and pepper.
3. Cook at 360°F for approximately 5minutes, until the edges begin to brown.

Honey-mustard Asparagus Puffs

Servings: 4 | Cooking Time: 35 Minutes

Ingredients:
- 8 asparagus spears
- ½ sheet puff pastry
- 2 tbsp honey mustard
- 1 egg, lightly beaten

Directions:
1. Preheat the air fryer to 375°F. Spread the pastry with honey mustard and cut it into 8 strips. Wrap the pastry, honey mustard–side in, around the asparagus. Put a rack in the frying basket and lay the asparagus spears on the rack. Brush all over pastries with beaten egg and Air Fry for 12-17 minutes or until the pastry is golden. Serve.

Corn On The Cob

Servings: 4 | Cooking Time: 12 Minutes

Ingredients:
- 2 large ears fresh corn
- olive oil for misting
- salt (optional)

Directions:
1. Shuck corn, remove silks, and wash.
2. Cut or break each ear in half crosswise.
3. Spray corn with olive oil.
4. Cook at 390°F for 12 minutes or until browned as much as you like.
5. Serve plain or with coarsely ground salt.

Smashed Fried Baby Potatoes

Servings: 3 | Cooking Time: 18 Minutes

Ingredients:
- 1½ pounds baby red or baby Yukon gold potatoes
- ¼ cup butter, melted
- 1 teaspoon olive oil
- ½ teaspoon paprika
- 1 teaspoon dried parsley
- salt and freshly ground black pepper
- 2 scallions, finely chopped

Directions:
1. Bring a large pot of salted water to a boil. Add the potatoes and boil for 18 minutes or until the potatoes are fork-tender.
2. Drain the potatoes and transfer them to a cutting board to cool slightly. Spray or brush the bottom of a drinking glass with a little oil. Smash or flatten the potatoes by pressing the glass down on each potato slowly. Try not to completely flatten the potato or smash it so hard that it breaks apart.
3. Combine the melted butter, olive oil, paprika, and parsley together.
4. Preheat the air fryer to 400°F.
5. Spray the bottom of the air fryer basket with oil and transfer one layer of the smashed potatoes into the basket. Brush with some of the butter mixture and season generously with salt and freshly ground black pepper.
6. Air-fry at 400°F for 10 minutes. Carefully flip the potatoes over and air-fry for an additional 8 minutes until crispy and lightly browned.
7. Keep the potatoes warm in a 170°F oven or tent with aluminum foil while you cook the second batch. Sprinkle minced scallions over the potatoes and serve warm.

Chili-oiled Brussels Sprouts

Servings: 4 | Cooking Time: 30 Minutes

Ingredients:
- 1 cup Brussels sprouts, quartered
- 1 tsp olive oil
- 1 tsp chili oil
- Salt and pepper to taste

Directions:
1. Preheat air fryer to 350°F. Coat the Brussels sprouts with olive oil, chili oil, salt, and black pepper in a bowl. Transfer to the frying basket. Bake for 20 minutes, shaking the basket several times throughout cooking until the sprouts are crispy, browned on the outside, and juicy inside. Serve and enjoy!

Foil Packet Lemon Butter Asparagus

Servings: 4 | Cooking Time: 15 Minutes

Ingredients:
- 1 pound asparagus, ends trimmed
- ¼ cup salted butter, cubed
- Zest and juice of ½ medium lemon
- ½ teaspoon salt
- ¼ teaspoon ground black pepper

Directions:
1. Preheat the air fryer to 375°F. Cut a 6" × 6" square of foil.
2. Place asparagus on foil square.
3. Dot asparagus with butter. Sprinkle lemon zest, salt, and pepper on top of asparagus. Drizzle lemon juice over asparagus.
4. Fold foil over asparagus and seal the edges closed to form a packet.
5. Place in the air fryer basket and cook 15 minutes until tender. Serve warm.

Mini Spinach And Sweet Pepper Poppers

Servings:16 | Cooking Time: 8 Minutes

Ingredients:
- 4 ounces cream cheese, softened
- 1 cup chopped fresh spinach leaves
- ½ teaspoon garlic powder
- 8 mini sweet bell peppers, tops removed, seeded, and halved lengthwise

Directions:
1. In a medium bowl, mix cream cheese, spinach, and garlic powder. Place 1 tablespoon mixture into each sweet pepper half and press down to smooth.
2. Place poppers into ungreased air fryer basket. Adjust the temperature to 400°F and set the timer for 8 minutes. Poppers will be done when cheese is browned on top and peppers are tender-crisp. Serve warm.

Grilled Lime Scallions

Servings:6 | Cooking Time: 15 Minutes

Ingredients:
- 2 bunches of scallions
- 1 tbsp olive oil
- 2 tsp lime juice
- Salt and pepper to taste
- ¼ tsp Italian seasoning
- 2 tsp lime zest

Directions:
1. Preheat air fryer to 370ºF. Trim the scallions and cut them in half lengthwise. Place them in a bowl and add olive oil and lime juice. Toss to coat. Place the mix in the frying basket and Air Fry for 7 minutes, tossing once. Transfer to a serving dish and stir in salt, pepper, Italian seasoning and lime zest. Serve immediately.

Cheesy Garlic Bread

Servings: 6 | Cooking Time: 12 Minutes

Ingredients:
- 1 cup self-rising flour
- 1 cup plain full-fat Greek yogurt
- ¼ cup salted butter, softened
- 1 tablespoon minced garlic
- 1 cup shredded mozzarella cheese

Directions:
1. Preheat the air fryer to 320°F. Cut parchment paper to fit the air fryer basket.
2. In a large bowl, mix flour and yogurt until a sticky, soft dough forms. Let sit 5 minutes.
3. Turn dough onto a lightly floured surface. Knead dough 1 minute, then transfer to prepared parchment. Press out into an 8" round.
4. In a small bowl, mix butter and garlic. Brush over dough. Sprinkle with mozzarella.
5. Place in the air fryer and cook 12 minutes until edges are golden and cheese is brown. Serve warm.

Steakhouse Baked Potatoes

Servings: 3 | Cooking Time: 55 Minutes

Ingredients:
- 3 10-ounce russet potatoes
- 2 tablespoons Olive oil
- 1 teaspoon Table salt

Directions:
1. Preheat the air fryer to 375°F.
2. Poke holes all over each potato with a fork. Rub the skin of each potato with 2 teaspoons of the olive oil, then sprinkle ¼ teaspoon salt all over each potato.
3. When the machine is at temperature, set the potatoes in the basket in one layer with as much air space between them as possible. Air-fry for 50 minutes, turning once, or until soft to the touch but with crunchy skins. If the machine is at 360°F, you may need to add up to 5 minutes to the cooking time.
4. Use kitchen tongs to gently transfer the baked potatoes to a wire rack. Cool for 5 or 10 minutes before serving.

Corn Muffins

Servings: 12 | Cooking Time: 10 Minutes

Ingredients:
- ½ cup all-purpose flour
- ½ cup cornmeal
- ¼ cup granulated sugar
- ½ teaspoon baking powder
- ¼ cup salted butter, melted
- ½ cup buttermilk
- 1 large egg

Directions:
1. Preheat the air fryer to 350°F.
2. In a large bowl, whisk together flour, cornmeal, sugar, and baking powder.
3. Add butter, buttermilk, and egg to dry mixture. Stir until well combined.
4. Divide batter evenly among twelve silicone or aluminum muffin cups, filling cups about halfway. Working in batches as needed, place in the air fryer and cook 10 minutes until golden brown. Let cool 5 minutes before serving.

Yellow Squash

Servings: 4 | Cooking Time: 10 Minutes

Ingredients:
- 1 large yellow squash
- 2 eggs
- ¼ cup buttermilk
- 1 cup panko breadcrumbs
- ¼ cup white cornmeal
- ½ teaspoon salt
- oil for misting or cooking spray

Directions:
1. Preheat air fryer to 390°F.
2. Cut the squash into ¼-inch slices.
3. In a shallow dish, beat together eggs and buttermilk.
4. In sealable plastic bag or container with lid, combine ¼ cup panko crumbs, white cornmeal, and salt. Shake to mix well.
5. Place the remaining ¾ cup panko crumbs in a separate shallow dish.
6. Dump all the squash slices into the egg/buttermilk mixture. Stir to coat.
7. Remove squash from buttermilk mixture with a slotted spoon, letting excess drip off, and transfer to the panko/cornmeal mixture. Close bag or container and shake well to coat.
8. Remove squash from crumb mixture, letting excess fall off. Return squash to egg/buttermilk mixture, stirring gently to coat. If you need more liquid to coat all the squash, add a little more buttermilk.
9. Remove each squash slice from egg wash and dip in a dish of ¾ cup panko crumbs.
10. Mist squash slices with oil or cooking spray and place in air fryer basket. Squash should be in a single layer, but it's okay if the slices crowd together and overlap a little.
11. Cook at 390°F for 5minutes. Shake basket to break up any that have stuck together. Mist again with oil or spray.
12. Cook 5minutes longer and check. If necessary, mist again with oil and cook an additional two minutes, until squash slices are golden brown and crisp.

Spicy Corn Fritters

Servings: 4 | Cooking Time: 22 Minutes

Ingredients:
- 1 can yellow corn, drained
- ½ cup all-purpose flour
- ¾ cup shredded pepper jack cheese
- 1 large egg
- ½ teaspoon chili powder
- ¼ teaspoon garlic powder
- ½ teaspoon salt
- ¼ teaspoon ground black pepper

Directions:
1. Cut parchment paper to fit the air fryer basket.
2. In a large bowl, mix all ingredients until well combined. Using a ½-cup scoop, separate mixture into four portions.
3. Gently press each into a 4" round and spritz with cooking spray. Place in freezer 10 minutes.
4. Preheat the air fryer to 400°F.
5. Place fritters in the air fryer basket and cook 12 minutes, turning halfway through cooking time, until fritters are brown on the top and edges and firm to the touch. Serve warm.

Chapter 9 Desserts And Sweets Recipes

Chapter 9 Desserts And Sweets Recipes

Nutty Fudge Muffins

Servings:10 | Cooking Time:10 Minutes

Ingredients:
- 1 package fudge brownie mix
- 1 egg
- 2 teaspoons water
- ¼ cup walnuts, chopped
- 1/3 cup vegetable oil

Directions:
1. Preheat the Air fryer to 300°F and grease 10 muffin tins lightly.
2. Mix brownie mix, egg, oil and water in a bowl.
3. Fold in the walnuts and pour the mixture in the muffin cups.
4. Transfer the muffin tins in the Air fryer basket and cook for about 10 minutes.
5. Dish out and serve immediately.

Lemon Mousse

Servings:6 | Cooking Time:10 Minutes

Ingredients:
- 12-ounces cream cheese, softened
- ¼ teaspoon salt
- 1 teaspoon lemon liquid stevia
- 1/3 cup fresh lemon juice
- 1½ cups heavy cream

Directions:
1. Preheat the Air fryer to 345°F and grease a large ramekin lightly.
2. Mix all the ingredients in a large bowl until well combined.
3. Pour into the ramekin and transfer into the Air fryer.
4. Cook for about 10 minutes and pour into the serving glasses.
5. Refrigerate to cool for about 3 hours and serve chilled.

Nutella And Banana Pastries

Servings:4 | Cooking Time:12 Minutes

Ingredients:
- 1 puff pastry sheet, cut into 4 equal squares
- ½ cup Nutella
- 2 bananas, sliced
- 2 tablespoons icing sugar

Directions:
1. Preheat the Air fryer to 375°F and grease an Air fryer basket.
2. Spread Nutella on each pastry square and top with banana slices and icing sugar.
3. Fold each square into a triangle and slightly press the edges with a fork.
4. Arrange the pastries in the Air fryer basket and cook for about 12 minutes.
5. Dish out and serve immediately.

Apple Pie Crumble

Servings:4 | Cooking Time:25 Minutes

Ingredients:
- 1 can apple pie
- ¼ cup butter, softened
- 9 tablespoons self-rising flour
- 7 tablespoons caster sugar
- Pinch of salt

Directions:
1. Preheat the Air fryer to 320°F and grease a baking dish.
2. Mix all the ingredients in a bowl until a crumbly mixture is formed.
3. Arrange the apple pie in the baking dish and top with the mixture.
4. Transfer the baking dish into the Air fryer basket and cook for about 25 minutes.
5. Dish out in a platter and serve.

Chocolate Soufflés

Servings:2 | Cooking Time: 15 Minutes

Ingredients:
- 2 large eggs, whites and yolks separated
- 1 teaspoon vanilla extract
- 2 ounces low-carb chocolate chips
- 2 teaspoons coconut oil, melted

Directions:
1. In a medium bowl, beat egg whites until stiff peaks form, about 2 minutes. Set aside. In a separate medium bowl, whisk egg yolks and vanilla together. Set aside.
2. In a separate medium microwave-safe bowl, place chocolate chips and drizzle with coconut oil. Microwave on high 20 seconds, then stir and continue cooking in 10-second increments until melted, being careful not to overheat chocolate. Let cool 1 minute.
3. Slowly pour melted chocolate into egg yolks and whisk until smooth. Then, slowly begin adding egg white mixture to chocolate mixture, about ¼ cup at a time, folding in gently.
4. Pour mixture into two 4" ramekins greased with cooking spray. Place ramekins into air fryer basket. Adjust the temperature to 400°F and set the timer for 15 minutes. Soufflés will puff up while cooking and deflate a little once cooled. The center will be set when done. Let cool 10 minutes, then serve warm.

Cranberry Jam

Servings: 8 | Cooking Time: 20 Minutes

Ingredients:
- 2 pounds cranberries
- 4 ounces black currant
- 2 pounds sugar
- Zest of 1 lime
- 3 tablespoons water

Directions:
1. In a pan that fits your air fryer, add all the ingredients and stir.
2. Place the pan in the fryer and cook at 360°F for 20 minutes.
3. Stir the jam well, divide into cups, refrigerate, and serve cold.

Peanut Butter Cookies

Servings:9 | Cooking Time: 27 Minutes

Ingredients:
- 2 tablespoons salted butter, melted
- 2 tablespoons all-natural, no-sugar-added peanut butter
- ⅓ cup granular brown erythritol
- 1 large egg
- ½ teaspoon vanilla extract
- 1 cup blanched finely ground almond flour
- ½ teaspoon baking powder

Directions:
1. In a large bowl, whisk together butter, peanut butter, erythritol, egg, and vanilla. Add flour and baking powder, and stir until combined.
2. Separate dough into nine equal pieces and roll each into a ball, about 2 tablespoons each.
3. Cut three pieces of parchment to fit your air fryer basket and place three cookies on each ungreased piece.
4. Place one piece of parchment with cookies into air fryer basket. Adjust the temperature to 300°F and set the timer for 9 minutes. Edges of cookies will be browned when done. Repeat with remaining cookies. Serve warm.

Pumpkin Cake

Servings:8 | Cooking Time: 25 Minutes

Ingredients:
- 4 tablespoons salted butter, melted
- ½ cup granular brown erythritol
- ¼ cup pure pumpkin puree
- 1 cup blanched finely ground almond flour
- ½ teaspoon baking powder
- ⅛ teaspoon salt
- 1 teaspoon pumpkin pie spice

Directions:
1. Mix all ingredients in a large bowl. Pour batter into an ungreased 6" round nonstick baking dish.
2. Place dish into air fryer basket. Adjust the temperature to 300°F and set the timer for 25 minutes. The top will be dark brown, and a toothpick inserted in the center should come out clean when done. Let cool 30 minutes before serving.

Roasted Pumpkin Seeds & Cinnamon

Servings: 2 | Cooking Time: 35 Minutes

Ingredients:
- 1 cup pumpkin raw seeds
- 1 tbsp. ground cinnamon
- 2 tbsp. sugar
- 1 cup water
- 1 tbsp. olive oil

Directions:
1. In a frying pan, combine the pumpkin seeds, cinnamon and water.
2. Boil the mixture over a high heat for 2 - 3 minutes.
3. Pour out the water and place the seeds on a clean kitchen towel, allowing them to dry for 20 - 30 minutes.
4. In a bowl, mix together the sugar, dried seeds, a pinch of cinnamon and one tablespoon of olive oil.
5. Pre-heat the Air Fryer to 340°F.
6. Place the seed mixture in the fryer basket and allow to cook for 15 minutes, shaking the basket periodically throughout.

Chilled Strawberry Pie

Servings:6 | Cooking Time: 10 Minutes

Ingredients:
- 1½ cups whole shelled pecans
- 1 tablespoon unsalted butter, softened
- 1 cup heavy whipping cream
- 12 medium fresh strawberries, hulled
- 2 tablespoons sour cream

Directions:
1. Place pecans and butter into a food processor and pulse ten times until a dough forms. Press dough into the bottom of an ungreased 6" round nonstick baking dish.
2. Place dish into air fryer basket. Adjust the temperature to 320°F and set the timer for 10 minutes. Crust will be firm and golden when done. Let cool 20 minutes.
3. In a large bowl, whisk cream until fluffy and doubled in size, about 2 minutes.
4. In a separate large bowl, mash strawberries until mostly liquid. Fold strawberries and sour cream into whipped cream.
5. Spoon mixture into cooled crust, cover, and place into refrigerator for at least 30 minutes to set. Serve chilled.

Fiesta Pastries

Servings:8 | Cooking Time:20 Minutes

Ingredients:
- ½ of apple, peeled, cored and chopped
- 1 teaspoon fresh orange zest, grated finely
- 7.05-ounce prepared frozen puff pastry, cut into 16 squares
- ½ tablespoon white sugar
- ½ teaspoon ground cinnamon

Directions:
1. Preheat the Air fryer to 390°F and grease an Air fryer basket.
2. Mix all ingredients in a bowl except puff pastry.
3. Arrange about 1 teaspoon of this mixture in the center of each square.
4. Fold each square into a triangle and slightly press the edges with a fork.
5. Arrange the pastries in the Air fryer basket and cook for about 10 minutes.
6. Dish out and serve immediately.

Fruit Turnovers

Servings: 6 | Cooking Time: 25 Minutes

Ingredients:
- 1 sheet puff pastry dough
- 6 tsp peach preserves
- 3 kiwi, sliced
- 1 large egg, beaten
- 1 tbsp icing sugar

Directions:
1. Prepare puff pastry by cutting it into 6 rectangles. Roll out the pastry with a rolling pin into 5-inch squares. On your workspace, position one square so that it looks like a diamond with points to the top and bottom. Spoon 1 tsp of the preserves on the bottom half and spread it, leaving a ½-inch border from the edge. Place half of one kiwi on top of the preserves. Brush the clean edges with the egg, then fold the top corner over the filling to make a triangle. Crimp with a fork to seal the pastry. Brush the top of the pastry with egg. Preheat air fryer to 350°F. Put the pastries in the greased frying basket. Air Fry for 10 minutes, flipping once until

golden and puffy. Remove from the fryer, let cool and dush with icing sugar. Serve.

Fried Banana S'mores

Servings: 4 | Cooking Time: 6 Minutes

Ingredients:
- 4 bananas
- 3 tablespoons mini semi-sweet chocolate chips
- 3 tablespoons mini peanut butter chips
- 3 tablespoons mini marshmallows
- 3 tablespoons graham cracker cereal

Directions:
1. Preheat the air fryer to 400°F.
2. Slice into the un-peeled bananas lengthwise along the inside of the curve, but do not slice through the bottom of the peel. Open the banana slightly to form a pocket.
3. Fill each pocket with chocolate chips, peanut butter chips and marshmallows. Poke the graham cracker cereal into the filling.
4. Place the bananas in the air fryer basket, resting them on the side of the basket and each other to keep them upright with the filling facing up. Air-fry for 6 minutes, or until the bananas are soft to the touch, the peels have blackened and the chocolate and marshmallows have melted and toasted.
5. Let them cool for a couple of minutes and then simply serve with a spoon to scoop out the filling.

Brownies For Two

Servings:2 | Cooking Time: 15 Minutes

Ingredients:
- ½ cup blanched finely ground almond flour
- 3 tablespoons granular erythritol
- 3 tablespoons unsweetened cocoa powder
- ½ teaspoon baking powder
- 1 teaspoon vanilla extract
- 2 large eggs, whisked
- 2 tablespoons salted butter, melted

Directions:
1. In a medium bowl, combine flour, erythritol, cocoa powder, and baking powder.
2. Add in vanilla, eggs, and butter, and stir until a thick batter forms.
3. Pour batter into two 4" ramekins greased with cooking spray and place ramekins into air fryer basket. Adjust the temperature to 325°F and set the timer for 15 minutes. Centers will be firm when done. Let ramekins cool 5 minutes before serving.

Fried Snickers Bars

Servings:8 | Cooking Time: 4 Minutes

Ingredients:
- ⅓ cup All-purpose flour
- 1 Large egg white(s), beaten until foamy
- 1½ cups Vanilla wafer cookie crumbs
- 8 Fun-size Snickers bars, frozen
- Vegetable oil spray

Directions:
1. Preheat the air fryer to 400°F.
2. Set up and fill three shallow soup plates or small pie plates on your counter: one for the flour, one for the beaten egg white(s), and one for the cookie crumbs.
3. Unwrap the frozen candy bars. Dip one in the flour, turning it

to coat on all sides. Gently shake off any excess, then set it in the beaten egg white(s). Turn it to coat all sides, even the ends, then let any excess egg white slip back into the rest. Set the candy bar in the cookie crumbs. Turn to coat on all sides, even the ends. Dip the candy bar back in the egg white(s) a second time, then into the cookie crumbs a second time, making sure you have an even coating all around. Coat the covered candy bar all over with vegetable oil spray. Set aside so you can dip and coat the remaining candy bars.
4. Set the coated candy bars in the basket with as much air space between them as possible. Air-fry undisturbed for 4 minutes, or until golden brown.
5. Remove the basket from the machine and let the candy bars cool in the basket for 10 minutes. Use a nonstick-safe spatula to transfer them to a wire rack and cool for 5 minutes more before chowing down.

Chocolate Brownie

Servings: 4 | Cooking Time: 16 Minutes

Ingredients:
- 1 cup bananas, overripe
- 1 scoop protein powder
- 2 tbsp unsweetened cocoa powder
- 1/2 cup almond butter, melted

Directions:
1. Preheat the air fryer to 325°F.
2. Spray air fryer baking pan with cooking spray.
3. Add all ingredients into the blender and blend until smooth.
4. Pour batter into the prepared pan and place in the air fryer basket.
5. Cook brownie for 16 minutes.
6. Serve and enjoy.

Monkey Bread

Servings:6 | Cooking Time: 20 Minutes

Ingredients:
- 1 can refrigerated biscuit dough
- ½ cup granulated sugar
- 1 tablespoon ground cinnamon
- ¼ cup salted butter, melted
- ¼ cup brown sugar
- Cooking spray

Directions:
1. Preheat the air fryer to 325°F. Spray a 6" round cake pan with cooking spray. Separate biscuits and cut each into four pieces.
2. In a large bowl, stir granulated sugar with cinnamon. Toss biscuit pieces in the cinnamon and sugar mixture until well coated. Place each biscuit piece in prepared pan.
3. In a medium bowl, stir together butter and brown sugar. Pour mixture evenly over the biscuit pieces.
4. Place pan in the air fryer basket and cook 20 minutes until brown. Let cool 10 minutes before flipping bread out of the pan and serving.

Cinnamon Pretzels

Servings:6 | Cooking Time: 10 Minutes

Ingredients:
- 1½ cups shredded mozzarella cheese
- 1 cup blanched finely ground almond flour
- 2 tablespoons salted butter, melted, divided
- ¼ cup granular erythritol, divided
- 1 teaspoon ground cinnamon

Directions:
1. Place mozzarella, flour, 1 tablespoon butter, and 2 tablespoons erythritol in a large microwave-safe bowl. Microwave on high 45 seconds, then stir with a fork until a smooth dough ball forms.
2. Separate dough into six equal sections. Gently roll each section into a 12" rope, then fold into a pretzel shape.
3. Place pretzels into ungreased air fryer basket. Adjust the temperature to 370°F and set the timer for 8 minutes, turning pretzels halfway through cooking.
4. In a small bowl, combine remaining butter, remaining erythritol, and cinnamon. Brush ½ mixture on both sides of pretzels.
5. Place pretzels back into air fryer and cook an additional 2 minutes at 370°F.
6. Transfer pretzels to a large plate. Brush on both sides with remaining butter mixture, then let cool 5 minutes before serving.

Cranberries Pudding

Servings: 6 | Cooking Time: 20 Minutes

Ingredients:
- 1 cup cauliflower rice
- 2 cups almond milk
- ½ cup cranberries
- 1 teaspoon vanilla extract

Directions:
1. In a pan that fits your air fryer, mix all the ingredients, whisk a bit, put the pan in the fryer and cook at 360°F for 20 minutes. Stir the pudding, divide into bowls and serve cold.

Midnight Nutella Banana Sandwich

Servings: 2 | Cooking Time: 8 Minutes

Ingredients:
- butter, softened
- 4 slices white bread
- ¼ cup chocolate hazelnut spread
- 1 banana

Directions:
1. Preheat the air fryer to 370°F.
2. Spread the softened butter on one side of all the slices of bread and place the slices buttered side down on the counter. Spread the chocolate hazelnut spread on the other side of the bread slices. Cut the banana in half and then slice each half into three slices lengthwise. Place the banana slices on two slices of bread and top with the remaining slices of bread to make two sandwiches. Cut the sandwiches in half – this will help them all fit in the air fryer at once. Transfer the sandwiches to the air fryer.
3. Air-fry at 370°F for 5 minutes. Flip the sandwiches over and air-fry for another 2 to 3 minutes, or until the top bread slices are nicely browned. Pour yourself a glass of milk or a midnight nightcap while the sandwiches cool slightly and enjoy!

Fried Oreos

Servings: 12 | Cooking Time: 6 Minutes Per Batch

Ingredients:
- oil for misting or nonstick spray
- 1 cup complete pancake and waffle mix
- 1 teaspoon vanilla extract
- ½ cup water, plus 2 tablespoons
- 12 Oreos or other chocolate sandwich cookies
- 1 tablespoon confectioners' sugar

Directions:
1. Spray baking pan with oil or nonstick spray and place in basket.
2. Preheat air fryer to 390°F.
3. In a medium bowl, mix together the pancake mix, vanilla, and water.
4. Dip 4 cookies in batter and place in baking pan.
5. Cook for 6minutes, until browned.
6. Repeat steps 4 and 5 for the remaining cookies.
7. Sift sugar over warm cookies.

Cherry Cheesecake Rolls

Servings: 6 | Cooking Time: 30 Minutes

Ingredients:
- 1 can crescent rolls
- 4 oz cream cheese
- 1 tbsp cherry preserves
- 1/3 cup sliced fresh cherries
- Cooking spray

Directions:
1. Roll out the dough into a large rectangle on a flat work surface. Cut the dough into 12 rectangles by cutting 3 cuts across and 2 cuts down. In a microwave-safe bowl, soften cream cheese for 15 seconds. Stir together with cherry preserves. Mound 2 tsp of the cherries-cheese mix on each piece of dough. Carefully spread the mixture but not on the edges. Top with 2 tsp of cherries each. Roll each triangle to make a cylinder.
2. Preheat air fryer to 350°F. Place the first batch of the rolls in the greased air fryer. Spray the rolls with cooking oil and Bake for 8 minutes. Let cool in the air fryer for 2-3 minutes before removing. Serve.

Almond Shortbread Cookies

Servings:8 | Cooking Time: 1 Hour 10 Minutes

Ingredients:
- ½ cup salted butter, softened
- ¼ cup granulated sugar
- 1 teaspoon almond extract
- 1 teaspoon vanilla extract
- 2 cups all-purpose flour

Directions:
1. In a large bowl, cream butter, sugar, and extracts. Gradually add flour, mixing until well combined.
2. Roll dough into a 12" x 2" log and wrap in plastic. Chill in refrigerator at least 1 hour.
3. Preheat the air fryer to 300°F.
4. Slice dough into ¼"-thick cookies. Place in the air fryer basket 2" apart, working in batches as needed, and cook 10 minutes until the edges start to brown. Let cool completely before serving.

Peanut Cookies

Servings: 4 | Cooking Time: 5 Minutes

Ingredients:
- 4 tablespoons peanut butter
- 4 teaspoons Erythritol
- 1 egg, beaten
- ¼ teaspoon vanilla extract

Directions:
1. In the mixing bowl mix up peanut butter, Erythritol, egg, and vanilla extract. Stir the mixture with the help of the fork. Then make 4 cookies. Preheat the air fryer to 355°F. Place the cookies in the air fryer and cook them for 5 minutes.

Mini Crustless Peanut Butter Cheesecake

Servings:2 | Cooking Time: 10 Minutes

Ingredients:
- 4 ounces cream cheese, softened
- 2 tablespoons confectioners' erythritol
- 1 tablespoon all-natural, no-sugar-added peanut butter
- ½ teaspoon vanilla extract
- 1 large egg, whisked

Directions:
1. In a medium bowl, mix cream cheese and erythritol until smooth. Add peanut butter and vanilla, mixing until smooth. Add egg and stir just until combined.
2. Spoon mixture into an ungreased 4" springform nonstick pan and place into air fryer basket. Adjust the temperature to 300°F and set the timer for 10 minutes. Edges will be firm, but center will be mostly set with only a small amount of jiggle when done.
3. Let pan cool at room temperature 30 minutes, cover with plastic wrap, then place into refrigerator at least 2 hours. Serve chilled.

Chocolate-covered Maple Bacon

Servings: 4 | Cooking Time: 25 Minutes

Ingredients:
- 8 slices sugar-free bacon
- 1 tbsp. granular erythritol
- 1/3 cup low-carb sugar-free chocolate chips
- 1 tsp. coconut oil
- ½ tsp. maple extract

Directions:
1. Place the bacon in the fryer's basket and add the erythritol on top. Cook for six minutes at 350°F and turn the bacon over. Leave to cook another six minutes or until the bacon is sufficiently crispy.
2. Take the bacon out of the fryer and leave it to cool.
3. Microwave the chocolate chips and coconut oil together for half a minute. Remove from the microwave and mix together before stirring in the maple extract.
4. Set the bacon flat on a piece of parchment paper and pour the mixture over. Allow to harden in the refrigerator for roughly five minutes before serving.

Baked Apple

Servings: 6 | Cooking Time: 20 Minutes

Ingredients:
- 3 small Honey Crisp or other baking apples
- 3 tablespoons maple syrup
- 3 tablespoons chopped pecans
- 1 tablespoon firm butter, cut into 6 pieces

Directions:
1. Put ½ cup water in the drawer of the air fryer.
2. Wash apples well and dry them.
3. Split apples in half. Remove core and a little of the flesh to make a cavity for the pecans.
4. Place apple halves in air fryer basket, cut side up.
5. Spoon 1½ teaspoons pecans into each cavity.
6. Spoon ½ tablespoon maple syrup over pecans in each apple.
7. Top each apple with ½ teaspoon butter.
8. Cook at 360°F for 20 minutes, until apples are tender.

Custard

Servings: 4 | Cooking Time: 45 Minutes

Ingredients:
- 2 cups whole milk
- 2 eggs
- ¼ cup sugar
- ⅛ teaspoon salt
- ¼ teaspoon vanilla
- cooking spray
- ⅛ teaspoon nutmeg

Directions:
1. In a blender, process milk, egg, sugar, salt, and vanilla until smooth.
2. Spray a 6 x 6-inch baking pan with nonstick spray and pour the custard into it.
3. Cook at 300°F for 45 minutes. Custard is done when the center sets.
4. Sprinkle top with the nutmeg.
5. Allow custard to cool slightly.
6. Serve it warm, at room temperature, or chilled.

Grape Stew

Servings: 4 | Cooking Time: 14 Minutes

Ingredients:
- 1 pound red grapes
- Juice and zest of 1 lemon
- 26 ounces grape juice

Directions:
1. In a pan that fits your air fryer, add all ingredients and toss.
2. Place the pan in the fryer and cook at 320°F for 14 minutes.
3. Divide into cups, refrigerate, and serve cold.

Crème Brulee

Servings:3 | Cooking Time: 60 Minutes

Ingredients:
- 1 cup milk
- 2 vanilla pods
- 10 egg yolks
- 4 tbsp sugar + extra for topping

Directions:
1. In a pan, add the milk and cream. Cut the vanilla pods open

and scrape the seeds into the pan with the vanilla pods also. Place the pan over medium heat on a stovetop until almost boiled while stirring regularly. Turn off the heat. Add the egg yolks to a bowl and beat it. Add the sugar and mix well but not too bubbly.

2. Remove the vanilla pods from the milk mixture; pour the mixture onto the eggs mixture while stirring constantly. Let it sit for 25 minutes. Fill 2 to 3 ramekins with the mixture. Place the ramekins in the fryer basket and cook them at 190°F for 50 minutes. Once ready, remove the ramekins and let sit to cool. Sprinkle the remaining sugar over and use a torch to melt the sugar, so it browns at the top.

Ricotta Stuffed Apples

Servings: 4 | Cooking Time: 25 Minutes

Ingredients:
- ½ cup cheddar cheese
- ¼ cup raisins
- 2 apples
- ½ tsp ground cinnamon

Directions:
1. Preheat air fryer to 350°F. Combine cheddar cheese and raisins in a bowl and set aside. Chop apples lengthwise and discard the core and stem. Sprinkle each half with cinnamon and stuff each half with 1/4 of the cheddar mixture. Bake for 7 minutes, turn, and Bake for 13 minutes more until the apples are soft. Serve immediately.

Merengues

Servings: 6 | Cooking Time: 65 Minutes

Ingredients:
- 2 egg whites
- 1 teaspoon lime zest, grated
- 1 teaspoon lime juice
- 4 tablespoons Erythritol

Directions:
1. Whisk the egg whites until soft peaks. Then add Erythritol and lime juice and whisk the egg whites until you get strong peaks. After this, add lime zest and carefully stir the egg white mixture. Preheat the air fryer to 275°F. Line the air fryer basket with baking paper. With the help of the spoon make the small merengues and put them in the air fryer in one layer. Cook the dessert for 65 minutes.

Grilled Banana Boats

Servings: 3 | Cooking Time: 15 Minutes

Ingredients:
- 3 large bananas
- 1 tablespoon ginger snaps
- 2 tablespoons mini chocolate chips
- 3 tablespoons mini marshmallows
- 3 tablespoons crushed vanilla wafers

Directions:
1. In the peel, slice your banana lengthwise; make sure not to slice all the way through the banana. Divide the remaining ingredients between the banana pockets.
2. Place in the Air Fryer grill pan. Cook at 395°F for 7 minutes.
3. Let the banana boats cool for 5 to 6 minutes, and then eat with a spoon. Bon appétit!

Lemon Berries Stew

Servings: 4 | Cooking Time: 20 Minutes

Ingredients:
- 1 pound strawberries, halved
- 4 tablespoons stevia
- 1 tablespoon lemon juice
- 1 and ½ cups water

Directions:
1. In a pan that fits your air fryer, mix all the ingredients, toss, put it in the fryer and cook at 340°F for 20 minutes. Divide the stew into cups and serve cold.

Cinnamon-sugar Pretzel Bites

Servings:4 | Cooking Time: 1 Hour 10 Minutes

Ingredients:
- 1 cup all-purpose flour
- 1 teaspoon quick-rise yeast
- 2 tablespoons granulated sugar, divided
- ¼ teaspoon salt
- 1 tablespoon olive oil
- ⅓ cup warm water
- 2 teaspoons baking soda
- 1 teaspoon ground cinnamon
- Cooking spray

Directions:
1. In a large bowl, mix flour, yeast, 2 teaspoons sugar, and salt until combined.
2. Pour in oil and water and stir until a dough begins to form and pull away from the edges of the bowl. Remove dough from the bowl and transfer to a lightly floured surface. Knead 10 minutes until dough is mostly smooth.
3. Spritz dough with cooking spray and place into a large clean bowl. Cover with plastic wrap and let rise 1 hour.
4. Preheat the air fryer to 400°F.
5. Press dough into a 6" × 4" rectangle. Cut dough into twenty-four even pieces.
6. Fill a medium saucepan over medium-high heat halfway with water and bring to a boil. Add baking soda and let it boil 1 minute, then add pretzel bites. You may need to work in batches. Cook 45 seconds, then remove from water and drain. They will be puffy but should have mostly maintained their shape.
7. Spritz pretzel bites with cooking spray. Place in the air fryer basket and cook 5 minutes until golden brown.
8. In a small bowl, mix remaining sugar and cinnamon. When pretzel bites are done cooking, immediately toss in cinnamon and sugar mixture and serve.

Fried Twinkies

Servings:6 | Cooking Time: 5 Minutes

Ingredients:
- 2 Large egg white(s)
- 2 tablespoons Water
- 1½ cups Ground gingersnap cookie crumbs
- 6 Twinkies
- Vegetable oil spray

Directions:
1. Preheat the air fryer to 400°F.
2. Set up and fill two shallow soup plates or small pie plates on your counter: one for the egg white(s), whisked with the water until foamy; and one for the gingersnap crumbs.

3. Dip a Twinkie in the egg white(s), turning it to coat on all sides, even the ends. Let the excess egg white mixture slip back into the rest, then set the Twinkie in the crumbs. Roll it to coat on all sides, even the ends, pressing gently to get an even coating. Then repeat this process: egg white(s), followed by crumbs. Lightly coat the prepared Twinkie on all sides with vegetable oil spray. Set aside and coat each of the remaining Twinkies with the same double-dipping technique, followed by spraying.

4. Set the Twinkies flat side up in the basket with as much air space between them as possible. Air-fry for 5 minutes, or until browned and crunchy.

5. Use a nonstick-safe spatula to gently transfer the Twinkies to a wire rack. Cool for at least 10 minutes before serving.

Cocoa Spread

Servings: 4 | Cooking Time: 5 Minutes

Ingredients:
- 2 oz walnuts, chopped
- 5 teaspoons coconut oil
- ½ teaspoon vanilla extract
- 1 tablespoon Erythritol
- 1 teaspoon of cocoa powder

Directions:
1. Preheat the air fryer to 350°F. Put the walnuts in the mason jar. Add coconut oil, vanilla extract, Erythritol, and cocoa powder. Stir the mixture until smooth with the help of the spoon. Then place the mason jar with Nutella in the preheated air fryer and cook it for 5 minutes. Stir Nutella before serving.

Glazed Chocolate Doughnut Holes

Servings: 5 | Cooking Time: 22 Minutes

Ingredients:
- 1 cup self-rising flour
- 1 ¼ cups plain full-fat Greek yogurt
- ¼ cup cocoa powder
- ½ cup granulated sugar
- 1 cup confectioners' sugar
- ¼ cup heavy cream
- 1 teaspoon vanilla extract

Directions:
1. Preheat the air fryer to 350°F. Spray the inside of the air fryer basket with cooking spray.
2. In a large bowl, combine flour, yogurt, cocoa powder, and granulated sugar. Knead by hand 5 minutes until a large, sticky ball of dough is formed.
3. Roll mixture into balls, about 2 tablespoons each, to make twenty doughnut holes. Place doughnut holes in the air fryer basket and cook 12 minutes, working in batches as necessary.
4. While doughnut holes are cooking, in a medium bowl, mix confectioners' sugar, cream, and vanilla. Allow doughnut holes 5 minutes to cool before rolling each in the glaze. Chill in the refrigerator 5 minutes to allow glaze to set before serving.

Pumpkin Pie–spiced Pork Rinds

Servings:4 | Cooking Time: 5 Minutes

Ingredients:
- 3 ounces plain pork rinds
- 2 tablespoons salted butter, melted
- 1 teaspoon pumpkin pie spice
- ¼ cup confectioners' erythritol

Directions:
1. In a large bowl, toss pork rinds in butter. Sprinkle with pumpkin pie spice, then toss to evenly coat.
2. Place pork rinds into ungreased air fryer basket. Adjust the temperature to 400°F and set the timer for 5 minutes. Pork rinds will be golden when done.
3. Transfer rinds to a medium serving bowl and sprinkle with erythritol. Serve immediately.

Easy Churros

Servings: 12 | Cooking Time: 10 Minutes

Ingredients:
- ½ cup Water
- 4 tablespoons (¼ cup/½ stick) Butter
- ¼ teaspoon Table salt
- ½ cup All-purpose flour
- 2 Large egg(s)
- ¼ cup Granulated white sugar
- 2 teaspoons Ground cinnamon

Directions:
1. Bring the water, butter, and salt to a boil in a small saucepan set over high heat, stirring occasionally.
2. When the butter has fully melted, reduce the heat to medium and stir in the flour to form a dough. Continue cooking, stirring constantly, to dry out the dough until it coats the bottom and sides of the pan with a film, even a crust. Remove the pan from the heat, scrape the dough into a bowl, and cool for 15 minutes.
3. Using an electric hand mixer at medium speed, beat in the egg, or eggs one at a time, until the dough is smooth and firm enough to hold its shape.
4. Mix the sugar and cinnamon in a small bowl. Scoop up 1 tablespoon of the dough and roll it in the sugar mixture to form a small, coated tube about ½ inch in diameter and 2 inches long. Set it aside and make 5 more tubes for the small batch or 11 more for the large one.
5. Set the tubes on a plate and freeze for 20 minutes. Meanwhile, Preheat the air fryer to 375°F .
6. Set 3 frozen tubes in the basket for a small batch or 6 for a large one with as much air space between them as possible. Air-fry undisturbed for 10 minutes, or until puffed, brown, and set.
7. Use kitchen tongs to transfer the churros to a wire rack to cool for at least 5 minutes. Meanwhile, air-fry and cool the second batch of churros in the same way.

Hot Coconut 'n Cocoa Buns

Servings:8 | Cooking Time: 15 Minutes

Ingredients:
- ¼ cup cacao nibs
- 1 cup coconut milk
- 1/3 cup coconut flour
- 3 tablespoons cacao powder
- 4 eggs, beaten

Directions:
1. Preheat the air fryer for 5 minutes.
2. Combine all ingredients in a mixing bowl.
3. Form buns using your hands and place in a baking dish that will fit in the air fryer.
4. Bake for 15 minutes for 375°F.
5. Once air fryer turns off, leave the buns in the air fryer until it cools completely.

S'mores Pockets

Servings: 6 | Cooking Time: 5 Minutes

Ingredients:
- 12 sheets phyllo dough, thawed
- 1½ cups butter, melted
- ¾ cup graham cracker crumbs
- 1 Giant Hershey's milk chocolate bar
- 12 marshmallows, cut in half

Directions:
1. Place one sheet of the phyllo on a large cutting board. Keep the rest of the phyllo sheets covered with a slightly damp, clean kitchen towel. Brush the phyllo sheet generously with some melted butter. Place a second phyllo sheet on top of the first and brush it with more butter. Repeat with one more phyllo sheet until you have a stack of 3 phyllo sheets with butter brushed between the layers. Cover the phyllo sheets with one quarter of the graham cracker crumbs leaving a 1-inch border on one of the short ends of the rectangle. Cut the phyllo sheets lengthwise into 3 strips.
2. Take 2 of the strips and crisscross them to form a cross with the empty borders at the top and to the left. Place 2 of the chocolate rectangles in the center of the cross. Place 4 of the marshmallow halves on top of the chocolate. Now fold the pocket together by folding the bottom phyllo strip up over the chocolate and marshmallows. Then fold the right side over, then the top strip down and finally the left side over. Brush all the edges generously with melted butter to seal shut. Repeat with the next three sheets of phyllo, until all the sheets have been used. You will be able to make 2 pockets with every second batch because you will have an extra graham cracker crumb strip from the previous set of sheets.
3. Preheat the air fryer to 350°F.
4. Transfer 3 pockets at a time to the air fryer basket. Air-fry at 350°F for 4 to 5 minutes, until the phyllo dough is light brown in color. Flip the pockets over halfway through the cooking process. Repeat with the remaining 3 pockets.
5. Serve warm.

Chocolate Macaroons

Servings: 16 | Cooking Time: 8 Minutes

Ingredients:
- 2 Large egg white(s), at room temperature
- ⅛ teaspoon Table salt
- ½ cup Granulated white sugar
- 1½ cups Unsweetened shredded coconut
- 3 tablespoons Unsweetened cocoa powder

Directions:
1. Preheat the air fryer to 375°F.
2. Using an electric mixer at high speed, beat the egg white(s) and salt in a medium or large bowl until stiff peaks can be formed when the turned-off beaters are dipped into the mixture.
3. Still working with the mixer at high speed, beat in the sugar in a slow stream until the meringue is shiny and thick.
4. Scrape down and remove the beaters. Fold in the coconut and cocoa with a rubber spatula until well combined, working carefully to deflate the meringue as little as possible.
5. Scoop up 2 tablespoons of the mixture. Wet your clean hands and roll that little bit of coconut bliss into a ball. Set it aside and continue making more balls: 7 more for a small batch, 15 more for a medium batch, or 23 more for a large one.
6. Line the bottom of the machine's basket or the basket attachment with parchment paper. Set the balls on the parchment with

as much air space between them as possible. Air-fry undisturbed for 8 minutes, or until dry, set, and lightly browned.
7. Use a nonstick-safe spatula to transfer the macaroons to a wire rack. Cool for at least 10 minutes before serving. Or cool to room temperature, about 30 minutes, then store in a sealed container at room temperature for up to 3 days.

Chocolate Lava Cakes

Servings:2 | Cooking Time: 15 Minutes

Ingredients:
- 2 large eggs, whisked
- ¼ cup blanched finely ground almond flour
- ½ teaspoon vanilla extract
- 2 ounces low-carb chocolate chips, melted

Directions:
1. In a medium bowl, mix eggs with flour and vanilla. Fold in chocolate until fully combined.
2. Pour batter into two 4" ramekins greased with cooking spray. Place ramekins into air fryer basket. Adjust the temperature to 320°F and set the timer for 15 minutes. Cakes will be set at the edges and firm in the center when done. Let cool 5 minutes before serving.

Brownies

Servings: 8 | Cooking Time: 20 Minutes

Ingredients:
- ½ cup all-purpose flour
- 1 cup granulated sugar
- ¼ cup cocoa powder
- ½ teaspoon baking powder
- 6 tablespoons salted butter, melted
- 1 large egg
- ½ cup semisweet chocolate chips

Directions:
1. Preheat the air fryer to 350°F. Generously grease two 6" round cake pans.
2. In a large bowl, combine flour, sugar, cocoa powder, and baking powder.
3. Add butter, egg, and chocolate chips to dry ingredients. Stir until well combined.
4. Divide batter between prepared pans. Place in the air fryer basket and cook 20 minutes until a toothpick inserted into the center comes out clean. Cool 5 minutes before serving.

Creamy Pudding

Servings: 6 | Cooking Time: 25 Minutes

Ingredients:
- 2 cups fresh cream
- 6 egg yolks, whisked
- 6 tablespoons white sugar
- Zest of 1 orange

Directions:
1. Combine all ingredients in a bowl and whisk well.
2. Divide the mixture between 6 small ramekins.
3. Place the ramekins in your air fryer and cook at 340°F for 25 minutes.
4. Place in the fridge for 1 hour before serving.

Dark Chocolate Peanut Butter S'mores

Servings: 4 | Cooking Time: 6 Minutes

Ingredients:
- 4 graham cracker sheets
- 4 marshmallows
- 4 teaspoons chunky peanut butter
- 4 ounces dark chocolate
- ½ teaspoon ground cinnamon

Directions:
1. Preheat the air fryer to 390°F. Break the graham crackers in half so you have 8 pieces.
2. Place 4 pieces of graham cracker on the bottom of the air fryer. Top each with one of the marshmallows and bake for 6 or 7 minutes, or until the marshmallows have a golden brown center.
3. While cooking, slather each of the remaining graham crackers with 1 teaspoon peanut butter.
4. When baking completes, carefully remove each of the graham crackers, add 1 ounce of dark chocolate on top of the marshmallow, and lightly sprinkle with cinnamon. Top with the remaining peanut butter graham cracker to make the sandwich. Serve immediately.

Tortilla Fried Pies

Servings: 12 | Cooking Time: 5 Minutes

Ingredients:
- 12 small flour tortillas
- ½ cup fig preserves
- ¼ cup sliced almonds
- 2 tablespoons shredded, unsweetened coconut
- oil for misting or cooking spray

Directions:
1. Wrap refrigerated tortillas in damp paper towels and heat in microwave 30 seconds to warm.
2. Working with one tortilla at a time, place 2 teaspoons fig preserves, 1 teaspoon sliced almonds, and ½ teaspoon coconut in the center of each.
3. Moisten outer edges of tortilla all around.
4. Fold one side of tortilla over filling to make a half-moon shape and press down lightly on center. Using the tines of a fork, press down firmly on edges of tortilla to seal in filling.
5. Mist both sides with oil or cooking spray.
6. Place hand pies in air fryer basket close but not overlapping. It's fine to lean some against the sides and corners of the basket. You may need to cook in 2 batches.
7. Cook at 390°F for 5 minutes or until lightly browned. Serve hot.
8. Refrigerate any leftover pies in a closed container. To serve later, toss them back in the air fryer basket and cook for 2 or 3 minutes to reheat.

Sage Cream

Servings: 4 | Cooking Time: 30 Minutes

Ingredients:
- 7 cups red currants
- 1 cup swerve
- 1 cup water
- 6 sage leaves

Directions:
1. In a pan that fits your air fryer, mix all the ingredients, toss, put the pan in the fryer and cook at 330°F for 30 minutes. Discard sage leaves, divide into cups and serve cold.

Fried Cannoli Wontons

Servings: 10 | Cooking Time: 8 Minutes

Ingredients:
- 8 ounces Neufchâtel cream cheese
- ¼ cup powdered sugar
- 1 teaspoon vanilla extract
- ¼ teaspoon salt
- ¼ cup mini chocolate chips
- 2 tablespoons chopped pecans (optional)
- 20 wonton wrappers
- ¼ cup filtered water

Directions:
1. Preheat the air fryer to 370°F.
2. In a large bowl, use a hand mixer to combine the cream cheese with the powdered sugar, vanilla, and salt. Fold in the chocolate chips and pecans. Set aside.
3. Lay the wonton wrappers out on a flat, smooth surface and place a bowl with the filtered water next to them.
4. Use a teaspoon to evenly divide the cream cheese mixture among the 20 wonton wrappers, placing the batter in the center of the wontons.
5. Wet the tip of your index finger, and gently moisten the outer edges of the wrapper. Then fold each wrapper until it creates a secure pocket.
6. Liberally spray the air fryer basket with olive oil mist.
7. Place the wontons into the basket, and cook for 5 to 8 minutes. When the outer edges begin to brown, remove the wontons from the air fryer basket. Repeat cooking with remaining wontons.
8. Serve warm.

Pineapple Sticks

Servings: 4 | Cooking Time: 20 Minutes

Ingredients:
- ½ fresh pineapple, cut into sticks
- ¼ cup desiccated coconut

Directions:
1. Pre-heat the Air Fryer to 400°F.
2. Coat the pineapple sticks in the desiccated coconut and put each one in the Air Fryer basket.
3. Air fry for 10 minutes.

Coconut Macaroons

Servings: 12 | Cooking Time: 8 Minutes

Ingredients:
- 1⅓ cups shredded, sweetened coconut
- 4½ teaspoons flour
- 2 tablespoons sugar
- 1 egg white
- ½ teaspoon almond extract

Directions:
1. Preheat air fryer to 330°F.
2. Mix all ingredients together.
3. Shape coconut mixture into 12 balls.
4. Place all 12 macaroons in air fryer basket. They won't expand, so you can place them close together, but they shouldn't touch.
5. Cook at 330°F for 8 minutes, until golden.

Fried Pineapple Chunks

Servings: 3 | Cooking Time: 10 Minutes

Ingredients:
- 3 tablespoons Cornstarch
- 1 Large egg white, beaten until foamy
- 1 cup Ground vanilla wafer cookies (not low-fat cookies)
- ¼ teaspoon Ground dried ginger
- 18 Fresh 1-inch chunks peeled and cored pineapple

Directions:
1. Preheat the air fryer to 400°F.
2. Put the cornstarch in a medium or large bowl. Put the beaten egg white in a small bowl. Pour the cookie crumbs and ground dried ginger into a large zip-closed plastic bag, shaking it a bit to combine them.
3. Dump the pineapple chunks into the bowl with the cornstarch. Toss and stir until well coated. Use your cleaned fingers or a large fork like a shovel to pick up a few pineapple chunks, shake off any excess cornstarch, and put them in the bowl with the egg white. Stir gently, then pick them up and let any excess egg white slip back into the rest. Put them in the bag with the crumb mixture. Repeat the cornstarch-then-egg process until all the pineapple chunks are in the bag. Seal the bag and shake gently, turning the bag this way and that, to coat the pieces well.
4. Set the coated pineapple chunks in the basket with as much air space between them as possible. Even a fraction of an inch will work, but they should not touch. Air-fry undisturbed for 10 minutes, or until golden brown and crisp.
5. Gently dump the contents of the basket onto a wire rack. Cool for at least 5 minutes or up to 15 minutes before serving.

Brown Sugar Cookies

Servings:9 | Cooking Time: 27 Minutes

Ingredients:
- 4 tablespoons salted butter, melted
- ⅓ cup granular brown erythritol
- 1 large egg
- ½ teaspoon vanilla extract
- 1 cup blanched finely ground almond flour
- ½ teaspoon baking powder

Directions:
1. In a large bowl, whisk together butter, erythritol, egg, and vanilla. Add flour and baking powder, and stir until combined.
2. Separate dough into nine pieces and roll into balls, about 2 tablespoons each.
3. Cut three pieces of parchment paper to fit your air fryer basket and place three cookies on each ungreased piece. Place one piece of parchment into air fryer basket. Adjust the temperature to 300°F and set the timer for 9 minutes. Edges of cookies will be browned when done. Repeat with remaining cookies. Serve warm.

Honey-roasted Mixed Nuts

Servings: 8 | Cooking Time: 15 Minutes

Ingredients:
- ½ cup raw, shelled pistachios
- ½ cup raw almonds
- 1 cup raw walnuts
- 2 tablespoons filtered water
- 2 tablespoons honey
- 1 tablespoon vegetable oil
- 2 tablespoons sugar
- ½ teaspoon salt

Directions:
1. Preheat the air fryer to 300°F.
2. Lightly spray an air-fryer-safe pan with olive oil; then place the pistachios, almonds, and walnuts inside the pan and place the pan inside the air fryer basket.
3. Cook for 15 minutes, shaking the basket every 5 minutes to rotate the nuts.
4. While the nuts are roasting, boil the water in a small pan and stir in the honey and oil. Continue to stir while cooking until the water begins to evaporate and a thick sauce is formed. Note: The sauce should stick to the back of a wooden spoon when mixed. Turn off the heat.
5. Remove the nuts from the air fryer and spoon the nuts into the stovetop pan. Use a spatula to coat the nuts with the honey syrup.
6. Line a baking sheet with parchment paper and spoon the nuts onto the sheet. Lightly sprinkle the sugar and salt over the nuts and let cool in the refrigerator for at least 2 hours.
7. When the honey and sugar have hardened, store the nuts in an airtight container in the refrigerator.

Appendix : Recipes Index

T

V

W

Y

Z

Printed in Great Britain
by Amazon

36915927R00059